ST ANDREWS CITIZENS

THEIR SOCIETIES, PAST AND PRESENT

Published by

Librario Publishing Ltd

ISBN: 1-904440-39-8

Copies can be ordered via the Internet
www.librario.com

or from:

Brough House, Milton Brodie, Kinloss
Moray IV36 2UA
Tel /Fax No 00 44 (0)1343 850 617

Cover Photograph: May morning 2002 at the Castle Pool
(Tom Finnie, The Alan Photograph Agency)

Printed and bound by Digisource GB Ltd

ST ANDREWS CITIZENS

THEIR SOCIETIES, PAST AND PRESENT

Betty Willsher

Librario

Previous publications by the Author

School Before Five	1959	Faber and Faber Ltd
Tales of Professor Popoff	1961	Pergamon Press
The Flying Jacket	1964	Blackie and Son
Call Me Person	1969	Pergamon Press
Stones (with Doreen Hunter)	1978	Canongate
Understanding Scottish Gravestones	1985	W & R Chambers & CSA (reprinted Canongate Books)
How to Record Scottish Graveyards	1985	CSA
Scottish Epitaphs	1996	Canongate Books
St Andrews – Ancient City in the Twentieth Century	2003	Librario

CONTENTS

FOREWORD

Many books have been written about St Andrews, its long history, its University, its golf links, golf clubs and golfing events. The University holds in its archives a collection of more than 300,000 old photographs and images, and the Preservation Trust an additional 8500. Five books have been published using a selection from these collections, with comments. They illustrate changes in the physical face of the city, and changes in the way of life. I wondered, too, about the other links – those between people and groups of people. It seemed that the history of the associations, societies and clubs might reveal these, and show changes as the twentieth century passed.

When I started this study, I had no idea what records survived, nor how much material there was to tackle. I discovered that many of the twentieth-century societies began in the nineteenth century or earlier, so I give outlines of each from its beginnings. I have confined the story to the associations of St Andrews and district, and excluded any which cover Fife, East Fife or North-East Fife, and likewise the political party associations, which for some time have not had headquarters here. Nor have I dealt with University clubs, except in Chapter 6 on music, because performances were attended by Town and Gown. In Chapter 4, I have included the University Ladies Club for reasons given in that section. The story of the St Andrews Preservation Trust is closely linked with the physical changes in the city, and the material has made a separate book.

My sources include the publications listed in the Bibliography, and material held in the Archives Department of the University Library, in the Kinburn Museum and in the Preservation Trust Museum.

Often I have had to extract information from handwritten minutes or reports, and have noted down names and dates given to me on the telephone; I apologise for any transcriptional and other unintentional errors. *Betty Willsher*

St Andrews, 2003

Acknowledgements

I would like to thank all those who are mentioned in the text for their help, and also the following: Peter Adamson, Mike Aitken, Revd Charles Armour, Heather Chisholm, Robin Constable, Beatrice Copson, David Donaldson, Ian Donaldson, Eileen Drever, Margaret Finlay, Gordon Christie, Hazel Gifford, Pat Harvey, Brian Jeffreys, John Johnson, C.K. Karsten, Susan Keracher, Cathy Kirkcaldy, Karen Latter, John Lindsey, Colin McAllister, Janet McGregor, Jim McIntosh, Marjorie Moncrieff, Ann Morrison, Colin Muir, Margaret Murray, Keith Neilson, Ian Palfrey, Molly Pirie, Edwina Proudfoot, Irene Redford, Alistair Reid, Sybil Scott, Andrew Soutar, Bill Sutherland, Diana Sykes, Penelope Walker, Revd James Whyte, Anne Williamson, Marion Woods, Julia Young, Michael Zochowsky, as well as many others who gave me information by telephone. Also, I much appreciate the assistance given to me by the staff of the University Library and of the Museums mentioned in the Foreword.

I would like also to thank the Preservation Trust and the University of St Andrews Library for permission to reproduce photographs from their collections, and Peter Adamson, Tom Finnie, Lyn Moir, Brian Jeffreys and John Tucker for the use of their photographs

I am most grateful to the following for their support and grants:

The Royal and Ancient Golf Club of St Andrews
(R&A Club Committee)

The Royal Borough of St Andrews Community Council

St Andrews Rotary Kilrymont

The Bart Burgess Trust

Dedication

To the public-spirited citizens of St Andrews,
past and present

Chapter 1

THE CHURCHES OF ST ANDREWS

One must acknowledge that the first and foremost societies have been the congregations of the various churches. Any newcomer to St Andrews in 1900 might have been surprised by the number of churches. At that time there were twelve places of worship: the church of St Salvator's, newly furbished as University Chapel; the ancient Holy Trinity, soon to be restored, and its acolyte, St Mary's; Hope Park; St Leonard's out west; St Andrews; the Congregational Church in Bell Street; the Baptist Church, and three which would soon be replaced by finer buildings: Martyrs' Church, St James Church and All Saints. There was also the Salvation Army Hall. The founding of each congregation and the struggles to continue may be signs of the stubborn independence, of determination to worship in the manner one preferred, of loyalty to a group. Besides the church services, there were (and are) societies within each congregation, such as the Women's guilds, youth clubs, dramatic clubs, badminton clubs – how well the church halls have served. From the separate and different stories of the beginnings of each church, one can build up a picture of the characters of the founder members and of the subsequent leaders. Added to this was a fresh-flowing stream of university lecturers and professors and their wives, and retired professional families with new ideas and interests.

All the churches above except two have continued into the twenty-first century. And there are three further congregations. At a time when church attendance throughout Britain has dropped, this is interesting.

Four Congregations of the Church of Scotland

Until 1412 the townsfolk of St Andrews worshipped in the small Church of the Holy Trinity, which stood beyond the east gable of the Cathedral. But by the fifteenth century St Andrews had become a market area and a civic centre, and there was need for a central parish church. The site of six riggs in South Street was given by Sir William Lindsay of the Byres, and in 1430 there was a further gift of a rigg to the west, for the enlarging of the graveyard. The church suited the increasingly prosperous medieval St Andrews. By 1500 it had twenty-seven altars; by 1559 the number may have increased to thirty-two, served by eighteen chaplains.

Holy Trinity was the centre of important events in our history. For part of the time when John Knox was with the Castilians in the Castle, as their elected preacher he preached in the Town Church on weekdays. On the Sabbath the Roman clergy and friars took over. Well known is the story of Knox's capture by the French, his gruelling time in the galleys, and his release in 1549. He went to England and returned to play his part in the Reformation.

The Reformation in Scotland

I quote from T.C. Smout's History of the Scottish People 1560-1830. 'In St Andrews on 11th June 1559 the citizens went to bed as Catholics and woke up as Protestants, because overnight the Lords of the Congregation – the Protestant army – had come into town, had gone into the parish church and ripped down all the Catholic ornaments, whitewashed the walls and turned it into a Protestant church'. Ronald Cant's account in The Parish Church of the Holy Trinity St Andrews differs somewhat. 'After the sermon ... the magistrates and the community agreed to remove all the monuments of idolatry. Archbishop Hamilton departed that same day, never to return. We can assume that the medieval furbishings would be dismantled and the main body of the church adapted to provide facilities for the administration of the Reformed sacraments of baptism and the Lord's Supper, and the preaching of the word in which the people might hear, see and participate intelligently'. This sounds like a reasonably peaceful process. I think that the current idea of the character of John Knox seems to be warped; in fact, while he was determined in his convictions and objectives, he was against war and against violence.

In August 1560 the Reformation Parliament passed a series of Acts. John Knox and five other ministers had drawn up a new Scots Confession of Faith; the objective was to have a qualified ministry in the parish churches. The problem was how to get money to pay the ministers so that the word of God could be preached. Knox was concerned about the financial situation because the riches of the church had been flowing back to the Protestant lords, whose ancestors had given land to the church. A reformed church based on The First Book of Discipline was authorised by the Scottish Parliament. Superintendents (mostly ministers) had the responsibility of planting churches and staffing them with ministers.

The growth of Presbyterianism is one that was complicated by politics and wars, by the Union of the Crowns and by difficulties caused by the Stuarts claiming the Divine Right of Kings. (When King James VI went south in 1603, he wanted to impose episcopacy on Scotland.) The form of Presbyterianism which developed was based mainly on The Second Book of Discipline which was drawn up by Andrew Melville. He had been a student at St Andrews. In 1574 he came back from Geneva, where he had studied under Calvin's successor. He became Rector of St Andrews University in 1580 and made St Marys into a school for the training of ministers. Just as Knox had remonstrated with Mary Queen of Scots, so Melville harried the 'tulchan bishops' (these were a device to get money for the churches). In 1597 Melville was deprived of his rectorship by a commission and later was sent to the tower. He died in exile in France. As Smout puts it: 'Finally in 1690 it emerged as the Presbyterian church of the 18th and 19th centuries with its elders, deacons and ministers, its kirk sessions, synods and general assemblies, its convictions of ecclesiastical parity and its frequent association with sabbatarianism and puritanism.'

Holy Trinity Church

At the important church of the Holy Trinity there were two ministers: a First Charge and a Second Charge. By the Act of 1690, the First Charge, who was nominated by the Archbishop or the Crown, was to be submitted to the whole congregation for approval or rejection. The Second Charge was appointed by the Town Council. In 1712 this Act was repealed by the English Parliament. In spite of protests from the General Assembly, patronage prevailed until 1874. This was the cause of several secessions over the years and of the 'Disruption' in 1843 when a large number of ministers and members left to form the Free Church.

In 1831 there were 5,621 citizens in the Parish of St Andrews. To accommodate the 2,000 communicants of the Parish Church of Holy Trinity, in 1840 St Mary's Church was erected at the western extension of Market Street (it is presently known as the Victory Memorial Hall). It was designed to hold 560 people. Between 1865 and 1899 the Holy Trinity congregation was distributed between the two places of worship; St Mary's was served by the two parish ministers in turn.

Holy Trinity Church is still the town church; it has been the centre for all important occasions and it contains the memorial to those who fell in the 1914-18 war. Its carillon is well known. Fifteen bells were installed in 1926 to the memory of Patrick Macdonald Playfair, who served as First Charge for twenty-five years. The carillon now numbers twenty-seven bells. To hear the curfew sound from the great tower, or to hear the familiar hymn tunes played on the carillon on Sunday before morning service, stirs the heart.

St Leonard's Church

St Leonards was a parish at the east of St Andrews. Under Bishop Robert a Culdee hospital, sited just off the Pends for the accommodation of six pilgrims, was enlarged and placed under the care of the Cathedral's Augustinian canons in 1144. By 1413 its chapel also served as a parish church dedicated to St Leonard. In 1512 the hospital, which had been used as a home for old women when the number of pilgrims decreased, was converted into a new college for the University, the College of the Poor Clerks of the church of St Andrew. These buildings were abandoned after the union of the colleges of St Leonards and St Salvators, and in 1747 the congregation of the St Leonards parish followed the students and held its services in St Salvator's Chapel. After this the old chapel was unroofed and became a ruin. Before 1900 the University intimated that it required sole use of its chapel, and so the St Leonards congregation had need for a church of its own. The site at the corner of Hepburn Gardens and Donaldson Gardens was some way from the parish; nevertheless it was agreed upon, and by 1902 P. Macgregor Chalmers' fine Romanesque church with its crow-stepped, saddle-backed tower was ready. The Manse was at 26 Hepburn Gardens. With the growth of houses to the west of St Andrews the site has proved a useful one, and the church has flourished.

Hope Park Church

Hope Park Church had its beginnings in the 'praying societies' of East Fife, which were the seed-bed of the secession church. I am grateful to Professor Whyte who has clarified my confusion about the secessions, in these words. 'At first these societies worshipped in the parish churches, but they were critical of the dry and moralistic preaching so often heard there. The first secession took place in 1733; four ministers, Erskine, Moncrieff, Wilson and Fisher had been outed from the Church of Scotland and had formed the Associate Presbytery. In 1737 the Correspondence petitioned the Associate Presbytery and on March 2nd 1738, at Balone Den they formed a Kirk Session.' Weekly a small group of men – who were to be the founders of Hope Park – walked to Abernethy to sit under the Rev Moncrieff (one of the four ministers above). It was forty-four miles in all. They left early on the Sabbath, attended the service and reached home in the early hours of Monday. It brings the story to life to know that they carried their boots, and put them on when they reached Abernethy. Then for a time they met in a house in Ceres, where they were able to build their own church. Unfortunately in 1749 there was a split in the Secession over the intention of the Burgess Oath; this required burgesses to acknowledge the true religion publicly preached in the realm and authorised by law. In East Fife the Anti-Burghers remained in Ceres, and the Burghers came to St Andrews. The place of worship was a rented cottage in Imrie's Close (today marked by a plaque). In 1774 the Burghers moved to larger premises in Burgher Close where they worshipped until 1827. In the space of almost a hundred years they were without an appointed minister for a total of twenty-one years.

The next Burgher chapel was in North Street (now 52 North Street) where five successive ministers of great ability brought an increase in numbers. Their faith, enthusiasm and courage led to the building of the present church which opened in 1865. They then took the name Hope Park Church. In 1929, with the union of the United Free and the Established Kirk, Hope Park was denominated Church of Scotland. T.T Fordyce heads one chapter in his history of Hope Park Church '18th century Morality' and writes: 'Briefly it appears that every conceivable sin was an everyday occurrence… On account of their universality and innumerable abominations it was decided there was a great need for a day of Fasting and Humiliation to stir the congregation out of their security. This was held on 20th April 1756'. Matters of discipline were prominent in those days.

Hope Park Church has had a succession of respected and well loved ministers. By 1986 the congregation had grown to 1100. The session consisted of over eighty elders, men and women. The manse had been the upper floors of 1 Howard Place, but a new manse was bought in 1987 at Priory Gardens. Hope Park has taken part in the training of ministers by having a newly licensed minister for the probationary year. In addition, it has prepared many girls of St Leonards School for church membership. Also, for thirty-six years a Hope Park group has made regular visits to the patients at Stratheden Hospital. There is a 'Caring and Sharing' campaign annually which raises money for three chosen good causes, and the church also supports missionary work in India.

In 1985-7 repairs were made to the steeple, and the Royal and Ancient Golf Club contributed £1000 to the expenses, 'because of the vital importance of the steeple as a landmark for golfers playing the 17th hole'. In 1993 more drastic stonework repairs on the tower cost £23,000. Today, as I write, the tower and steeple are again covered in scaffolding – some tiles are being replaced.

Martyrs' Church

A short history of this Church was written in 1978 by Robert A. Warren, and it was revised in 1992. In February of 1843 a group of twenty-five men and five women met in the Congregational Chapel and decided to form an association within the Free Church. Some of the founding members were well known local people – Alexander Meldrum of Kincaple, Sir David Brewster, Mrs Playfair, Captain Dalgleish, David Anderson and others. In the minutes of the Free Presbytery of St Andrews is an item of 21 June 1843 whereby Mr Brown was appointed to constitute the first Kirk Session. The first services of this congregation were held in the Secession Church; although the churches had split, they helped one another in a Christian spirit. Mr Hetherington was appointed as Minister. By June 1844 they were able to hold services in their own new church in North Street. Additions were made to the church in 1851, and in 1857 a large manse (now Rathelpie) was built in Kennedy Gardens and served for a hundred years. In November 1900, with the union of the Free and United Presbyterian churches, this congregation became Martyrs' Church. The first church was replaced by the present building in 1928; the North Street facade which belongs to John Milne's reconstruction of 1851 was kept; the Hall was added in 1933. In 1964 during the ministry of the Revd John Patterson the congregation numbered 694, and the Sunday School (now the Young People's Church) reached almost 150 with 19 teachers, and a further 24 young people in the Bible Class. Martyrs' Church has a long tradition of supporting overseas missionary work.

St Andrew's Church and All Saints Church

There are two Episcopalian churches. Not long before his death John Thompson, who was Rector of Madras College, wrote a book *St Andrew's, St Andrews 1689-1993*. In tracing the history of the Episcopal church he says, 'It is misleading to suggest that this church began as a sect which split away from the main stream of the Church of Scotland in 1689. In fact the first episcopal congregations formed round those ministers of the Church of Scotland who had been forced to leave their charges and their livings for political reasons.' On 4 April 1688 the Scottish Convention offered the Crown to William and Mary; on 13 April all clergy were ordered to pray for William and Mary as king and queen of Scotland. The two ministers of Holy Trinity at this time were Archdeacon Richard Waddell and John Wood. Both were summoned before a committee of the Estates on 11 May and required to take an oath of loyalty to William and Mary and abjure King James. As loyal to the Stuart cause they refused, and both were deprived. Some of the congregation followed Dr Waddell who was banished in 1691 but returned and ministered to 'the faithful remnant'. The Act of Toleration of 1712 allowed them to exist as a separate denomination, with freedom to worship and form congregations. They found a meeting place in a house on the south side of South Street, and later moved to a succession of rooms. This congregation survived although it was hampered by penal laws; the first in 1719 (although only short-lived), aimed at curbing Episcopalians because of their Jacobite sympathies, forbad an episcopalian clergyman who had not taken the oath of loyalty to the Hanovers to officiate over a gathering of more than nine persons. As a result of the second Jacobite Rebellion, the penal laws were renewed in 1746 and 1748 with stronger penalties. However, evidence shows that the Episcopalian group was tolerated in St Andrews. Pre-1843 records of baptisms and marriages, all performed in private houses, all with Scottish names, were salvaged from a tobacconist's shop (some had been used for wrapping up snuff); many of the members were from outlying places.

With the 1792 Act of Relief the Epsicopalians were freed from restrictions. By the beginning of the nineteenth century the congregation of St Andrew's Church had grown to about 3000. In July 1821 the first vestry was formed, and two years later a decision was taken to build a church. A piece of ground in North Street, which is now occupied by the extension to College Gate, was obtained. The church was built and was dedicated to St Andrew on 29 September 1825. It was designed by William Burn at a cost of £1486, a huge sum which was raised from gifts by members of the congregation and by well-wishers in Scotland and England; one benefactor was Dr Andrew Bell. An organ was gifted and a choir formed. A house in Playfair Terrace was obtained for a parsonage. By 1853 it was necessary to enlarge the church. Thompson tells us that the ladies organised a 'Fancy Fair' in the Town Hall and employed a German band to enliven it.

Numbers continued to increase, and it was decided to build a new church, so a site was acquired at the south end of Queens Gardens. This (the present) church was designed by Robert Rowan Anderson; the first services took place on 8 April 1869. It took eight years of effort to pay off the debt; the ladies worked valiantly, holding bazaars and sales of work. Money was needed as the tower was still to be built; it was completed in 1892 from Strathkinness stone and was eighty feet high. (Sadly this landmark showed structural faults, and in 1938 it was necessary to bring the tower down to the level of the chancel eaves.) The building programme continued: first vestries and a hall were built, and then a handsome rectory. Over the years this congregation was notably outlooking. A small congregation was formed at Guardbridge for whom a mission church, St Saviour's, was built in 1901; the St Saviour's congregation established a mission in Strathkinness.

The financially successful system of pew rents in St Andrew's church had come to mean that there were no seats for poor people, so the vestry of St Andrew's decided to provide a mission church at the east end of North Street, where the fisher families lived. In 1903 an iron church, purchased from the Glasgow firm of Spiers, was erected on the site of the present All Saints. There was free seating for 150 people. It was known among the Fisherfolk as the 'Bundle Kirk', as gifts of clothing and goods were handed out from time to time. Castle Wynd House was acquired as a residence for the priest in charge. A stone chancel and a tower and vestry were donated four years later. In 1918 a handsome benefaction by Mrs Annie Younger of Mount Melville brought about the replacement of the iron church by stone buildings to Paul Waterhouse's design. A chapel, vestry, large hall, gymnasium and Guild Hall were in the plan, together with complete furnishings. Castle Wynd House was extended and fitted out for two clubs, one for women, and one for men with a billiard room (later a Men's Temperance Association met here); there was also a library. This congregation, as All Saints, became independent in 1920. The church was consecrated on 1 November 1923. Among many other activities church members run 'The Ladyhead', a bookshop and café in North Street.

The Independent Congregational Church

This congregation was formed in 1805 by a small group of people who were influenced by the preaching of two Englishmen, and seceded from the Holy Trinity Church. By the mid century they were able to commission the St Andrews architect, Jesse Hall, to design a chapel for them in Bell Street. This was ready for use in 1854.

There are Sunday School records dating from 1846, and books of carefully kept accounts. Money was short, but somehow enough was raised by 1922 to buy an organ which cost £355-7-6d. Many people will remember Revd Helen Woods who came to the Baptist Church in 1934. She was the first woman minister at this church, and in St Andrews. In the summer of 1937, 20 Queens Gardens was leased as a Manse, but Dr Woods – in order to save the church's money – bought a house for herself in Park Street, and the rent for the Manse went to the church. At the end of each year she completed her personal accounts and gave the surplus balance to a charity. She was an ardent Scottish Nationalist, and had strong views on many things. When she left her ministry here in 1959 she went to a teaching appointment in England, but returned to St Andrews in the early 1960s and became a member of All Saints.

The Revd John Geyer was called in April 1961, and in an address said, 'The fechtin church is still battling on.' There were active groups within the church: Christian Endeavour involving teenagers, a Women's Meeting, Junior Church and of course Family Worship. Mr Geyer left in August 1963, and the induction of Revd John A.L. Cheyne was not until 3 September 1964. After a year the numbers of the congregation had dropped, and the financial situation was not promising. Mrs Cheyne became ill, and Mr Cheyne had to make the decision to leave and train to become a teacher. The mood of the congregation was described as 'one of despondency'. Great efforts were made, but at the end of 1965 the decision had to be for dissolution. The closing service was held on 8 February 1966. There were many warm letters of appreciation and of concern for this sad ending. Going through the records of this church, one appreciates the warmth and loyalty of its close-knit congregation, and the amount of work undertaken. Dr Donald Watt, the Treasurer, must have spent a great deal of time over the years, and in the business of the sale of the church and hall, and the disposal of the contents. Some of these were gifted to other congregational churches. The church was bought by the University to offer to The Order of the Eastern Star, who had a meeting house on the land in North Street where the University was going to build the new Library.

The Order of the Eastern Star was originally founded for the wives, daughters and other female relatives of Freemasons. It was *not* the equivalent of a branch of the masons. The aim was to provide fellowship and the benefits which would come from this. Perhaps one might say that it was a caring society on a Christian foundation. The Order was founded in 1956 and celebrated its Diamond Jubilee in its Hall in Bell Street. Soon after this, the former property of the Congregational Church was sold and was demolished in order to build flats and shops on the site. The Eastern Star came to an end.

The Baptist Church

Ian Docherty wrote a history of the Baptist Church 1841-1991, and from this we learn that the founders were originally members of the Independent Congregational Church. In 1840 the Revd William Lothian, who was Minister of this church, gave a series of lectures, one of which was on the subject of baptism. A man whose name was William Stobie became leader of a small group who felt it was their duty to be baptised as believers. The nearest Baptist Church was in Cupar, so William Stobie went to see Revd J. Watson, the minister, who agreed to baptise him. However, Stobie felt he was received coldly on returning to services at Mr Lothian's church. Letters passed between the two ministers. Mr Lothian was determined to quash any debate on the matter of baptism, and asked the baptist group to exercise forbearance. He suggested that if this was against their consciences they should withdraw. On 1 June 1841 a small group of eight men and four women reluctantly left the Congregational

Church. It was hard to do, but with permission from the Town Council they began meetings in the Town Hall.

The story of this brave and determined congregation is a heartening one. In October 1842 Lt. Col. Playfair, who admired the courage of these Baptists, offered for the sum of £600 a piece of land with a building; this was on the site of the present Baptist Church in South Street, between Madras College and Rose Lane. After renovation of the building, the church opened on 13 October 1842. In January of the next year Brother Thomas Henderson accepted the call as pastor, there then being seven men and eleven women members.

When Mr Henderson resigned two years later, there were thirty-eight members. The debt was not yet cleared. There was a vacancy for two years, but services continued. This was to be the pattern. Because the membership was small the pastor's salary was limited. There were other years without full pastoral coverage. A succession of good and loved pastors came, young and elderly, and went on to larger congregations or retired from ill health. In 1849 a fellowship fund was started to give support to any member who should need it. In 1870 the founder, William Stobie, died, and the resignation of Mrs and Miss Stobie was a further blow. Mrs Stobie wrote: 'There may yet be days of prosperity for the little church that has struggled bravely against many difficulties and discouragements'. There were seventy-two members, but numbers decreased in the following seven years when the Baptists were without a pastor. The Revd Sim Hirst served from 1890 to 1902 (and he returned 1910-25), and the congregation slowly built up to 29 in 1892 and 62 in 1895. There was soon a Sunday School of 93 children, a Band of Hope of 150, and a Christian Education Society of 53. It was at last possible to pay the pastor a salary of £100. Deacons and deaconesses were appointed; part of their duties was to make home visits.

For twenty-five years Mr Gourlay was the faithful organist. In 1901 the building of a new church began, and services were held in the Good Templar Hall until 20 July 1902, the day of the opening of the new church. Finances were helped by the proceeds of a two-day bazaar in the Town Hall. It was opened by Lady Griselda Cheape, and among the attractions were marionettes, a conjuring entertainment, 'Grand Kinematograph', and 'A Ladies Monkey Brand Polishing Competition'!

The congregation has always been concerned with Outreach. It began to hold services in Kinburn Park. In 1934 the numbers were up to 127, which was to be the peak. Over the years the Geddes family and the Docherty family were staunch workers. In 1962 Robert Docherty, Church Treasurer, went to a new job in Banff; he was followed by his brother who had been a deacon since 1907. George Geddes was superintendent of the Sunday School for twenty-two years. Throughout the year the University Christian Union brought in new members. In 1964 education for all ages was introduced, and an Adult Sunday School was started. In 1968 a holiday Bible Class was run. In 1974 number 2 Rose Lane was acquired and alterations made; it has since served as a centre for service and outreach, including Sunday School, Age Concern, a Fellowship group, and Family Conciliation. As there was no church building south of the Kinnessburn, in 1978 Sunday services were started at Langlands School during term time, and in holiday times these were held at the homes of two families of the congregation who lived in the area. Under Pastor Willie Wright (1981-91) an assistant pastor was appointed to take on the Langlands work, and a second manse was acquired at 65 Lamond Drive. The Langlands Fellowship continues to thrive. The Sunday morning services are now held at Madras Kilrymont; the congregation (in 2002) was over 300, almost all of them young people. A series of committees was set up with different responsibilites: Missionary, Evangelism, Youth Co-ordinating, and Social Concern.

St James' Church

In 1983 Peter King wrote a short history of the Catholic Church in St Andrews which gives the following information. After the

Reformation there were hardly any Catholics in St Andrews until, in the nineteenth century, some Irishmen came to Fife to get work. In 1849 there was a Catholic mission in Cupar, and in 1878 a place of worship there. John Strain, a priest, came from Cupar to St Andrews on the first Wednesday of each month to say Mass and hear confession, and subsequently the Clergy of the Catholic Cathedral in Edinburgh sent priests to take Mass twice monthly in the summer, and once a month in the winter,

In 1846 James Hope bought a field known as Colonel Holcroft's Park; the building of his overall plan, which comprised Abbotsford Crescent, Howard Place and Hope Street, began in 1860 and was completed in the 1890s. He married Charlotte Lockhart, the granddaughter of Sir Walter Scott, and inherited Abbotsford. In 1851 he became a Catholic. He had also bought a large area of ground in the Scores, which he gave to the Catholic Eastern District so that a mission might be built on it. About 1870 permission was given to set up a roller-skating rink on the site, with the condition that it must in time make way for a church. It was it was used for flower shows from 1877 to 1882.

In 1878 the Catholic hierarchy was restored, and John Strain of Cupar asked for a collection for a church in St Andrews. However, he died and at this point the 5th Marquess of Bute stepped in and offered to meet the costs. When in England he met a young Scot, George Angus, who had been in the Army in India, and in 1870 had been received into the Catholic church in Dundee, and ordained in 1876. He was willing to leave London to become a pastor in St Andrews. He came in September 1884 to a house which the Marquis had acquired at 22 Queen Street (Queens Gardens). A large room was made into a chapel and the first Mass was held on 5 October. Sixty-eight people were present, and a hundred people came in the evening when those of other denominations were welcome.

Lord Bute had grandiose and impractical ambitions about the building of a Catholic cathedral in St Andrews. He had to face reality, and eventually agreed to pay for a temporary building. This was a small corrugated iron and wooden church, with a little belfry, ecclesiastical windows and a porch. The first service in it was after Easter 1885. In 1886 the stone Presbytery was built, and Father Angus moved in. There was a daily mass, and the church was open all day to any comer. The whole congregation was Irish, fifty-eight from St Andrews and another twenty-five from Dura Den, Crail and Kilconquahar. Fr Angus took part in a controversy over the Irish Nationalists and bombings, making it plain that the Catholic Church dissociated itself from these. He became friendly with Dr A. K. H. Boyd of Holy Trinity; he was elected to the R. and A. and was held in deep affection in the town. When he was confined to a wheelchair a friend of his, Father Herbert Laughton, came to help. Fr Angus died on 17 March 1907, and Fr Laughton was the priest at St James from 1909 to 1922.

In 1908 the Catholic Church was subjected to the normal government of the church, and St James became a properly constituted parish, stretching from the River Eden to Earlsferry. The time had come to build a stone church. First the temporary church, known locally as 'The Tin Tabernacle' was removed. Many of us will have seen the fine photograph of its dramatic removal in 1910, taken with the old Station Hotel in the background: the church is mounted on an enormous float, which is towed by a steam engine! It was taken to James Street (off Bridge Street) and re-erected there. David Lyle recorded that regular dances were held on the polished wooden floor of 'La Scala'; there used to be community singing, social events and roller-skating. On Sundays evenings the first silent films were shown. The audience had to sing a hymn to make the gathering legal, and had to pay a penny for their entrance fee.

The money for the new stone church came partly from Fr Laughton and partly from a relative of his, Mrs Annette Elizabeth Harmer, who had come to live at Canmore (on the corner of Murray Place and The Scores). The architect was Reginald Fairlie of Myres, who also re-ordered St Salvator's Chapel and designed All Saints Rectory. The spire of St James' Church echoes that of St Salvators. The new St James' was consecrated by Archbishop James Smith on 2 August 1910.

Fr Laughton died in the Cottage Hospital in 1924, and was succeeded by Canon John Gray, whose ministry was from 1929 to 1955. He was 'a countryman, a gardener, a beekeeper, a skilful craftsman and a mechanic'. He enjoyed pastoral work and was very popular. He said weekly masses at Crail and Pittenweem, and two curates came to assist him in the increasing work. During the war the Poles in this area attended St James. A tradition arose from that time and is still kept up: before the Christmas night mass, Polish carols are sung. I find this very moving,

In 1947 the White Fathers bought Canmore as a house of studies for their order. Here three or four men lived who were studying for degrees at the University. Many will remember Father Hugh Gordon (and his friendly black spaniel dog) who came to St James' in 1955. Up to this time all religious instruction to children was given in school or out of school hours. In 1956 with Canon Gray leading, plans for a school began to crystallise. In September 1957 this was embarked upon; the present St James' Church Hall was built as a school. A lot of the building work, which took four years, was done by Fr Gordon and his parishioners. The school was staffed by the Poor Clares of Newby, who lived in a convent in Queens Terrace. At first only 5-7 year-olds attended, but soon it was possible to have all grades. The school moved out of the Church Hall to a large house in Queens Terrace, opposite the Convent (now a student annexe for St Regulus). Fr Gordon used his car to collect the country children and return them to their homes. This involved driving fifty miles a day, but soon offers to help came along. In 1968 Fife Education Authorities agreed to take over the school, and the next year it was moved to the old Borough School in Abbey Street, where it continues. The Catholic School is a testimony to Fr Gordon.

In 1958 the White Fathers sold Canmore to the Brothers of Christian Instruction; a year later the University took it over, and it became a Catholic University Chaplaincy. Father Engelen came as sole priest to St James' in 1969. There the story can rest – it is within living memory. St James' is one of the group of churches which come under the St Andrews Council of Churches.

St Salvator's Church

This was built in 1450-60 as the church for St Salvator's College. It was, however, not the usual college chapel. The doors were open, and all might enter and take the sacrament and listen to the preaching. By 1475 thirty chaplainries were endowed whose holders could study at the University. There were seven altars and many treasures. At the shrine of the Holy Rude was a silver image of the Saviour. The tomb of the founder, Bishop Kennedy, was said to be the finest example of medieval funeral art in Scotland. It is still remarkable, though the carved stonework has been badly damaged. (In the 18th century it was thought that the splendid barrel roof was unsafe, and workmen used gunpowder to dislodge it.)

In 1563 the chapel was taken over by the Burgh and used as a Commissary Court. In 1754-7 the church was restored for ecclesiastical use for parishioners of St Leonards. Since 1902, when it was restored by Reginald Fairlie, it has been 'University Chapel'; in my student days 'Pop Sawyer' sat at the organ. On a Sunday there was choir practice first thing, a stroll along North Street for some fresh air, and then return for morning service – followed, of course, by the pier walk. Cedric Thorpe Davie succeeded Dr Sawyer and had a great effect on music in St Andrews. A degree course was initiated, only to be curtailed to a year course some thirty years later.

Ecumenical services are held in Chapel on Sundays in term time, and the public are welcomed. We had a strange unprecedented experience last year when we went to morning service taken by the

Chaplain, with the Moderator as guest preacher. It was good to see the students wearing their red gowns (they have gone out of fashion). When the first hymn had just begun, there seemed to be a brief announcement which we could not decipher. This happened again during the next hymn. When the Moderator ascended the historic pulpit and began his sermon, he referred to the dwindling numbers in congregations, a matter of great concern. 'There are those who say that this is the time when God should give some sign – should speak …'. He stopped; a loud voice rang through the Chapel, 'Will you now turn to hymn...'. Everyone was taken aback, and afterwards no one could remember the number of the hymn. For a few moments there was a dead silence, and then the Chaplain came forward, 'I must explain what has happened', he said, 'We are on the same loop sound system as the church across the road. Last week I was told they received three messages from us. So now, after three interruptions here today we are level. I can assure you it is now switched off.' The Moderator looked doubtful. 'Well', he said, 'so long as you are sure it wasn't the voice of the Lord you have switched off.'

On Charities Day in 1958 the students dreamed up a unique prank. The first citizens in the street were amazed by the sight of large white footprints running to the top of St Salvator's tower which dominates North Street. At the request of the Questor, Willie Fulton came to remove the paper footprints. A crowd gathered as Willie was hoisted up in his bosun's chair and began his work. The students appealed to him to stop, but he continued. Another man was holding the rope, and some students bribed him to let them take it over. Willie was left suspended in space when the students disappeared with the rope into the Union, and locked the doors. Word flies fast in St Andrews, so the crowd soon increased, and a photographer arrived and captured the best-ever Charities Day caper!

Other Worshippers

The Christian Society of Friends (the Quakers) in St Andrews was started by Robin Waterston, grandson of the University's distinguished Professor Waterston (chair of Anatomy). One of the Professor's sons had been a pupil at the Quaker school Bootham's at York, and his sons, Robin and Tony, also attended this school. As a student at St Andrews, Robin met American students who were Quakers, and they formed a group. This group first met in 1964, and it still continues, having had various meeting rooms.

The Eden Fellowship is a comparatively recent foundation. The Rev. Ted Collington tells me that the St Andrews congregation was started in 1983 and has flourished. There is a core of stalwarts, with a number of students and other young people. The style of worship is not structured; members are encouraged to offer prayers spontaneously, and there is a band.

Finally, there are three other small, faithful congregations. In the early part of the twentieth century the Salvation Army had a Barracks in South Castle Street and subsequently moved to a building beside Martyrs' Church in North Street. The Gospel opened in rooms above a shop in North Castle Street after the First World War; the Gospel Hall is now at 39-41 Market Street. In Greenside Place a sect of Brethren spends the Sabbath Day at worship in their Meeting Hall.

Two items as a single donation were received by the University Library in July 2001, and are held in the Archives.

(1) Papers of the St Andrews Christian Council (1948). This short-lived Council was formed by the ecclesiastical and theological establishment of the town to approach secular issues from a Christian perspective.

(2) Papers of the St Andrews Ecumenical Council (1951-1974) which cover the full life-term of this fellowship.

* * *

I hope that these bare summaries may serve to indicate the religious traditions and the character of the people of St Andrews. The Reformation brought a new experience of great value to Scotland: that each man, whatever his birth, had an equal chance of salvation. The leaders had the courage of their convictions; members learned to work as a group, and to endure times when things were difficult. Many of them had good experience of debating, of drawing up rules and revising them. They became accustomed to considering and helping others. Importantly, women played a large part in the work of the churches, although in the Church of Scotland it was not until 1966 that eldership was opened to them, and the ministry in 1968. In the Episcopal Church women are now eligible for the diaconate and the priesthood.

Chapter 2

HELPING OTHERS

The congregations of all the churches have done much to contribute to local and national charities, and it would take a deal of space to list the various ways in which they help those in need. Two small examples might be: the early setting up of a Temperance Club in All Saints, and the current Stratheden Group from Hope Park Church who weekly visit patients at the hospital there. It will be apparent that almost all of the societies described in this book subscribe to charities, even if this is not their main objective. In this chapter I will mention only those charitable organisations based in St Andrews and district (not Fife or North East Fife branches).

There is scarcely a Saturday when the streets are not manned by collectors with their tins and the stickers of the cause. The church halls, the Town Hall and the Victory Memorial Hall are heavily booked for coffee mornings in aid of a string of good causes, local and national. Over more than a hundred years, thousands of good ladies have baked millions of cakes and scones and goodies, and poured out millions of cups of coffee and tea. Jumble sales, book sales, the student charities and Kate Kennedy Day have all subscribed to good causes.

Services and other voluntary organizations

Womens Voluntary Service

How much can you remember about this eminent service? Most people reply, 'They wore green uniform.' I recall my mother going from her home in County Durham at the height of the air-raids to spend a week in London, assisting in the shelters to give some relief to

WVS workers there. I myself have vivid memories of evenings helping in a canteen for Polish soldiers in Suffolk.

In 1938, on the brink of war, Home Secretary Samuel Hoare approached Stella, Lady Reading, to ask if she would take a leading role in the formation of a large national force of women volunteers to aid the Air Raid Precautions Department. The new organisation, named the 'WVS for Air Raid Precautions' was founded on 16 May 1938; by 3 September 1939 there were 165,000 members. The name was soon changed to the 'WVS for Civil Defence'. Its role diversified, and members were involved with evacuation of children, pregnant women and the disabled. Throughout the war they also ran hostels, sick bays, and clubs and restaurants for evacuees, and provided school meals for evacuees. They looked after the welfare of refugees from Europe, distributed 40 million ration books and explained how to use them, and distributed and fitted gas masks. They collected materials for recycling, organised the 'Make-do and Mend' scheme and dealt with the millions of pounds worth of Overseas Gifts. In addition, they wove thousands of camouflage nets.

When the air-raids began, the WVS opened rest centres for those who had lost their homes, supplied mobile canteens for the rescue workers, drove ambulances and acted as emergency cycle couriers. They set up clubs and canteens (some mobile) and Welcome Clubs for American Troops in 1943. I quote: 'There was nothing that the WVS would not take on as a job. The only question was, "Will it help to win the war?" Their unofficial motto became "Not why we can't but how we can."'

When the war came to an end, it was decided to carry on for another two years. Over sixty years later, the Women's Royal Voluntary Service (as it is now called) is still going strong.

In the immediate post-war years the WVS set up Darby and Joan Clubs for the elderly, and Residential Clubs for those of limited means. The Meals on Wheels scheme was officially launched in Welwyn Garden City in 1947, and this service spread to all branches. In 1948 when the National Health Service was set up, the WVS extended its already existing services to hospitals, including making and mending clothes and running the popular trolley shops. In 1951 a memorial to the 241 WVS members killed on duty during the war was unveiled in Westminster Abbey in the presence of the Queen. On her accession to the throne, Queen Elizabeth agreed to become Patron, and in 1966 awarded the WVS the great honour of adding Royal to its title.

Members now worked as auxiliary nurses in hospitals, as drivers taking patients to and from hospitals. They also took on interviewing in prisons. Whenever help was need they came to the rescue – in floods, air crashes, the Piper Alpha air disaster and so on. They assisted with refugees when they came pouring into Britain.

There is little information about the St Andrews Branch. It began as a Savings Group in June 1941. By March 1942 there were seventeen Street Groups which collected money: £1040 in the first forty weeks, £4139 by February 1943, and £9541 by December 1943. This was sent to the WVS War Savings Association. They had an office and collected knitted garments, etc., for the 'Comforts to Russia'. At this time they took part in the distribution of vitamins. The leaders were Mrs Scott of Westview House and Mrs Austin of Kilrule.

The WVS here met essential needs. During the war they stocked the Red Cross Centre at Deanscourt. Then they provided Meals on Wheels. Mrs Lorraine Smith remembers that in the 1960s she helped with a Tufty Club for small children which was held at the Louden's Close Hall. Mrs Martineau was regional organiser and remembers that St Andrews was fairly self-sufficient. In time, many of the obvious needs (such as Meals on Wheels) were taken over by the Council's Social Work Department. In 1994 the Council decided to withdraw funding. Some of the WRVS members volunteered to help with a new Hard of Hearing Club.

The Sixty Club

In 1941 Felicity Irvine assisted by Anne Sutherland, Alison Hopwood, and Avril Moir-Gray (now Avril Sloan) started a club for men in the

Forces. Mr Charles Grace of the Grange handed over, rent free, his empty house at 60 South Street. An appeal in the paper brought almost all they needed to furnish and equip it. They held dances to raise money.

It was open every day from 2.30 to 10 p.m., and the helpers worked in three shifts of 2½ hours, six on each shift. The canteen offered an unusual variety of good food, there was peace for letter writing or reading, billiards, and companionship – the club was a great success. A Polish ballet dancer gave dancing lessons and a dancing team was formed. Men in the Forces were able, in their spare time, to attend classes given by the University.

Some of the Polish soldiers stayed on in St Andrews after the war and married local girls. They eventually formed the Polish Club which has lasted for many years.

Royal National Lifeboat Institution, St Andrews Branch

St Andrews has had cause in the past to respect and be grateful for the lifeboat crews who went to the rescue of a good number of ships in distress in the 19th and early 20th centuries. There was no lifeboat in 1800 when the 'Janet' was wrecked, but in the course of the following years, four St Andrews lifeboats (all rowing boats) were bought. The first was launched in 1801. The third (1873) was called 'The Ladies Own', and the last was 'The John and Sarah Hatfield'; this amazing boat was launched at the East Sands (where the lifeboat station was) in 1910. One of the later and well-known coxwains was Davy Fenton. The RNLI closed down the lifeboat service at St Andrews in 1939.

There seems to have been a St Andrews Branch of RNLI which ceased for a time and was re-founded after the 1939-45 war. Air Marshal Sir Brian Baker, Mrs Underwood and Mrs Stewart Meiklejohn were very involved. Mrs Jean Tynte did 43 years service, many as President, and received the Silver Award. Mrs Barbro Scott was President from 1967 to 1993 and continued to be on the committee. In the 1960s and 1970s as much as £10,000 was raised annually; in the last five years the average has been about £7000.

Age Concern

Age Concern St Andrews Branch was started in 1953. Dr Rankin and Colonel Hawes were prime movers. The churches and many of the clubs such as Rotary contributed to an active service, and for many years volunteers carried out the Meals on Wheels delivery service. The chiropodists of the town offered free services to old people. There was a café, social events and an annual Christmas dinner. However, the Council has now taken over many of the services. Volunteers no longer participate in Meals on Wheels, and there is free chiropody for pensioners at the Health Centre.

The St Andrews Community Service

In the late 1960s a young woman called Jenny Sherwood came to live in St Andrews with her husband, who travelled a lot in his work, and their three young children who were under school age. She became ill soon after she arrived, and realised she did not know where to turn for help – her family lived far away and there had not been time to make friends. When she was able to get about again and meet up with other young mums, Jenny found she was not alone in this sort of problem. So a group set up a baby-sitting circle, and then a mothers' and toddlers' group at the Cosmos Centre.

The organisation St Andrews Community Service (always known as STACS) started officially in April 1972. Jenny felt there was still a need for more help, information and advice, so the '4848' phone line came into being. Here a team of volunteers were each on phone duty one day in fourteen. The phone line was transferred for twenty-four hours to that of the person on duty. The emphasis was on a Link service – what was to be done when on duty was to stay in for the day and answer all calls. Margaret Murray writes,

> At first the volunteers were apprehensive lest they received nothing but Samaritan-type calls – which they would have to transfer to Dundee Samaritans or elsewhere. However, the pattern turned out to be more mundane – baby sitting, lifts to hospital for visits or appointments, and general advice. The members of this group were Jenny Sherwood, Veronica Sullivan, Julie Poole, Jean Pumford, Isla Ashcroft, Linda Adamson, Kate Jackson, Elizabeth Wiffen, and Father Jock Dalrymple. As well as telephone volunteers there were other helpers who took a great pleasure in sorting out challenging requests and were prepared to tackle almost any problem.

As the years went by, other agencies took over some aspects of what was required. A Citizens' Advice Bureau was set up in St Andrews, and also Cruse (a North East Fife branch) for bereavement counselling. It became clear to STACS that lifts were the biggest need, so more volunteer drivers were recruited. Margaret MacGregor tells me that the current aim is to supply volunteer drivers who will take people with transport problems to hospital, for appointments or visiting. The driver waits to see his/her passengers home. There are also requests to be taken to airports. Margaret writes, 'I see our function as supplying a "friend" who will talk or listen, help in finding the place of the appointment in the vastness of Ninewells, and generally offer reassurance to people who are worried/lonely. There are about ten people who act as committee and in turn man the phone from 9 to 5. At present there are thirty drivers, but more are always needed.'

I think that this service is invaluable and is greatly appreciated. Hospital appointments may be at Kirkcaldy or Ninewells; the time involved may be lengthy, and the Hours STACS drivers devote to this duty must often be a real sacrifice. I have been very thankful on one occasion, not only for the practical help, but also for the kindness and support.

Charity shops

The first charity shop to be opened in St Andrews was Oxfam in Bell Street (1971); it was run by volunteers only, one of them being the organiser. In turn the excellent organisers were Nana Kerr, followed by Jill Thompson (wife of the Rector of Madras College), Mary Lindsay and then Pam Glencross.

This is an excerpt from a short article in The Citizen of 18 January 1978 when someone from Oxfam HQ paid a visit and reported: 'This is a splendid operation. If every Oxfam shop was as efficient and attractive as the St Andrews one is, we should have no worries. Mrs Glencross and her team have done excellent work.' The shop was noted for its teamwork. Most of the volunteers worked there regularly year after year. Nor was it staffed by people who had little else to do. One volunteer asked if she could come on Wednesday afternoons; she was a university lecturer and it was her only free time. In the 1980s the Woodwards did great service over many years, Joan being an expert in sorting and pricing bric-a-brac and Ferdy in pricing books. In 1997 Oxfam HQ decided to put in a paid supervisor, and as a result a number of the volunteers left. A string of other charity shops was set up, each staffed by volunteers: Dr Barnardos, Save the Children, Sue Ryder, Shelter, Imperial Cancer Research Fund, Cancer Research Campaign Scotland and British Heart Foundation. After running well for years, these shops are now finding it difficult to get sufficient volunteers. In addition to this, a National Trust for Scotland shop was opened in 1977, started by June Baxter and assisted by Gillian Falconer. It is open 10 a.m.-5 p.m. on six days a week from Easter to Christmas. It is staffed by a volunteer supervisor/ organiser and shifts of two volunteers. There was also a Red Cross Office in Burghers Close, but it shut down in the late 1990s; the office is now a room in the Town Hall, where medical aids are issued and first aid classes are held.

Citizens' Advice Bureau

This was set up in the Council Offices (in the old West Infants School) in January 1981 with Isla Ashcroft as Organiser on a part-time salary. She had previously trained for this in Edinburgh and elsewhere. In turn, she trained a team of volunteer assistants, some of whom had specialist knowledge. CAB was open five days a week from 10 a.m to 2 p.m. Every Monday evening there was a legal clinic at which the solicitors in the town gave their services on a rota. An initial interview and advice were free; if the enquirer wished to pursue the matter further, he/she went to a solicitor in the usual way. CAB was such a success that the opening hours were extended to 4 p.m. every weekday, with four staff there for each session. I recall having excellent advice from John Evans, a retired income tax inspector.

In summer 1986 a CAB branch office opened in Cupar, and in the autumn another was set up at Anstruther. The latter started slowly but then became busy; it was manned by a volunteer, Liz Thirkell. The St Andrews office was moved to 158 South Street, which was more comfortable, and warmer, but the premises were upstairs. A large amount of field information had been collated, and volunteers had gained expertise. At the time of the miners' strike (1973-4) the Council set up Rights Offices in Fife towns, with paid staff. When the strike and its effects were over, it seemed that the Council was offering a duplicate service and that, in the case of St Andrews, CAB and Rights offices should amalgamate at Cupar. There was an outcry in St Andrews, and a petition for CAB to stay here was signed by 4,000 people. The outcome was that in this area two offices were set up, one in Cupar and one in St Andrews under the name 'Citizens Advice and

Rights'. Some of the volunteers left, but among those who stayed on were John Hunter and Rosalind Hind. The office is now at St Mary's Place and, with volunteers and paid workers, offers the same services as CAB had so ably done for many years.

Enable

This is the name for the old Society for the Mentally Handicapped. The St Andrews Branch was inaugurated in 1971 by Keith and Isobel Neilson. Keith was Chairman for 21 years, and has been succeeded by Mrs Annal. The members met first in the Congregational Hall, then in the Victory Memorial Hall, and they now meet in the Holy Trinity Church Hall in Greenside Place.

Rymonth Housing

Keith Neilson led a campaign for a small complex for those needing a form of sheltered housing and care. Attractive premises were put up by the banks of the Kinnessburn, east of the bridge leading to Langlands Road. There is a house for fourteen residents of mixed ages from over sixteen to elderly. In addition there are two houses on the site for people who are semi-independent, one with three residents and the other with four. The Duchess of Kent opened Rymonth Housing in 1986. It is financed by the Department of Social Services, and residents pay towards their keep. Some of the residents go daily to a Centre at Dalgairn House, Cupar. Keith's wife, Isobel, is Chairman of the Friends of Rymonth Hostel. The Friends take residents out, and raise funds for such things as birthday and Christmas presents.

The St Andrews Committee for the Blind (Partially Sighted)

This Committee runs a weekly afternoon meeting for the Blind/Partially Sighted in Hope Park Church Hall. About thirty people come. The meetings take the form of social afternoons, with talks, table games and tea. In the summer there is an afternoon session of bowling at Kinburn. There is a Christmas party. The Social Work Department of Fife Council run St David's Centre in St Andrews as a training centre for the Blind.

The Hard of Hearing Club

Cecile Anderson gives the following report:

> In the Autumn of 1988 Mr Tom Gibson, who was a social worker based in Cupar, wrote to all the deaf or hard of hearing people in North East Fife who had previously contacted the Social Services for help with equipment. He felt that deaf people were often isolated because of their disablity and that having social contact with others in the same situation would be beneficial.
>
> He organised a meeting in the Victory Hall and about fourteen people turned up. It was decided to meet once a month, and he arranged for speakers to come and, with the help of the WRVS, a snack lunch was supplied. The Victory Hall was not a suitable venue, and others were tried before Mr Gibson obtained permission to meet in the Community Centre at Scooniehill.
>
> The numbers increased, and the talks were often related to problems that the deaf experience. Mr Gibson dropped a bombshell one day when he announced that he would not be able to continue with us much longer, and that we would have to elect a committee to run the club ourselves. Eventually a Chairperson, Secretary and Treasurer were found. The WRVS agreed to supervise the arrangements and without their help it would have been impossible to continue. The Hard of Hearing Club

meets on the second Wednesday of each month at noon. The average attendance is about twenty. The speaker talks for about thirty minutes before the WRVS serve lunch. A very wide range of topics has been covered.

St Andrews Branch Heartstart

This branch was begun in 1987 and has two objectives: to supply equipment such as defibrilators, and to train members to give basic help in cases of emergency.

Arthritis Care

The St Andrews group started ten years ago. There are about eighty members, and weekly meetings are held, mainly in the form of social events.

Other groups

The Pilgrim Foundation

This was set up by the late Patrick Cassells who had been a Fife Councillor. The purpose of this charity was to preserve the historic core of St Andrews, and Patrick's intention was to run the charity without overheads. He died in 1999, and the work has been continued by an able executive working group: Maries Cassells and Mary Freeborn (Trustees), and Isla Ashcroft, Sylvia Donaldson, Michael Tabert and Graham Smith, Secretary Ian Donald, Co-ordinator Michael Bonallack. A series of auctions has been held, both here and in the USA. In summer 2001 an internet golf package was very successful; £13,000 was raised through a gesture from Dunhill – an auction of a playing slot for an amateur to join the pros during the inaugural Dunhill Links Championship. The next package had some attractive lots, including short stays at prestigious hotels with a round of golf thrown in; Ryder Cup Captain Sam Torrance's putter with signature; and 'a significant bottle of Springbank Malt whisky'. Local businesses have given invaluable support.

Since October 2001 the Pilgrim Foundation has presented to Madras College Rector, Lindsay Matheson, cheques to the value of £12,000 towards the £60,000 needed to pay for the restoration of the handsome pillars in Madras College quadrangle. The work, undertaken by the well known firm of stonemasons, William Watson and Sons, is at present (end June 2002) more than one-third complete. The Foundation has donated sums amounting to £25,000 towards the Harbour Trust repairs.

Friends of the Pier

When St Andrews lost its Town Council, it retained the Harbour Trust. There is a long history of damage to the pier, and with difficulty the Trust had managed to find enough to meet the costs. However, the latest crisis came in 1997 when the Harbour Trust faced a huge estimate for extensive repairs. The pier was unsafe and was closed. An application was made to the Lottery Fund, which was willing to give an award providing the appeal and effort came from the community. In 1998 Donald McGregor of the Community Council organised sponsored St Andrews Day Celebrations, and the majority of those involved wanted the money raised to be given to the repair of the pier. Nan Taylor, who had been a councillor, organised The Pier Project by instituting a new body, Friends of the Pier. She envisaged a sort of Blue Peter Appeal; £17,000 was raised, with many local bodies giving generous amounts. Fife Environmental Trust donated £50,000 and Historic Scotland £2943; the Lottery Fund completed the package with £350,000. It is now November 2002 and most of the repairs are completed. Surely this is one of the most valuable and successful efforts.

Chapter 3

BRANCHES OF NATIONAL ASSOCIATIONS

Many of the St Andrews societies are branches of national or international bodies.

The Freemasons

I am indebted to the Grand Secretary and the Archivist of the High Lodge Edinburgh for information about Freemasonry at St Andrews, and to Mr J.E. McIntosh of Lodge St Andrew No. 25 for his help.

There is a letter in the minute book of the Lodge of Edinburgh dated 29 November 1599 stating that a general meeting of Masons was to be held in St Andrews on 12 January 1600. There are no subsequent records until 1720, but it seems that this Lodge of stonemasons was the predecessor to the Lodge St Andrew – although there is no evidence of direct lineage. From 1160, when the building of the Cathedral began, lodges of masons had been at work here.

Lodge St Andrew No. 25 (originally and briefly entitled Lodge 27), which still continues to meet in St Andrews, was a founder member of the Grand Lodge of Scotland; the meeting above was one of a series which subscribed to the first St Clair Charter. The meetings were held successively in Edinburgh, St Andrews, Haddington, Atcheson-Haven and Dunfermline, and as a result The Grand Lodge of Scotland was instituted in 1736. Lodge St Andrew was registered in the roll. There is interesting information in a rare book by George R.T.E. Wilson, *History of the Lodge St Andrew No. 25*, published by Joseph Cook and Son in 1894. Wilson, who was Secretary, states that 'early papers of the Lodge have gone a-missing'. The extant minute books date from

October 1720 when there were thirty members; within the next hundred years a total of seven hundred names were entered, and continuing up to 1894 Wilson worked out that nearly two thousand brethren were recorded.

A well-known Brother was the Earl of Mar and Kellie (1824), and 19th-century officials were: Masters (Royal Worshipful Masters, usually abbreviated in reports to RWM) – Stuart Grace (1795-96 and 1810) and his son Charles Grace (1813-14 and 1823-24), Cathcart Dempster (1799), Hugh Lyon Playfair (1818), William Moncrieff (1821-22), George Cruikshanks (1841-53 and 1858-61), Walter Thomas Milton (1862-65), John McPherson (1866-69), David Stevenson Ireland (1872-74 and 1881-86), John Whyte-Melville (Provincial Grand Master of Fife and Kinross); Depute Masters – William Rusack (1890), who was also Treasurer, John Paterson (ex-Provost), and John MacGregor (Provost 1894). However, the Lodge has always been an artisan Lodge; there are records over many of the earlier years of the difficulties in obtaining officials who were sufficiently literate.

Up to 1858 the identified meeting places were The Black Bull, at the east end of South Street on the corner of Huckster's Wynd, at the old Town Hall, also a Lodge at 110 South Street. On 23 May 1781 the Lodge St Andrew, together with eight other Lodges met at the Town Hall and processed to the ceremony of laying the foundation stone of St Leonards Hall (the house later bought by Provost Playfair and then to become part of St Leonards School). This is part of a poem written by a Brother who was present:

We marched off slow time, while the bells did ring
And music most softly did play,
Till we came to the ground where we all stood around
While our Master the first stone did lay.

He continues with lines rejoicing that the Brethren were so fortunate as to have this meeting place (i.e. St Leonards Hall) of their own. In

1810 they sold all their property and, by making a payment of £10 to the Council, acquired rights and privileges to meet at the Town Hall for all time.

When the new Town Hall was built in 1857, according their rights the Brethren were permitted to have premises above the Council Chamber of the Town Hall, but to be provided at their own expense. They held a bazaar and raised £42, but the Lodge and its fine furbishings cost as much as £1249-0-1d. The dome of the Lodge may be seen if you stand in South Street by the door which leads to the Sharp aisle of Holy Trinity church. Lodge St Andrew No. 25 is open to the public on St Andrew's Day. Mounting first fifteen steps and then fifty winding steps, you reach the 'new' Lodge, which has now been in use for almost 150 years. The ceiling of the dome is unique. It was painted by Wilkie Graham of Dundee and completed in 1904. In the centre of the blue sky is a depiction of the All Seeing Eye. Below, in a circle, are the following representations: part of St Andrews Cathedral, St Mark's Venice, Rome, the Tiber River, the Sphinx, Ancient Egyptian prehistoric dwelling, Jacob's Ladder, Solomon's Temple, Indian Temple, Japanese buildings, Chinese buildings, and so round to St Andrew. There are stained-glass windows and many objects of interest. When the Town Hall was altered in 1957, a separate entrance was made to the Lodge, and it also serves as a fire escape.

Aims and practices

George Cruikshanks was a member of Lodge St Andrew No. 25 for over fifty years and Royal Worshipful Master for fifteen years. On 18 July 1862 after 'an excellent supper provided by Brother Davidson of the Royal Hotel' there was a presentation to Brother George of a testimonial in the form of a silver jug and inkstand. In his speech of acknowledgement Brother Cruikshanks expressed succinctly the primary aims of the Masons: 'to promote the practice of every moral and social virtue calculated to promote human happiness in the world, and inspiring the hope of a more perfect felicity in the next.'

Quoting from Wilson: 'As an apprentice passed to a fellowship, and for his zeal, diligence and capacity was raised to the sublime degree of Master Mason' he was presented with a diploma which carried at the top a view of the Cathedral ruins and at the foot a representation of St Andrew on the Cross.

There is good information about the uniform of the brethren. They wore elaborate aprons and sashes, the colours of which changed in time from dark blue with gold frieze to light blue with silver trimmings and then to dark blue with silver. In 1847 new jewels were procured (and at other times donated) for the office bearers, and were worn on special occasions. Other gifts were received: 'A bible printed in 1640 was presented by Bro. James Carstaris [*sic*] merchant and was still in use in 1894'. The Brethren, dressed 'in full masonic costume, with clothing and jewels draped with crape' appeared at the funerals of the late Lord Dalhousie and the late Lord Murray, and they attended many funerals in St Andrews and other parts of Fife. At the funeral of Bro. William Jamieson, brother for over fifty years and Chaplain for twenty-eight years, 'on the coffin were placed a handsome jewel, and a silver compass set with jewels'. At another funeral of a mason, each of the Brethren dropped a white flower into the grave.

On 16 October 1845 a deputation 'in proper masonic costume – viz: black clothes, white cravat, white gloves and white vest – journeyed to Cupar to assist the P.G.M. to open his Lodge in the County Hall there.' In 1866 the costume of the Tyler is described as 'an elaborately braided coat, velvet knee-breeches, white silk stockings, silver-buckled shoes, and bear-skin helmet. On the front of the headgear the number and name of the Lodge is lettered in gold.' The Tyler was the outside watchman of the Lodge and carried a snake-shaped sword with a pointed end so that he could ensure that no one was hiding in the eaves (eaves-dropping).

The charitable nature of the Society is shown in the minutes; for example, 'In 1880s on instigation of Bro. D.S. Ireland R.W.M., a fund was set up (apart from the ordinary funds) and invested'; from the annual interest, annual payments were made 'to necessitous and deserving members of the Lodge, their widows and children'. In 1801 a resolution was passed 'to subscribe £100 sterling to the fund that lately appeared in this place for the purpose buying up a stock of corns [*sic*] to be manufactured into malt and to be sold to the inhabitants at the Market Place.' The benevolence of the Lodge and of other organisations was greatly affected when the 1808 Act was passed for the regulation of Friendly Societies.

For a century the Lodge met annually to celebrate the Festival of St John on 27 December. They held a torchlight procession through the city, accompanied by the Band of the Local Militia. They then adjourned to the Lodge for a dinner 'in the shape of twopenny pies and bottles of punch'; musicians were hired to play at the dinner. Later this event was held on St Andrew's Day instead of St John's Day. Another special event was an annual ball. Wilson refers to 'a very successful revival' of the ball in 1889. There were constantly communications with other Lodges. Members were sent as representatives to occasions elsewhere and likewise representatives came to St Andrews.

Special occasions in St Andrews

In 1809 the Brethren took part in the ceremony of laying the foundation stone of the Ladies Hot and Cold Baths. Theses public baths were a financial venture by Captain Jackson; they were built in the Scores, west of the Castle (where the house 'Ladies Lake' now stands). They were an amazingly early innovation: marine baths supplying hot and cold sea water, with accommodation for visiting parties.

25 October 1809: His Majesty's Jubilee was marked by a torchlight procession and celebration at the Lodge.

21 July 1848: The Brethren patronised the theatre. They walked in procession from the Town Hall to the theatre accompanied by a Band of Music and 'were highly gratified by the night's entertainment, the house being crowded to over-flowing'. Again, in July 1855 and in August 1857 the Brothers visited the Theatre, described as the 'Queen's Theatre' and 'managed by the Brothers Gomersal and Morton'. (If only there had been a note of where the theatre was and what was played!)

13 July 1853: The foundation stone of the New Club House (the Royal and Ancient) was laid with Masonic honours. The Brethren met in City Hall, processed three hundred strong to Madras College accompanied by three bands of music, and via South Street and North Street to the site of the Club House. The ceremony of the laying of the stone then took place. First there was a blessing on the undertaking from the Chaplain; then a bottle of current coins and newspapers was placed in the cavity. The stone was lowered;

> the usual implements having been placed on the stone it was declared perfect and the PGM gave it three knocks and implored the God Almighty to shower his blessing on the work. Agreeable to the very ancient usage of masonry on such occasions, the corn, wine and oil were then poured on the stone. [The corn symbolised nourishment, the wine refreshment and the oil joy.] The cheers of the vast assembly rent the air, and the bands adding to the heartstrung strains at the same time, the view of the assembled multitude was divine.

2 June 1858: The foundation stone of the New Town Hall was laid. Previous to this ceremony the Lodge assisted in the opening of the Provincial Grand Lodge of Fife at Madras College. Then, accompanied by four instrumental bands, the members of the

Lodge processed to the Town Hall site. Here the foundation stone was laid by Brother John Whyte-Melville (now Grand Mason of Scotland). Later a company of 250 masons sat down to dinner at Madras College.

24 June 1861: Twenty of the Brethren accompanied by the City Instrumental Band went to Stirling to assist in the laying of the foundation stone for the National Wallace Memorial at Abbey Craig.

26 April 1867: At St Andrews the laying of the foundation stone for College Hall took place with masonic honours. Sixty of the Lodge St Andrew and representatives from other Lodges brought the number of brethren to 277.

In 1873 the Lodge joined in a procession to do honour to the launching of the new lifeboat, 'The Ladies Own'.

19 July 1882: The foundation stone for the Gibson Hospital was laid. The building was bequeathed by James Gibson of Duloch who ordained that it would be built to the standard of his own house, and by its terms was to provide a home and care for elderly and indigent citizens of St Andrews who had been born in the city. (These terms can no longer be observed.) The Brethren processed from Madras College,

> attending (in order) were The St Andrews Brass Band, the Provost, Magistrates and Town Council, The Ancient City Court of Foresters, St Andrews Golf Club, St Regulus Lodge of Good Templars, the Masonic Lodges in order – the junior first, the St Andrews Flute Band, and last J. Whyte-Melville who was to lay the stone.

The Royal Arch, Chapter Josiah 1780-1830

In 1970 a small manuscript was found in the Lodge, edited with comments by Cecil Hill, under the title of 'The Masonic

Commonplace book of John Gourlay'. Gourlay was initiated into the Lodge of St Andrew on 27 March 1778, and it seems he was well respected among the Brethren. He was initiated into the Royal Arch Chapter of Dundee on 16 October 1780. Along with James Methven and John Braid he was one of the founder masters of the Royal Arch Chapter in St Andrews on 26 October 1780. This Lodge took the name Josiah. John Gourlay's book is $4^{1}/_{2}$in x $7^{1}/_{2}$in., and there are 104 pages. We learn that 'singing was greatly enjoyed at ceremonies and meetings'; he has given us the words of a number of songs. He has also recorded the format, the costume worn, the procedure, the addresses and the prayers used on masonic occasions: for the Ceremonies of Consecration and Dedication, of installation, of funerals, at the admission of a brother and at the constitution of a Lodge.

One of the last entries he made was 'The Chapter being closed with the usual solemnities and anthem sung, The Grand Master and other deputations accompanied by Josiah's Principals and a number of Companions retired to the Black Bull and enjoyed themselves with that harmony and brotherly love which ever distinguished masons.' On 22 January 1830 John Gourlay, who was by then a sick man, signed the motion dissolving the Lodge benefit society. He died on 13 February 1831. The discovery of his commonplace book was valuable as there seem to be few old records of the Royal Arch Chapter Josiah, but it continues to meet.

Lodge Union No. 542 lasted only a short time (28 November 1873 to 1881). It is said that Sir Hugh Lyon Playfair wanted his own Lodge and formed it with his friends from the R. and A., using the Lodge Room in St Leonards. The Lodge failed to continue after the death of Sir Hugh Lyon Playfair, and the office-bearers' jewels were purchased and presented to Lodge St Andrew 25 by Bro. Milton, past Master and ex-Provost of St Andrews. Mr McIntosh writes,

> Lodge St Andrew 25 in the twentieth century continued to be a central figure in St Andrews with a continual

growth in membership, but with the introduction of alternative organisations, i.e. the Rotary Club, Round Table and the like, the proportion of membership from the town has steadily declined. The reduction of local members has been greatly offset by an influx of members from the surrounding towns and cities. The membership from Dundee continues to rise (Lodge St Andrew sticking to the old standards?) – a reversal of when Gourlay went to Dundee!

The Town Hall keeps us engaged in looking after the premises. The benevolent works of the Lodge still continue. The Lodges in Fife support C.H.A.S. in Kinross and many other charitable causes during each financial year. Lodge St Andrew will have disbursed a figure of something near £1000 by the end of the financial year to causes outwith Masonic Charities.

Looking back on these records, one is impressed by the great days of ceremony and brotherhood, of loyalty and pride in the city, and of Christian faith.

Thistle and Rose Free Gardeners of St Andrews

Recently, a small packet of papers was discovered in the Town Hall and is now in the Archivist Department there. It seems that this Lodge had split off from the freemasons and formed an independent Lodge. Letters written between 1823 and 1834 show the Thistle and Rose acting as a benefit society to its members and their families. There is one from a doctor telling the society of the death of a member, 'leaving a poor widow'. One from a surgeon reports the injury of John Peattie, gardener. Some letters are concerned with requests for loans from the Lodge, or the repayment of loans. One who had to repay gave over his land and wrote, 'I am left with scarcely a farthing.' On a happier note, there is an invitation from the Olive Lodge at Cupar to its annual

Festival on 5 July: 'the procession leaves at 3 o'clock.

The Thistle and Rose was disbanded when the National Insurance Act was passed.

The St Andrews Branch of the British Legion

This was formed in 1932, and the first report is of its participation in the British Legion Silver Poppy Trophy Competition. Its headquarters were hired rooms at 105 South Street; then it rented an old malt barn at Wilson's Brewery in Argyle Street. Here the British Legion had room for social events and also to set up a rifle range. Over one doorway was painted 'The Better 'Ole'. In 1937 the first Conference of the British Legion was held in St Andrews. The St Andrews Branch eventually acquired St Mary's Church in St Mary's Place. In 1959 the Legion announced that they had spent £11,500 on converting it to the Victory Memorial Hall, and it was handed over to the Town Council.

The British Legion was very active between the two world wars. In the University Library archives there is a photograph of the St Andrews Branch in the early 1930s, marching along South Street. Heading the procession is the President who carries the insignia on a cushion, with standard bearers on either side of him. I think the central figure may be Captain David Rusack, who inaugurated the branch here.

One year, representatives paid a visit to St George's Church at Ypres. Back in St Andrews they gave lunches for the unemployed and held social events for ex-servicemen. They have constantly raised money and siphoned it through SSAFA (Soldiers Sailors Air Force Association) to help families in need. They are also at the heart of the annual event of the Remembrance Day service at the War Memorial. The Prince of Wales came to St Andrews in 1932 and held an inspection. By 1935 the numbers were up to a hundred and forty. The British Legion was in abeyance during the World War II, but re-formed when it was over. In 1991 Andrew Brown, who had been a staunch member, was made a life member. The present President is Dr A.H. McKerrow, who has been a member for fifty years, and the Chairman is John Rankin, son of the late Dr Rankin, Minister of Holy Trinity.

It surprised me to know that the British Legion had a Women's Section, but I have no information on this.

Rotary Clubs and Inner Wheel

Rotary International was founded in Chicago in 1905 by a lawyer, Paul Harris. He discussed his plan to form a club with three men, a coal merchant, a mining engineer and a merchant tailor. The first two years of activities were entirely social. In 1907 Paul agreed to be President and outlined his plans for the future: to increase the size of the Chicago Club; to set up a Rotary Club in every important town in the USA; to change the emphasis of the club so that it became outward-looking and gave service to those in need. It is incredible that this small beginning could have spread to the establishment of flourishing Rotary clubs in cities and towns in countries all over the world, and that these clubs could have achieved such important results. A summary gives this information:

> Rotary is a service organisation of business and professional leaders united world-wide who help those in need, encourage high ethical standards in all vocations, and work towards understanding and peace. Rotary is more than 1.2 million service-minded men and women (women were admitted after a change in the constitution in 1989) belonging to 27,000 Rotary Clubs in 150 countries. Rotarians meet weekly to enjoy each other's fellowship and discuss ways to serve others. Rotary is compassion for the underprivileged, the ill and the disabled who benefit from over 50,000 Rotary Club service projects in the world each year. Rotary foundation gives more than £21 million every year to

educational and humanitarian programmes which promote international understanding.

St Andrews Rotary

The first Rotary Club in Scotland was formed in Glasgow in March 1912. Subsequently Rotary clubs were founded in Edinburgh (1912), Perth (1917), Dundee, Inverness and Kirkcaldy (1922), Cowdenbeath (1923). On 21 October 1927 a party of gentlemen met in the Victoria Café, St Andrews. They were Peter L. Forgan, cabinet maker, David C. Mackie, ladies outfitter, Andrew D. Peddie, gentlemen's outfitter, William Watson, burgh surveyor, and Alfred Scott, architect. Two Rotarians from Dundee had agreed to discuss the aims of Rotary. It was decided to form a branch at St Andrews, and they drew up a list of twenty-five possible members. There was a good response, and the first meeting was held at Rusacks Hotel with D.C. Mackie in the chair and Andrew Peddie acting secretary. The first Rotarian lunch was held at Fisher's Hotel (Imperial/Argyl) on 24 November, and Dr Orr was elected President. The speaker was W.S. Draffen from Dundee. On that day the St Andrews Branch of Rotary International was inaugurated. Since then, many well-known St Andreans such as Johnston Paton, Peter Swankie, Hunter Scott, George Caithness and Colin Risk have contributed to the series of fundraising efforts. One significant local one has been the endowment of University bursaries for young Americans, and making contact with these students. The first sight of Father Christmas in the lives of many children who have lived in St Andrews may have been in South Street when Rotary made their collection annually (now done by Round Table).

Rotary Club of St Andrews Kilrymont

This Club was inaugurated on 23 August 1996 at the St Andrews Golf Hotel with a membership of twenty-five. Colin Risk and Dr George

Caithness of the St Andrews Rotary, the mother club, oversaw its foundation. Office bearers elected were President Angus Peter, S.U.P. George Donaldson, Secretary Don Walker and Treasurer Ian Lumsdaine. The Charter dinner was held at the Golf Hotel on 28 November, and the Club continues to meet there weekly on Tuesday evenings.

All its fund-raising events are independent projects, and George Donaldson tells me that up to date (i.e. in five years) Rotary Kilrymont has raised over £50,000 for various causes and groups. Of those he has listed, the following are described elsewhere in this book: Duke of Edinburgh Award Scheme Madras College; Boys Brigade; St Andrews Pipe Band; St Andrews Youth Club Project; 8th Fife Scouts; St Andrews Colts FC; Dogs for the Hard of Hearing; Enable; The Byre Theatre and also Gibson House; the St Andrews Youth Café project, and cancer research. In many cases the donation was put to a specific cause – for instance, the one to the Pipe Band was a bale of tartan for kilts. Donations were given to Operation Inasmuch (an ecumenical charity run by the churches); RNLI Anstruther, the Earl Haig Fund, North-east Fife Home Start, the Flic Flac Gymnasium Club, the Carolyn Burns School of Dancing, Blind Bowlers, Ninewells Hospital Childrens Ward for Easter gifts, and playgroups. In addition, in its involvement with the work within Rotary International, this new Club has contributed to appeals resulting from disasters, earthquakes and floods, and also Polio Plus.

Inner Wheel, St Andrews and District Club

This international club originated through Rotary in Manchester in 1924. Membership was restricted to wives or unmarried sisters of Rotarians, but it is now open to female partners or relatives of Rotarians. Today there are 110,000 members in a hundred countries. The aims are to promote true friendship, encourage personal service and to foster international understanding.

In the summer of 1948 Mr and Mrs Winkler visited St Andrews; he gave an address to the Rotarians and Mrs Winkler, the Chairman of Inner Wheel District 1 & 2, met wives of the Rotarians. As a result of this The St Andrews Inner Wheel Club was formed on 27 October 1948. There were twenty-two founder members; Mrs A.G Scott (wife of the architect) was elected President, and Mrs L. Auchterlonie Secretary. Mrs T. Black, Mrs J.B.Armit, Mrs A.M. Ness, Mrs Milne (Station Hotel), Mrs Cooper and Mrs Buick were the other committee members. The Charter was presented at an afternoon function in the Victoria Cafe on 3 June 1949. The Presidential Badge was presented by Tom Morrow, and the reading desk by Aly Ness. The gavel was made and presented by Laurie Auchterlonie, and the visitors' book was given by Mrs Auchterlonie. There were fifty members and guests present.

Margaret Murray became a member in 1970 and was President for a number of years. I quote some significant words from her: 'The Club started in a quiet and unassuming way, but being a university town we had ample opportunity to give hospitality to overseas students. Our members were involved in other organisations. This enabled us to help each other with local charities and to give much service. This is still the pattern in the Club. We work closely with the Rotarians, and they are ever helpful to us. Coffee mornings with stalls, whist drives, evening work parties, raffles, etc., helped us to build up a Charities Fund which was opened in the bank in 1959/60.'

Margaret Murray also gave me some recent examples of the ways in which the aims of the Club have been fulfilled.

> Last year we held a fund-raising coffee morning for Badaguish Holiday Centre near Aviemore, where disabled young people can experience an outdoor holiday; a soup lunch raised money for Rachel House, a children's Hospice. Stamps have been collected for 'Hearing Dogs', clothes for Blythswood to go to Eastern

> Europe, and money raised for Water Aid. Locally we help with a trolley service at the Hospital and arrange flowers on the wards. We had a very successful party in March for the elderly. Many of us help to entertain students from overseas. Since 2000 we have a link with a newly chartered club in Bulgaria. E-mail makes corresponding with them easy and we are learning about life in Bulgaria.

The following is revealing: 'Our members are involved in a wide variety of organisations in the town and call on other members to help from time to time. Because of the comparatively small size of the town, people from all sorts of groups get to know each other.' My comments are that, in the past, although church congregations were – on the whole – existing and worshipping and working separately, the town societies brought together a cross-section of people. In addition, because there has been, over the years, a stream of newcomers settling here, whether as members of the University staff or to live here in retirement, fresh support and fresh ideas have kept the societies alive.

The Club had its fiftieth birthday in June 1999. There were fifty members. They no longer wore hats and gloves, which were obligatory in the early days.

Lastly Margaret Murray refers to 'the friendship and fun obvious at our meetings', and the many activities of the club, such as outings, golf, curling, bridge, and even a recent frisbee match against Rotarians! The pattern of monthly afternoon meetings, tea and speaker has been changed to evenings to accommodate members who work. This brought an increase in the numbers.

St Andrews and District Branch of the National Association of Round Tables of Great Britain and Ireland

At the British Industries Fair at Birmingham in 1927 the Prince of Wales said, 'The young business and professional men of this country must get together round the table, adopt methods that have proved so sound in the past, adapt them to the changing needs of the times and, where-ever possible, improve them.' One young man took note of this. He was Erminio William Louis Marchesi, born in January 1898 of an Irish mother and a Swiss father. He had joined the Army in 1914 when he was under-age, had been torpedoed off the Cape of Good Hope and then spent ten hours in the sea. In 1927 he became a member of the Norwich Rotary, and giving his maiden speech he developed the idea of a club for young men only. So 'Mark', as he was always known, began the RTBI, which fast spread to all regions of Britain and, as Round Table International, to over forty countries. As Secretary to Norwich RT, Mark started the magazine *News and Views.* He was President 1935-36, and made contact with twenty to thirty other clubs. He served in the 1939-45 war and then continued his devoted work for the Tablers. He died in December 1968.

There are at present 900 active Tables across the British Isles, with 12,000 members spread across the regions. The lower age limit is 18, and until recently the retiring age was 40; in May 1998 it was extended to 45. A branch meets regularly twice a month. The Aims and Objects are as follows:

1. To develop the acquaintance of young men through the medium of their various occupations.
2. To emphasise the fact that one's calling offers an excellent medium of service to the community.
3. To cultivate the highest ideals in business, professional and civic traditions.
4. To recognise the worthiness of all legitimate occupations and to dignify each by his own precept and example.
5. To further the establishment of peace and goodwill in international relationships.
6. To further these objects by meetings, lectures, discussions and other activities.

The first Round Table in Scotland was formed in Glasgow in 1938. St Andrews Round Table was inaugurated on 9 November 1962, and the charter was granted on 9 September 1963. There is a list of founder members and their occupations, among them Dr Delaney, Alistair Matheson, Grant Milne, Glen Pride and Alexander Gilchrist. The first elected officials were Chairman William Smith (dental surgeon), George Watson, Robert Murray (accountant), Graham McNicol (solicitor). Although Tables prefer to support local and regional charities, the 60th Anniversary appeal in 1987 raised, nationally, £800,000 for the Anthony Nolan Bone Marrow Clinic, and later another £300,000 for the same cause. Round Table is one of the largest contributors to Children in Need.

XT Club

This mysterious name turns out to be a continuation Club of the Round Table, for members who have reached the age limit and wish to continue the fellowship. Ideals and activities remain the same.

Ladies Circle

This is the female counter part of the Tablers. It was started in St Andrews by Moira Delaney and Mary Wilson on 13 November 1964. It continues to meet fortnightly with only a small membership.

Soroptomist International St Andrews and District

Mr Stewart Morrow, a professional organiser who had established many branches of Rotary in America, was challenged to set up a club for women and did so in Oakland in 1921. It was given the name Soroptomist from the Latin words *soror* (sister) and *optimus* (the best). The first meeting of the St Andrews and District Club was held on 12 October 1960 at the Athol Hotel. The first President of the Club was

Susan Solman, physiotherapist, then Molly Cumming, University Accommodation Officer. The occupations of those who were Presidents shows a good mix: a doctor, a psychologist, a social worker, teachers, shop owners, and others.

Meetings are held fortnightly and a varied syllabus is arranged. Topics range from health care and environmental awareness to education issues. One of the objectives is to strive for human rights and in particular to advance the status of women (it was founded at the time when women had gained the right to vote.) The members strive to contribute to international understanding and universal friendship. The Club has made a link with Latvia, and locally holds regular international nights. Some of the projects have been studies of recycling, of water facilities in Fife, and of well women/breast-screening. This is a service organisation and raises funds for various causes; it raised £1000 for the renal unit at Ninewells, and also money for funding Macmillan nurses, and has contributed to many local and national causes.

St Andrews Probus

In early 1976 the Convener of the Rotary Club of St Andrews Vocational Service Committee wrote to various people explaining that he had been notified of a possible need of a club for retired business and professional men in the St Andrews area. The name PROBUS came from PROfessional and BUSiness Men. Clubs under the name of 'Probus' had already been formed in various places in Fife. The object of the club is to provide a regular meeting place during winter months, where good fellowship can be enjoyed, together with the stimulation and interest of a talk from a local or visiting speaker. The Rotary Club invited those interested to a preliminary meeting on 23 March 1976 at MacArthur's restaurant, South Street, when members of the Leven and District Branch of Probus would speak about Probus and answer questions. At this meeting it was decided to start a branch in St Andrews, and a steering committee was formed, with Dr Alan Fordyce as Chairman and six others including Donald Macrae.

A notice was put in *The St Andrews Citizen*, and the response was tremendous. The first meeting of the St Andrews Probus was held at MacArthur's on Tuesday 27 April 1976, and the subscription rates were fixed and business arrangements made. In the first year fortnightly morning meetings were held for ten months, but this changed to monthly meetings from October through to April. The venue moved from MacArthur's to Rusacks and finally in 1994 to the St Andrews Golf Hotel. In 1978 Pitlochry Theatre outings were started and proved to be very popular. In 1981 the first golf outing is recorded, and the Club joined the Probus Club Golfing Society in 1986. In 1985 the first luncheon was established and there have been many prominent speakers over the years.

Although Probus is not a fund-raising organisation, for many years an annual donation has been made to various worthwhile causes. Roger Chick writes: 'It is a thriving club with members enjoying the fellowship of friends and like-minded people. At each meeting, after coffee and biscuits, a speaker gives a talk on one of many far-ranging topics, increasing the bounds of knowledge.'

St Andrews Branch of the United Nations

In 1933 a branch of the League of Nations was formed in St Andrews. It may have been initiated by Professor Turnbull. The first President was Sir James Irvine, who was succeeded in 1935 by J.D. Mc Petrie, Rector of Madras College, and in 1939 by the Revd W.L. Coulthard of St Leonard's church. There is no further information, but I am told that subsequently there was a branch of the United Nations, presumably in place of the above. When Lavinia Hunter settled in St Andrews in 1981 she found this had faltered and, together with Margot Waterston and others, she re-formed it. There are some student members, and in the present state of world affairs the members are seeking support. Bulletins are received from headquarters in London, and a main conference is held annually.

St Andrews Merchants' Association

Gordon Christie, son of James Christie, merchant, was born 'within an iron shot of the West Port', and is a fifth-generation St Andrean. He recalls attending, with his father, the first St Andrews civil air display at the West Sands in 1919. He was proprietor of the well-known cycle and toy-shop in Market Street, and retired in 1975 to allow himself more time for research into the history of St Andrews in which he has a deep interest and wide knowledge. He became a member of the Merchants' Association in May 1941. From his collection of papers and cuttings comes the following brief summary.

On 3 December 1903 a meeting was held in the Council Chambers with ex-Bailie Aikman called to the chair. After discussion a motion was put forward by Mr R. Officer in favour of forming a St Andrews Shopkeepers' Association. This was seconded by Mr D. Brown and was passed unanimously. Ex-Bailie Aikman was elected President, Mr A. Haxton Treasurer and Mr William MacDougall Secretary. The name was changed to 'The St Andrews Merchants' Association' at the February 1914 AGM. The annual subscription was ls. The objects of the Association were:

- to promote the principles of sound business
- to consult with and advise any members on any subjects which would advance the general interest of the Association
- to become affiliated with the Chamber of Trade and any other similar organisation
- to promote such functions as are deemed conducive to the increase of social inter-course between all members.

Some of the concerns of the Association and matters which have been taken up are as follows. The Government Shop Act of 1912 was complex and necessitated calling a great many meetings. In 1921 and for many years after that, protests on the high prices of electricity were made. In 1933 the need for a Tourist Guide was first discussed. This Guide was published in 1934. It includes a plan of the golf courses, a street plan by architect John Cunningham, and some of the features of the town. Tourist leaflets and revised guides were published at intervals over the years. The Tourist Office in St Andrews was, of course, important to the Merchants, and in the 1950s was manned by Senior Citizens. There is a close liaison between the Association and the present Council's Tourist Board. In November 1977 Gordon Christie suggested that St Andrews should issue a free street map, and this met with approval. This objective was achieved when the Saint Andrews Society was inaugurated at Gordon Christie's instigation. In 1980 the founder members of this society had the expertise to lay out the history of St Andrews, which was printed on the reverse of the map, and the Merchants gave permission to use their 1936 map with some alterations to update it. This history sheet with map has been a great boon. By 1982 70,000 had been produced and, and reprinting has continued at intervals.

In the early days the topic of the shop holidays was discussed, and a suggestion was made that Christmas Day should be a half-holiday, but this was not agreed. When I came here in 1950 the shops were closed on Christmas Day, all day Sunday, on Thursday afternoons (shop half-day holiday) and on local holidays. Nowadays most shops are open on Thursday afternoons, and a large number are open on local holidays and on Sundays.

For centuries the Lammas Market has been held annually on the second week in August, in my time in the Market Place, Church Street, Church Square and the length of South Street. Periodically, it has been a topic of discussion and complaint by the Merchants' Association. The same applies to the question of street traders.

As a result of the Business Premises Order 1941, a Fire Watching

Order was instituted; meetings were held about Fire Prevention. In 1943 there were discussions on the siting of shops on the new housing area. After 1960 strong protests were made from time to time regarding applications by various building societies for premises which were considered prime sites for shops.

A useful film was shown on the question of security, and an early warning system was made available. There is great concern today about vandalism, particularly the breaking of shop windows, and there is pressure for security cameras to be installed.

But by far the greatest concerns have been the questions of traffic, of one-way traffic systems, and of parking. More recently the possibility of traffic-free zones had arisen; many merchants feel this would lead to a loss of trade.

In the last decades there have been recurrent protests over the Council's assessments of rateable values in St Andrews. This affects not only merchants who own the property from which they trade, but also those who lease it. The advent of supermarkets hit the small shops hard, but high rates and rents have been even more damaging. The rates here are higher per square foot than in Rose Street, Edinburgh. One family business after another in St Andrews has been forced to close down, and has usually been replaced by a branch of a multiple store. The character of the town as a shopping centre has changed more rapidly in the last decade than ever before.

As for the social side, the first excursion took place in 1905, to Inverness with dinner at the Royal Hotel. In 1909 a three-day golf tournament was held; there were forty-eight entrants. Golf professional Harry Vardon won the first prize, and L.B. Ayton took sixth prize. In 1924 the members went to the Wembley Exhibition. The total cost per person was 35/- which included rail fare, breakfast, lunch, a drive to places of interest and entry to the Exhibition.

Andrew Aikman died in 1932; as founder and President of the Association and Provost of St Andrews 1914-1918, due honours were paid to him. From 1920 Mr John B. Armit took a leading part in the affairs of the Association, in particular arrangements for the annual excursions from 1925 to 1933. He retired from business in 1951 and received a handsome tribute. In 1941 Mr W.D. Campbell, the Secretary, was obliged to resign and he was presented with a gold watch, a token of gratitude for his work over thirty years. He was made the first Life Member of the Association. In 1976 Mr Gordon Christie, who joined the Association in 1941, was made an Honorary Life Member.

St Andrews Business Club

I have my information from Mr R.A. Murphy who has been Secretary since 1980 and was President 1991-92. This Club, which is a member of the Association of Business Clubs, was founded on 28 January 1950 through the Dundee Business Club, primarily through one of its members, a Mr William Paterson. I have a note of its fourth annual dinner in February 1966 when Mr S.R.F. (Stan) Robertson was President. This function continues to be the major event of the Club; the attendance is usually about one hundred. In 1983 the constitution was amended to allow ladies to join the Club.

The Club usually met at MacArthurs in South Street, then it moved to the Four Woods Restaurant and since 1997 has met at the Old Course Hotel. Recently, so that more members might attend, the meetings have alternated between a breakfast or lunch meeting and an evening meeting. One speaker is usually a prominent businessman and the second gives a humorous talk. I have a list of the Presidents from 1950 to 2001, which includes many well-known names. The first was George Bruce; the Revd Charles Armour was President from 1958-59. Mr Kenneth Smith was Secretary for many years and also President.

The Club continues, but Mr Murphy tells me he learned recently that the Dundee and the Edinburgh City Business Clubs have been wound up.

Moving the Old Catholic Church, October 1901.

(Cowie Collection, courtesy St Andrews University Library)

St Andrews Archery Club, c. 1895.

(Courtesy St Andrews Preservation Trust)

Ladies' Swimming Pool, c. 1911
(Courtesy St Andrews Preservation Trust)

The Bute Medical and Bell Pettigrew Museum, c. 1915.
(Courtesy St Andrews University Library)

St Andrews Ladies' Golf Club, c. 1890.
(Courtesy St Andrews Preservation Trust)

Royal and Ancient Clubhouse.
(Courtesy Peter Adamson)

Church Parade, Lodge St Andrews no 25, c. 1900.
(Courtesy St Andrews Preservation Trust)

A selection of Masonic emblems. (Courtesy J.E. MacIntosh)

Sailing Club, East Sands, 2002.
(Courtesy Lyn Moir)

Professor Bell Pettigrew's Flying Machine – reproduced by Professor John Tucker from Bell Pettigrew's article in 9th edition of Enclyopedia Britannica.

Kinburn Bowling Club. (Courtesy Brian Jeffreys)

Renaissance Group, November 1974.
(Courtesy Peter Adamson)

St Andrews Pipe Band, St Andrew's Day 1980.
(Courtesy St Andrews Preservation Trust)

May Morning, 2002, at the Castle Pool. (Courtesy Tom Finnie)

St Andrews Angling Club. (Courtesy Keith Neilson)

Chapter 4

WOMEN'S ASSOCIATIONS

Women's Suffrage

To understand what happened in St Andrews in relation to this movement, it is necessary to describe the background briefly.

Leah Leneman's book *A Guid Cause: The Women's Suffrage Movement in Scotland* was published in 1991 (Aberdeen University Press). 'The story illuminates an aspect of Scottish history which few knew about'. Leneman gives a comprehensive account of the beginnings of the movement. The agitation over parliamentary reform was common to England and Scotland in the 1860s. The causes for which Victorian women in Scotland fought were many: the Scottish Chartist Movement, Anti-Slavery, the struggle for higher education for women, for the right of entry to the professions, for married women's legal rights, for the election of women on school boards and for the municipal franchise. One by one these demands were met.

However, the cause of parliamentary franchise for women involved a disappointingly long battle. There were many societies in Scotland which were allies. The first branch of the National Society for Women's Suffrage was constituted in Edinburgh in November 1867. By January 1871 there were branches in Aberdeen, Glasgow, St Andrews and Galloway. In 1909 all non-militant local suffrage societies were invited to join the National Society for Women's Suffrage Scotland. There was a close liaison with the English counterpart. The campaigning was vigorous, partly led by individuals who toured the country, and mainly took the form of annual conventions, rallies and meetings, as well as through publications, and by deputations to 10 Downing Street and to both Houses of Parliament. The NSWSS gained the support from their local MPs and from ministers of the Church. As well as these women's freedom movements, there were men's groups who petitioned for women's suffrage. By 1869, petitions with 16,000 signatures had been sent to London, and in the next nine years two million more signatures were collected,

In 1903 the Women's Social and Political Union was formed in Manchester on the instigation of Emmeline Pankhurst and her daughter Christabel. The work done in Lanarkshire among women textile workers inspired the Scottish Society to get up meetings in the industrial towns in Fife and Angus which met with great response and further signed petitions.

The first act of militancy was in Manchester in October 1905, when Christabel Pankhurst caused herself to be arrested at a large Liberal meeting. The women of the militant WSPU were named 'suffragettes' to distinguish them from those of the suffrage associations. The first branch of the WSPU in Scotland was the Glasgow and the West of Scotland. In 1907 Helen Fraser accepted the office of Scottish organiser of this Union and was a speaker at meetings all over the country. In 1908 a suffrage procession in London was a failure, and Emmeline Pankhurst announced that greater militancy was the only answer. Stones were thrown at the windows of the house of a cabinet minister. This caused Helen Fraser to resign from the WSPU and join what was then the NUWSS. She explained later that her view was, 'You don't use violence you use reason to get the vote'. The extent and the activity of both movements brought increasing support for the cause. The campaign continued; sufragettes committed breaches of the peace and were sent to Holloway. At the end of 1911 it seemed that hope of success was receding,

The next chapters in the book are titled 'Coming to the Boil – 1912' and the chapter for 1914 'The Heather on Fire'. Between March 1912 and July 1918 there were seventy militant acts ascribed to suffragettes in Scotland with seventeen arrests. When imprisonment was followed by hunger strike a new bill, commonly known as 'The Cat and Mouse Act', allowed the discharge of such women prisoners on health grounds, but when better they were rearrested to finish their sentences. In August 1913 Arabella Scott, who had taken part in a WSPU protest in London, was jailed in the Calton on her return to Scotland. She employed a new tactic, a hunger and thirst strike, 'a far harder thing to endure and far more damaging to the health', and was force fed until her release. She refused to go and had to be forcibly ejected.

When hunger and thirst strike was dealt with by force feeding, many people must have been overwhelmed by feelings of admiration for the courage of the campaigners and with horror for the treatment they met. In 1914 it was resolved to send all suffragettes to Perth prison. Dr Ferguson Watson, who had forcibly fed Ethel Moorhead at Calton jail, was now posted to Perth. Arabella Scott was sent to Perth and force fed for five weeks. On 23 July she had to be released because of her condition. Fanny Parker, an untried prisoner on hunger strike, was transferred to Perth prison on 13 July; she had been without food or water since 9 July. At Perth she was forcibly fed until her release on the 16th. She was taken by her brother to a nursing home in Edinburgh and was examined by Dr Chalmers Watson. He found her to be 'a very thin woman in a state of pronounced collapse'. She complained of pain in the genital regions, and the medical examination revealed swelling and rawness. Dr Chalmers Watson attributed this to 'rough and faulty introduction of instruments'. Fanny Parker referred not only to rectal feeding but to 'a grosser and more indecent outrage'. The doctor expressed his distaste for the whole business with the words, 'I sincerely hope I will have no more experience of forcibly fed women.'

What of the part played by women in St Andrews? One prominent leader in the movement was Louisa Lumsden who was born in Aberdeen in 1840. When she was twenty-four she joined a lecture course given by a professor in Edinburgh. Subsequently she went to Girton College, Cambridge, and was one of three women to take the honours examination in classics and receive an LL D. From 1877 to 1882 she was Headmistress of St Leonards School, St Andrews, and successfully founded a new system for girls' boarding schools. She returned to Aberdeen and later became president of the Aberdeen Suffrage Society. In 1897 she accepted the post of Warden of University Hall, the first residence for women at St Andrews University. In 1913 the NUWSS organised a suffrage pilgrimage; the participants converged on London on 26 July. There was a big rally with twenty platforms: Louisa Lumsden was one of the speakers. In April 1914 the Scottish Federation of the NUWSS included 63 societies, making a membership of 7,370. Suffrage summer schools, in which Louisa Lumsden played a prominent role, were held in University Hall in 1913 and 1914.

On the other side of the coin was Lady Griselda Cheape of Strathtyrum. She was the daughter of the seventh Earl of Airlie, and before her marriage to James Cheape of Strathtyrum she trained and worked with children in hospital. She was the president of the St Andrews branch of the Scottish National Anti-Suffrage League from 1909 to 1912. She was also president of the British Women's Temperance Association. In September 1913 she formed her local anti-suffrage organisation, The Beehive. She was intensely religious and based her opposition to women's involvement in politics on biblical injunctions concerning women's rightful place in relation to man. She is described as 'the pillar of the anti-suffrage movement'. In October 1911 she was at the conference of the National Union of Women Workers in Glasgow. Here she made an allegation against the suffrage movement, which she later withdrew, saying, 'It is not that I object to women's suffrage, it is from the point of view of morality and not of politics.' One can imagine the debates and discussions and heart-searching among the women in St Andrews. Dame Louisa Lumsden was highly regarded; Lady Griselda was considered a 'little eccentric'.

In 1913 there were two serious local incidents. Militancy was now in full flood. On 4 June Emily Wilding Davison threw herself in front of the King's horse at the Derby and died from the injuries. A memorial service was held in Dundee. Leneman writes, 'As a bastion of anti-suffragism St Andrews was an obvious target'. There were threats to damage the golf links prior to the Amateur Championship. The Green Committee of the R. and A., the Links Committee and the local Ratepayers Association organised a round-the-clock watch, involving 330 volunteers. There was no sign of any women intruders.

On the last day of June the railway station at Leuchars was set on fire and burnt down. On 23 June the east wing of the Gatty Marine laboratory was destroyed by fire. Professor McIntosh, appointed to the chair of Natural History in 1882, was the first Director of the Gatty Marine laboratory, opened in 1896. Not long before the attack he had acted as Chairman at an anti-suffrage meeting, so that might have been the motive. The question of whether these fires were the work of local suffragettes, or indeed of any suffragettes, remained unsolved. The following is an extract from *The St Andrews Citizen* of 28 June 1913.

> A meeting of the St Andrews Branch of the Women's Suffrage Association was held at St Margaret's, home of Mrs Houston, Vice-President. Agnes Anstruther, Charlton, President, was in the chair. Members deprecated violent methods as violating the law and justice. A motion was passed, 'This association condemns in the most emphatic manner the damage done to the Gatty Marine Laboratory which is alleged to have been caused by a member or members who have adopted militant methods. The NUWSS has repudiated and condemned all militant action at its annual meetings from 1908 to 1913… This Society believes that violent action is both derogatory to those who take it and those who support it.'

In a letter which bears only the initials of the writer, the following opinion is expressed. 'There cannot be the slightest doubt that the women who commit these outrages are for the moment suffering from derangement of mind, which is induced by hysteria. Unless these women were wrought up to the pitch of highly-strung hysterical Nerve Tension, they would never have dared to commit such outrages.' He (she?) advocates that they are sent to a special type of nursing home and not to prison.

In August 1914 the Pankhursts suspended all acts of militancy. They dropped all suffrage work and threw themselves into the war effort. The Scottish branches of the suffrage societies undertook all sorts of relief work. Dr Elsie Inglis had the idea of setting up special hospital units of female doctors, nurses and drivers to work at the front. The NUWSS supported this and raised money and helped to organise it.

In December 1916 Asquith, who had always opposed women's enfranchisement, was superseded as Prime Minister by Lloyd George. The Representation of the People Bill passed its second reading on 19 June, and the House was to debate the women's suffrage clause. In Edinburgh there was a huge mass meeting on the Mound in support of the inclusion of women in the Bill. When the division came, 385 MPs voted in favour of the clause and only 55 against it. The vote for women was given to those over 30 who were female householders and to the wives of householders. A bill was rushed through in 1918 allowing women to stand for Parliament. There was still the cause for universal suffrage to work for. Many members of the disbanded suffrage societies joined newly-created Women Citizens' Associations.

The St Andrews Women Citizens' Association

In 1912 The Representation of the People Act was followed by the establishment of branches of the Women Citizens' Association of Scotland. The aims are given in a small, brown, printed handbook as:

(1) the organisation of women on non-party and democratic lines, to foster a sense of citizenship in women, and by lectures and discussions to encourage the decisions of civic, economic, industrial and social questions including local government, national and international politics.
(2) the encouragement of women to take their due share in local and parliamentary government, and so to use their citizenship as to secure such social reforms as were considered beneficial to the community.

By the end of 1919 fourteen towns in Scotland had Women Citizens' Associations. A central council was established; it would hold an annual conference which delegates from the autonomous associations would attend to decide on a united programme. In the early post-war years there were many obvious needs to supply: soup kitchens were set up, and centres in towns for women to take their produce to sell. There was concern about the welfare of children. There was need to set up nursery schools in the slums, and causes to support such as the campaign for a pure milk supply, and the legalisation of adoption.

St Andrews WCA was founded in 1919, but the minute book from then to 1925 is not with the collection, now held by North-East Fife Museums. After the Sex Discrimination Act in 1919 there was no sudden change in the lives of women. There was still a lot to be fought for, and the early committees of the WCA set to work to do this. The St Andrews WCA records begin in 1925 with a committee meeting at Craigard, The Scores home of Professor and Mrs Stout. Present were Mrs Laing (President), Miss Ketelbey (St Leonards), Mrs Carmichael, Mrs Wilson, Miss Barnet, Miss Fotheringham, Mrs Read, Miss Forgan, Lady Herkless, Mrs Martineau, Mrs A.G. Scott, Mrs Waterston, and Mrs Galloway. Two concerts which they had organised had raised £65-17-10. From time to time the Association gave donations to a cause, often connected with a lecture they had arranged. From the early days they held a Sunday service at the Home of Rest, which was at 36 North Street. They gave an annual tea party for the Blind, and gave much support to this cause.

The Kinburn Museum St Andrews has the banner of the St Andrews Women Citizens' Association. It was presented to them by Mrs Stout who had been given it when the St Andrews Suffrage group was disbanded, having won their cause. The banner was designed and executed by Miss Cruttwell of St Leonards School.

Letters were sent to the authorities on subjects which the members had learned about, discussed and on which they had taken a stance. Those on local matters were sent to the Town Council or relevant authorities. Among these in the years 1925-1940 were:

1. Should the new 'humane killer' be used at the slaughter house? The RSPCA was also addressed. A visit to see animals killed was offered, but I doubt whether it was accepted.
2. Effective objections were made to the proposed erection of a public lavatory beside the East Infants' School.
3. The matter of the distribution of unwrapped bread was taken up.
4. Objections were made about the admittance of children to 'A' films. It seemed that the Cinema House was disregarding a League of Nations edict that children could only be admitted to 'A' films if accompanied by an adult.
5. In 1937 rates for the Step Rock Pool season tickets were 'women and girls 12s 6d, men 7s 1d, boys 3s 6d'. They sought to have this remedied.
6. The need for one-apartment houses for single people.
7. Protests were made about the unsanitary conditions of the pavements through dog mess. (It took another thirty years to have this remedied by creating a post of a vigilant Dog Warden – no dogs running loose – and a system of 'poop scoops' and fines.)
8. An investigation into the situation re emergency beds, and booking of beds (not private beds) at the Cottage hospital.

The other active work was for national causes, and involved arranging lectures and getting information, then lobbying the local M.P. or the Secretary of State for Scotland. Among the subjects were:

1. Support for a Scottish mental deficiency act with clauses similar to the English one and for changes in the conditions of mentally deficient people in institutions.
2. Demands for women's pensions to be given at age 60.
3. Objections made about the present ruling on the nationality of married women.
4. Demands for equal opportunities for women working in industry and in professional jobs.
5. Changes should be made regarding the position of unmarried mothers claiming alimony and custody of children.
6. Investigation into the working conditions of nurses.
7. Support for permanent segregation of older men who committed sexual offences against the young.
8. Support for the Smoke Abatement Act.
9. Requests for the raising of the legal age of marriage for girls to sixteen.
10. Demands for the provision of training for unemployed women and girls.

Miss Frances Warrack was the first woman to have a place on the St Andrews Town Council, from 1919 to 1926 and from 1932 to 1934. When she was due to resign the WCA Committee wrote congratulating her. Each election year the Committee drew up a list of women who might stand, and tried to persuade them to do so, but for some time there was little response.

Delegates were sent to the annual conference. In 1927 it was held at St Andrews and the topic was 'Changing Conditions for Women'. Some also attended the conferences of the National Union of Social and Equal Citizenship.

Mrs Waterston was succeeded as President by Mrs Stout. In 1928 there were 392 members – a strong force, with several wives of professors and ladies of standing in the town. Dr Dorothy Douglas was Vice-President. The programme for the meetings was varied; some topics were on the handicapped and on health, some rather 'housewifely' (e.g. 'Bottling Fruit'), and many were on travel. Dr A.R.C. McKerrow's lectures on roses were popular. By 1934 there were 464 members.

I was interested to read that in 1927 Miss McMillan came to lecture to St Andrews WCA on Nursery Schools. In 1936 I went to Deptford to the Rachel McMillan Nursery School Training College. Lady Astor, who was the first woman member of Parliament (1919), came on one of her regular visits to the College, her son Bill accompanying her. She was a good friend of the McMillan sisters and to their cause. Rachel had died in March 1913, and Margaret had retired in the mid-twenties. In 1920 Miss Mabel Brydie and Miss Jessie Porter, who had been students at the Rachel McMillan Nursery School College, developed a new nursery school which had been started by a small group of people in St Agnes Road, Dundee. Tragically Miss Brydie died in December 1922 from a disease contracted at her work with some of the poorest children. Miss Porter carried on, and the school was a great success, gaining the friendship and support of the parents who were mostly jute workers. I remember the slums in Deptford in the 1930s – it would be hard to forget the horror of them. There were such conditions in all the industrial cities,

Some of the presidents of the St Andrews WCA in the fifties and sixties were Mrs Eleanor Scott, Mrs T.T. Fordyce, Mrs A.R.C. McKerrow, Mrs Molly Cumming, Miss Jessie Macfarlane, Mrs Christie, and Miss Isobel Brown.

On Armistice Day the members used to assemble 'outside Boots' and join the parade to the service at the War Memorial in North Street. Annually delegates were elected to attend the United Nations

Assembly Association, the Women's Economic Conference, besides the National WCA conference. Here in St Andrews the WCA was represented on the old People's Welfare committee. In the run-up to each election the WCA held a session in the Town Hall where members of each party addressed a large gathering and answered questions. I remember these as useful and exciting affairs.

In 1957 at a St Andrews Night Dinner Conference, the speaker was Mr Andrew Soutar, BBC controller who asked members to let him know any incidents of violence, blasphemy, or indecency on television. I think some comments were sent, as he wrote asking for specific programmes and exact details. (Maybe today we need another Mr Soutar?) In 1960 the WCA sent representations about the dangers to the gullible of the personal credit scheme; also on the question of lower moral standards among young people.

The above outline may give an idea of the lines which were followed in subsequent years. There was a fund-raising effort for the Hungarian Relief Fund, and support was given to many other causes. The Preservation Trust was taking notice of matters concerning St Andrews, though I did note an entry in the WCA minutes of 1956 'it was agreed to keep a watching brief on the traffic of St Andrews'. There were also Christmas parties and summer outings.

In 1993 Miss Jessie Robertson was President, and there were one hundred and seventeen members. The number of members continued to fall, and it proved impossible to get committee members. This was a difficulty many societies experienced in the last quarter of the twentieth century. With sadness and regret the St Andrews Women Citizens' Association was wound up on 10 October 1994.

The St Andrews Townswomen's Guild

On 10 October 1956 a meeting was held in the Tudor Café in order to start a Townswomen's Guild. From then until the present day this Guild has continued successfully to fulfil its aims. They are:

1. To advance the education of women, irrespective of race, creed and party, to enable them to make the best contribution towards the common good.
2. To educate such women in the principles of good citizenship.
3. To provide and assist in the provision of facilities for recreation and other leisure-time occupations for such women, in the interests of social welfare and with a view to improving the conditions of life.

Recent concerns have been to consider the Council's proposals for the establishment of a cycle network in Fife. This is a demanding issue, involving the safety of pedestrians and the handicapped. At the last meeting Mr Craig Stockton, general executive of the Scottish Motor Neurone Disease, gave a talk on this little-known disease. The President handed over to him a cheque for £120 towards this Association.

The University of St Andrews Ladies' Club

I did not intend to write about clubs which are restricted to members of the University, but for some time now this Ladies' Club has accepted alumni, graduates of other universities, and associate members, and also guests may attend the evening lectures.

The story begins on 3 December 1918, when a meeting of wives of professors, held in the Principal's room, formed 'The University Ladies' Committee'. Those present were Mrs Galloway (wife of the Principal of St Mary's), Mrs Stout, Mrs Main, Mrs Herring, Mrs Waterston, and Mrs Herkless who took the chair. They decided that two functions would take place annually: a party for bejants (men and women) in the form of an 'At Home' with tea, music and dancing, and also a party to which the wives of the professors at Queen's College, Dundee, would be invited.

In 1921 Mrs Irvine chaired the meeting; Mrs D'Arcy Thompson, Mrs Blyth Webster and Miss Lindsay (sister of Professor Lindsay) were now in the group. The programme for the 1922 Bejant party, held in November in Lower College Hall, was: 3.45 arrive; 4.00 tea; 4.30 music; 4.45 Arts League of Service; 5.00 a play. In 1930 the Younger Hall was used for the Bejant party, That year Mrs Waterston's suggestion that the wives of junior staff be invited to the parties was agreed. These parties continued annually until 1932. The expenses were increasing, so the Committee decided to ask the University Court to make grants for both parties. This request was declined, and there are no further minutes.

However, at the back of the minute book are the records of what seems to have been a sub-committee. In 1916 it met to consider the lodgings available for women students. On the committee's initiative the Court sent out letters to landladies. Miss Dobson (Warden of Hall) agreed to inspect the lodgings, and a list was published and renewed annually. Those assisting Miss Dobson were Mrs Herkless, Mrs Stout and Mrs Hodge. This group also sent out Christmas cards and gifts to graduates in the Forces in 1916 and 1917.

On 7 March 1916 accounts were received regarding the behaviour of certain women students (unfortunately there is no mention of what was going on!). The Committee met representatives of the women students, who did not accept the Ladies' offer to take action, but said they would call a mass meeting and make an appeal for high standards of behaviour. The Ladies' Committee compiled a list of eleven women students for each professor's wife, so that all those in Residence or lodgings would be asked out to tea. Maybe this was one way of supervision.

A New University Ladies' Club

There is no more information until 1955. A letter was sent to the University Court by Mrs Copson and Mrs Knox (wife of the new Principal) advising that they intended to form a University Ladies' Club. A meeting was held on 3 May, and a Committee was appointed: Mrs Knox, Mrs Copson, Mrs Jack, Mrs Graham, Mrs J.A.

MacDonald, Mrs Mitford, Mrs Ritchie, Mrs Cole and Mrs Read. Note that there are names of wives of 'Junior Staff' included here. The proposal was that, as an annual event, the Club would invite the members of the Queen's College Tea Club over to St Andrews on Kate Kennedy Day. It was hoped that some of the lady hostesses might offer lunch. After the procession there would be a tea party. At least one year this took place at University House; the invitations went out, and there were 152 acceptances: 69 St Andrews and 63 Dundee. This party continued as an annual event until 1964; as Dundee was now an independent university, it was decided to call a halt – there would be no more joint events.

In 1956 a Christmas party was organised for staff children who were under nine years old. This was attended by 67 children and 39 adults. There were games, tea, an entertainment by a conjuror, and then Professor Dickie took the role of Father Christmas and gave out presents. Some years later Professor J.A. MacDonald became Father Christmas. Eventually there was also a party for teenagers. Each year in October a tea-party was held to welcome the wives of new members of staff. Wives of 'Junior Staff' were very involved in these activities and in later additional ones.

In 1963 a new constitution was drawn up. Women members of staff were now eligible for membership. There would also be 'temporary members' such as the wife of the Provost. Later, membership was open to wives of university technicians; social barriers were breaking down. A programme of coffee mornings and lectures was arranged annually. In 1966 a creche for toddlers was organised by Mrs Callan. The Club was offered the use of the St Leonards School swimming pool. In 1968 there was a summer outing which remains an annual event. Classes in bridge were available (tutor: Mrs Copson) and classes in French, German, Italian and Spanish.

The University of St Andrews Ladies' Club continues to flourish. There are now three separate Book Discussion Groups, a Walking Group, and a Bridge Improvers' Class, all of which involve associate members. A supper is held in the early summer, with superb catering by the members of the committee. For the last few years the membership was about a hundred, with a small dip recently. The real difficulty is that young people are no longer joining. Most young wives have jobs – changed times!

Chapter 5

THEATRE: PROFESSIONAL AND AMATEUR

The St Andrews 1920 Club

There are three reasons for giving a fuller account of this Club than I have of many others. First, it is a good example of an élite club, the members being carefully elected by the committee. There are indications of changes in the late 1950s and the 1960s. Second, most of the minutes are safely deposited in the University Library Archives Department. Third, I found it a very enjoyable social club. Fuller details of the Club's productions are given in my report deposited at the Library of the University of St Andrews.

The Opening Scene

Date: 9 March 1920. The place: University House, The Scores, St Andrews.

Dramatis Personae:

Sir John Herkless, formerly Professor of Ecclesiastical History at St Mary's, Principal of St Andrews University from 1915.

Lady Herkless, the hostess.

Mrs Burnet, the wife of Professor Burnet, eminent classical scholar. (They had lived in the large and elegant house, 1 Hope Street, today the only one in the street which remains undivided into flats. Professor Burnet got into financial difficulties, but received generous help from the Principal, Sir James Donaldson who retired in 1914. The Burnet family moved to Balfour House beside the bridge over the Kinnessburn.)

Mrs Irvine, wife of the Professor of Chemistry, and living at Edgecliffe East, The Scores, near University House.

Mrs Waterston, wife of the Professor of Anatomy. (He abstained from the general acclamation at the discovery of the Piltdown Man, and was the first to recognise it as a fraud.)

Mr Curran who lived with his family at 9 Abbotsford Crescent; he was a talented musician and scholar. (The Currans and the Grimond family, who lived next door, were on very friendly terms.)

Mr Morrison, Castle House, who was to become Professor of Classics.

Mr Blyth Webster of 56 South Street, soon to be Professor of English.

Mrs Williams, wife of Mr Williams (later Professor of Ecclesiastical and Mediaeval History) of Inglewood and later of The Roundel, at the east end of South Street. Mr Williams was a brother of Mrs Irvine.

From St Leonards School: Miss Pelham Pearson, House Mistress of Day Girls.

(*Comment*: In a small and beautiful university city of 10,000 inhabitants, you will realise that this is an élite gathering of cultured and intellectual people. Note that the mistresses of St Leonards School, a well established and fee-paying boarding school for girls, are represented.)

The scene is set in the beautiful ground-floor drawing-room at University House. The walls are silver-grey, the carpet is rose pink and china blue. The grey satin curtains at the seven great windows are drawn; one is conscious that beyond them the lawn stretches to the edge of the cliff and, deep down below, the North Sea rolls in.

The action begins: Lady Herkless welcomes the guests and, everyone settled, a reading is given of the play 'The Two Mr Wetherbys' by St John Hankin. There follows a discussion on the reason for this meeting, the plan to start a Literary and Dramatic Club. It is decided that the name be 'The St Andrews 1920 Club'. Meetings are to be held in private houses every three weeks, at 8.30 p.m.; evening dress is to be worn. Books for readings will be purchased; the subscription is (optimistically) set at 2/6d. Miss Esme MacDonald agrees to be secretary. In addition to the General

Committee there is to be a Plays Committee which will select and cast plays from a list made by the General Committee.

Refreshments are served, and eventually the guests take their leave, and go forth to walk home, lighting the dark mediaeval streets with their pleasure and excitement.

The first official meeting was held later in March at Mr Curran's house; to this were invited an additional galaxy of stars – in addition to Sir John and Lady Herkless, and others described above:

Principal Galloway, of St Marys, the Divinity College, and Mrs Galloway

Professor Stout, Logic and Metaphysics

Mr Roy of the Department of English, who was the first President of the committee

Miss Ketelbey, Lecturer in History

Miss Riddell Webster, who lived at Priorsgate and was an eminent local figure.

It was agreed to invite the following to be members: Miss Bentinck Smith, the Head Mistress of St Leonards School, Miss Dobson, the Warden of University Hall, and Dr and Mrs Playfair, Minister of Holy Trinity (they lived at Wyvern, the house that stands high on the skyline on the junction of City Road and North Street). This added to the already potential number of venues for the meetings. At that time St Andrews abounded in houses with large drawing rooms; in addition there were the drawing rooms of the St Leonards School boarding houses.

But back to the meeting at Mr Curran's, Abbotsford Place. It was recorded that 'the Club was founded to afford those interested in Literature and Art a medium of expression and aesthetic enjoyment'; that the founders 'expressly disclaimed any deliberate purpose to educate or improve its members, being satisfied with such a means of pleasant intercourse, as well as at the same time affording them a right enjoyment of their leisure'.

(*An off-stage aside*: It was said many years later one aim was that the Club would afford social opportunities for 'The School' to meet 'The College'.)

The committee would decide on who was to be invited to membership. (Before long it was announced that the names of those wishing to join must be given to the Secretary three days before the meeting and circulated to the committee; a ballot took place at the committee meeting.

Principal Herkless was invited to be Hon. President, and agreed. The first real-life drama to shake the members of the newly-founded club was his sudden and unexpected death in the summer of 1920. He had held the office of Principal for five difficult years, most of which ran during the war.

The 1920 Club was swiftly successful. The initial limit set on the membership was 50 (including the committee), which was raised to 60 in May 1920, to 80 in March 1922, to 100 in February 1925, and to 125 in June 1938. In the next 44 years it rarely dipped below 100, and was up to 120 at one time. Members wore evening dress for the meetings, and the Secretary sent out RSVP cards.

It had been agreed that an occasional paper might be received, but this soon ceased. So, at the November 1920 meeting held at St Mary's, Professor Taylor (Moral Philosophy) gave a paper on Herbert French's 'Napoleon'.

(Recently I was at an evening meeting of the Saltire Society; it was held in the Senior Common Room at St Marys College; this was previously the Drawing Room of the residence of the Principal of the College. The lecture we heard was on Scottish Drama; my mind was stirred with images of a 1920 Club meeting held in that very room seventy-nine years earlier.)

The minutes of the Plays sub-committee from 19 March 1920 to January 1926 are in a separate book; this was recovered for the archives when part of the library of Professor Morrison was bought by the University Library. The joy is that we have a record of those who took parts in the readings and productions in early years, from 1920-1927, but only for that time.

At a committee meeting at University House on 9 May 1923, a suggestion was made that some readings might be accompanied by actions. (This idea was brought up again two years later and it was agreed that, in cases where the committee and the producer thought this suited to the play, the reading might be presented with actions.) It seems that there were two rehearsals for each reading. The enthusiasm was obvious from the long list of plays which were considered.

1920-30

Plays

In the first ten years, G.B. Shaw's plays *The Devil's Disciple*, *Major Barbara*, *Back to Methusela* and *St Joan* were selected. Nineteen men and five women took part in the performance of *St Joan.* Imagine a dramatic club with such a number of men available! Shakespeare's *Love's Labours Lost* and *Richard III* were read. The policy stated by Mrs Irvine initially was 'to select the more modern developments of Drama and Literature'. Ibsen, Chekov, Galsworthy, Laurence Houseman, and several of J.M. Barrie's plays were read/performed.

The list of plays read or acted by the members of the 1920 Club from its beginning to its end in 1969 is lengthy – and almost complete; it is given in my report kept in the Library of the University of St Andrews. It may be of interest, in that the choice reflects the tastes of an academically orientated group, the changes in taste as the years went by, and the difficulties and the successes.

The players: leading lights

Sir James and Lady Irvine

Mr and Mrs Norman Boase. (The family of Boase were active members of the 1920 Club. Mr Norman Boase was to become Provost of St Andrews. He paid for the refurbishments of the furniture at the Town Hall where his portrait hangs. He and Mrs Boase lived at the White House, Hepburn Gardens; the Boase family owned a prosperous flax-spinning business in Leven and Dundee. Mr Philip Boase – Norman's brother – and family lived at Law Park at the end of Hepburn Gardens and joined the 1920 Club; Mrs Philip Boase was President in 1930-1931. (Mrs Norman Boase and Mrs Philip Boase were sisters; their maiden name was Leadbetter). Another brother Mr Alan Boase joined later. They were cultured people and made a valuable impact on the life of St Andrews. We will meet these Boase families in other sections.)

Mrs Burnet, wife of Professor Burnet, and her daughter, Regula, who took the female lead many times. (Regula produced many readings. She was elected President in 1935 and wrote plays for Guest Night 1931 and Guest Night 1936. Sadly, she died in 1948; the notice in *The Citizen* of 28 June read: 'Suddenly at Balfour House as the result of an accident, Regula Burnet daughter of the Late Professor John and Mrs Mary Burnet'. This was a tragic death: there had been a fault in a gas pipe, and she was gassed by the leak. Previously she had not been well and so was not active in the Club for a few months.)

Professor and Mrs Waterston

Miss E. Aitken

Mr Lorimer (Classics Department)

Mr and Mrs Warren Wynne

Dr and Mrs Paton

Professor and Mrs Read

Professor and Mrs J. Wright

Miss Steele

Mr and Mrs Donald Mills

Miss M. Kidston

Mr Price

List of early Presidents

1920-21	Mr James Roy
1921-22	Prof. Blyth Webster
1922-23	Prof. Morrison
1923-24	Lady Irvine
1924-25	Mr Norman Boase
1925-26	Prof. J.D. Mackie
1926-27	Miss Chapman
1927-28	Mrs Warren Wynne
1928-29	Prof. Waterston
1929-30	Rev. Nowell Price

1930-39

Plays

In addition to further plays by J.M. Barrie, G. B. Shaw, Shakespeare, John Galsworthy and A.A. Milne, the Club performed plays by Synge, Chekhov, Laurence Houseman, J.B. Priestley, James Bridie, Ibsen and Quintero.

Presidents

1930-31	Mr Norman Boase
1931-32	The Rev. Slater Dunlop
1932-33	Mr C. Mayne
1933-34	Miss Pridden
1934-35	Prof. F.J. Charteris
1935-36	Miss Regula Burnet
1936-37	Miss M. Kidston
1937-38	Mrs Harrison
1938-39	Col. A.R. MacAllan
1939-45	in abeyance

Extracts from committee meetings and ABMs

ABM 1930: A revised constitution was drawn up, and this and the records of the first ten years of the Club were printed in a booklet. {*Sadly I can find no copy.*}

The committee in May 1930 was Mrs N. Boase, Mr Price (The Rectory), Mrs Burnet, Mrs Dunlop, Mrs Paton, Mrs Mills, Mr Orr, and Miss Aitken and Miss Steele who were joint secretaries. It had been found that the work of Secretary was heavy and needed to be shared. R.S.V.P. cards were sent to members for each meeting. (Miss Steele was secretary to Principal Irvine and later Dr Steele, Warden of Chattan. Miss Eleanora Aitken lived in the old house with the forestair, 19 North Street. {*I remember her well; she was active in the Preservation Trust and other causes.*}

Casting committee: Dr J.A. Macdonald (later Professor of Botany), Mrs Read (wife of the Professor of Chemistry), Dr E.T. Copson.

In June 1930 two new members were Dr Copson (to be Professor of Mathematics) and in December 1931 Mrs Copson and Dr J.A. Macdonald, and soon also his wife, Connie. So the Club was attracting younger people. {*Both Connie and Jay Macdonald read many parts. Jay told me that he had such a run of playing the villain that old ladies crossed the road in fear when they saw him coming!*}

Sir James and Lady Irvine resigned in October 1933 and must have been greatly missed; Miss Veronica Irvine continued to be a member for a time. Mr Bruce Mitford (classicist and archaeologist) was a new member, and later Mrs Mitford (1936), also Mr Arthur Taylor (Guardbridge Paper Mill) and his wife Simone in 1937. Both gave long service to the Club, as did Miss Margaret Kidston and Miss Annabel Kidston.

The committee members read and considered an amazing number of plays, and in 1934 the President stated that they tried to cater for a large variety of tastes. At one meeting they were faced with thirty-one suggestions! To deal with this they divided the committee into two halves, thus speeding up the circulation of the books. In the 1950s a screening committee was elected to cut down the work. One of my memories is of constantly cycling to and from various houses with the swiftly circulating books in my bicycle basket. The meetings had taken place at St Leonards School Houses, but by 1937 when the membership was up to 100, meetings were held in St Regulus Club until 1946.

A custom was to use selected unrehearsed one-act plays by holding an annual 'Hat Night'. (In 1955 it was endorsed that this practice would continue.)

ABM 14 June 1938: The Membership was up to full strength, i.e. 100 members. The subscription to be raised to 10s. The books of the Club Library were to be sold (some were sold to the Play Club). Miss Moir, who was later to become Provost, joined.

ABM 23 June 1939: The President stated that it had been a difficult year after the call for National Service. Because of the crisis people had less time for clubs such as the 1920 Club. Nevertheless in a period of difficulty and anxiety the Club had a successful year. All the plays were read at St Regulus Club. The membership stood at 104 – 38 men and 66 women. There had been 15 resignations. In view of the emergency, suggestions were put forward for the possible suspension of the Club for a year, or alternatively a reduction in the number of Readings and no Guest Night, together with a reduction of subscriptions to 5s. With the outbreak of war, the Club was in abeyance until 1946.

1946-55

Plays

The choice of plays was very much the same as before the war.

Presidents

1946-47	Dr J.Y. Macdonald
1947-48	Dr Steele
1948-49	Mrs Barry
1949-50	Mrs Skinner
1951-52	Brigadier Soutar
1952-53	Mr A.P. Taylor
1953-54	Mrs Harrison
1954-55	Mrs Cunninghan
1955-56	Mrs Hawes

Extracts from meetings

An Extraordinary General Meeting was held on 27 February 1946. Mrs Harrison was in the Chair. There was a balance of £35 in Defence Bonds and the interest had gone to paying the subscription to the British Drama League. There was a unanimous vote that the Club should continue. (By July 1946 the membership stood at 96.) There were various suggestions about accommodation for the meetings

The committee said there was a need for younger members. Mr David Grace (St Andrews solicitor) and Mrs Grace joined in 1948. They lived at 60 South Street and later at 'The Grange'. David was an excellent reader and actor (and later a most useful Treasurer). Mr Derek Macleod, Headmaster of New Park School, joined; he was a very accomplished reader and also took a turn as Secretary. Two young members, Miss Bromley of St Katherine's School (to become Mrs Caird), and Mrs Alfred Cole (Biddy, 1951), who had been on the London stage, took leading roles on many occasions. Biddy is long remembered for her role in Noel Coward's *Hay Fever*. Other new members were: Mr and Mrs Mitford, Mr and Mrs Arthur Taylor (Guardbridge Paper Mill), Miss Annabel Kidston, Mr and Mrs George Milligan (New Park School), Mr and Mrs H.B. Pirie (West House), and Professor and Mrs Woodward.

ABM 30 March 1947 was held in the Grand Hotel. The President reported that the committee had continued to run the Club on the lines which had proved so successful before the War. St Regulus Club was no longer available for meetings, but in 1946 good facilities had been provided by Mrs Donington Smith at the Grand Hotel at a cost of £l-ls for the Ballroom. The membership stood at 88 (36 had been elected during the year), and there were 12 vacancies. The Club had joined the Scottish Community Drama Centre at Kirkcaldy and this eased the difficulties of getting sets of books for fixed dates.

ABM 14 May 1948: Mr Macleod agreed to become Secretary. Meetings were all held at the Grand Hotel, but it was reported that it was to be closed for the winter; MacArthur's Café in Golf Place was to be used instead. After the winter, when it was decided not to use the Grand Hotel again, the Victoria Café was chosen and remained the meeting place for all future readings.

ABM 9 May 1949: New to the committee were Mrs Pirie of West House, an invaluable member, Miss McKendrick, Dr Steele, Mrs Mair.

ABM 11 May 1950: David Grace was elected Treasurer. There were some new names on the committee: Mrs Skinner, Dr Mair, Brig. Soutar, Mrs Rennie, Mrs Hawes, Mr McCurrach. (Mr and Mrs McCurrach were gifted readers and actors; they lived at Netherburn but when the Madras extension was erected they moved to North Fife.) Mrs Rennie became Mrs Hugh Richardson and was Secretary for some years, as was Mrs Cunningham (wife of John Cunningham the architect), Mr A.P. Taylor and Mrs Taylor. There was a suggestion that the Club's custom of wearing evening dress might be relaxed; this was brought up at a reading in January 1951 and overwhelmingly rejected.

Many people have memories of lady members hitching up and

securing their long skirts with elastic bands, as they had to cycle to the meetings. I remember, when we were all arriving and taking off our coats in the cloakroom at the Victoria Café, the flurries from dresses as they were released to assume their full lengths. In the winter some of the older ladies retained their fur coats, or wore fur capes, and the air was heavy with the smell of moth balls. Miss Osman, retired House Mistress of Abbey Park 'The School', and her friend Miss Stewart were always there in good time.

ABM 8 May 1952: The membership was 111. New committee members were Mrs Willsher, Mr Taylor.

At the committee meeting on 22 May 1953, nineteen plays were suggested; five of these were by Molière! Miss Margaret Kidston was made an Honorary Member. Meetings were being held downstairs in the Victoria Café. Fourteen plays were suggested. New Members were Dr and Mrs Sommerville. Mr and Mrs Williams, Miss Greenwell of St Leonards School who later married The Reverend John Thornton, also a member of the Club. (*The Thorntons went to Oxford and my two daughters – who went to Somerville College – both met their future husbands through his church group.*)

ABM 1954: The casting secretaries were Mrs Willsher and Mrs Pirie. Ten plays were suggested. Among new members were Mrs Barbara Carstairs, and Miss Daphne Swindells, Drama teacher at St Leonards, who both played many parts.

1956-69

Plays

New names were Pinero, Henry James, Agatha Christie, Terence Rattigan, Pamela Hansford Johnson, John Mortimer, Peter Ustinov, Charles Morgan, Christopher Fry and Noel Coward. In 1966-67 there was some criticism by older members of the choice of John Osborne's *Look Back in Anger*, Harold Pinter's *The Dumb Waiter* and Arnold Wesker's *Roots.* Times were changing fast!

Presidents

1956-57	Mrs Hawes
1957-58	Mr David Grace
1958-59	Mrs J.A. Macdonald
1959-60	Mrs Willsher
1965-66	Dr Ouston
1960-61	Mr Prytz
1961-62	Mrs Willsher

Chairmen

1962-63	Mrs Willsher
1963-64	Mrs Willsher
1964-65	Mr Milligan
1966-67	Mr A.P.Taylor
1967-68	Professor Dover
1968-69	Mrs Macgregor

Extracts from meetings

ABM 8 May 1956: Secretary, Mr A.P. Taylor. New committee members: Mrs Cole, Mr Woodward (Professor of Spanish), Mr Bell. New Members were Miss Macauley, Headmistress of St Leonards, and Miss Cochrane (a new lady doctor in the town).

ABM 1957:There were 112 members (during the years there had been several resignations owing to members leaving the area, but there was always a demand for places.) New members to the committee: Mrs Shaw, Mrs Hall Stewart, Mr Watt. New members: Professor Butler (Medieval History) and Mrs Butler, Mr Carstairs (Economics Department) and Mrs Carstairs. Honorary Member: Mrs Waterston, who had been a member of the Club from its early days.

ABM 1960: A subcommittee was elected to 'filter' plays. Difficulties over obtaining sets of plays continued. Mr Taylor who was Book Secretary 'had wrestled with a chaotic body of individuals who kept sending with persistence the wrong books'.

Committee meeting, 13 January 1961: There was a discussion on the difficulties of running the Club. It was becoming hard to find a cast who could give three evenings in a week for the rehearsals and performances. It was suggested that a new policy should be worked out: the readings simplified, and Guest Night abolished except as a reading. This was not agreed.

Guest Nights

A Guest Night was held annually in the early spring. A three-act play or two one-act plays were fully produced and acted in costume, and each member could bring a guest. The first Guest Night was held at University Hall in 1921. Miss Dobson was to invite all the Hall students to the Dress Rehearsal. There is no record of the casting, but the chosen plays were *The Pigeon* by Galsworthy and *The Proposal* by Chekhov; also, 'there was Music in the Interval', no doubt organised by Mr Curran.

Guest Night became one of the events in the social life of St Andrews, and there were up to 200 people at some of them. Guest Nights were held at various places: Upper College Hall (until information came that the stage had collapsed!), University Hall in both Miss Dobson's and Mrs Graham's days, The Imperial Hotel, the Students' Union Diner, the Town Hall and All Saints Church Hall. The responsibility of the President for Guest Night became too heavy, and it was decided that whoever was producing the play would do the casting. There was by tradition the option of having a well-rehearsed reading for Guest Night, but this rarely happened. Another matter arose more than once about readings. Was it not preferable to have all readings performed with actions? This was settled when Mrs Harrison 'came on the scene' in 1946, and there were always two rehearsals, giving some fine performances with essential 'props' and scenery.

Guest Night, 30 January 1924, was held in Upper College Hall with refreshments in Lower College Hall. The Play was J.M. Barrie's *Shall We Join the Ladies.* Principal Irvine, who became a close friend of J.M. Barrie, had his permission for the performance; J.M Barrie was

Rector of the University 1922-1925. The cast was:

The Host – Principal Irvine
The Butler – Dr McGavin
Lady Wrathie – Mrs Irvine
Miss Isit – Mrs McEuan
Miss Vaila – Miss Burnet
Sir Joseph Wrathie – Mr Mackie
Policeman – Professor Read.

Guest Night (1951) was six Scenes from *Victoria Regina* by Lawrence Housman produced by Mr Eliot Playfair of the eminent Playfair family, St Andrews. (He was an actor and producer, and had returned to St Andrews to do some work at the Byre Theatre; he had recently joined the Club, and offered to do this production. He was subsequently elected to the committee, but after some months as he had attended no meetings he was replaced.)

In 1953 the plays were *Shall We Join the Ladies* by J.M. Barrie and *A Hundred Years Old* by Quintero. (Professor Woodward (Ferdy) told me he played the centenarian and David Grace took the part of his son. Ferdy forgot David's name in the play, but asked him in Spanish and got a reply.)

At the 1956 Guest Night in All Saints Hall, *The Ghost Train* was performed, produced by Mrs Harrison. (David Borwein, now Emeritus Professor of Mathematics at London, Ontario, tells me he took the part of The Detective.)

Vivid in my mind, and often mentioned, is the Guest Night of 1960 which I produced. The play was *Autumn Crocus* by Dodie Smith, with Barbara Carstairs and Victor Dixon. (I am told that after it several ladies changed their hair-style to the one that Barbara wore.)

The Final Years

At the ABM 1961 there was a long discussion about the survival of the Club. The main difficulty was in finding casts for the plays.

Guest Night was 'the same, only worse'. In addition nobody was willing to accept the Presidency. Mrs J.Y. Macdonald said she had been a member of the Club for thirty two years; she thought it had been a real social asset, had been very lively and helped the people of St Andrews to mix. Mrs Willsher asked whether it might be possible for a committee to have a meeting with the Dramatic Society with a view to an amalgamation. This was not agreed. (*On thinking it over now, I do not think it was feasible; there were few members who belonged to both; the Societies had different aims. In fact the Dramatic Society was wound up two years after the 1920 Club.*) Mrs Harrison suggested we might hire sets of books for a longer period and spread out the rehearsals. She suggested that the office of President might be replaced by one of Chairman of the committee, and the duties delegated. This was agreed. In fact, as will be seen above, the Club continued with a few helpful alterations and a lot of hard work. The crisis came in February 1969. A questionnaire was sent out to all members.

1. I want the Club to continue.
2. I hope to attend regularly.
3. I hope to attend occasionally.
4. I would like to read if asked.
5. I don't object to the Club being wound up.
6. I think the Club should be wound up.

The results were confusing. Most people would be sorry see the Club's end, but not enough had offered to take part in readings. The ABM was held on the 19 March 1969. The Chairman stated that the general view of the committee was that the questionnaire confirmed the view that had already been formed, that there would be regret at the demise of the Club, but that there was not sufficient enthusiasm to keep it alive. The resolution was proposed that the Club would wind up at the end of the present season. Mrs J.Y. Macdonald proposed a counter-motion that it might be kept going another year, to make its fiftieth anniversary, and 'go out with a blaze of glory'. This was defeated and so the motion was carried. It was decided that the present funds should be donated to the Byre Theatre.

So the last meeting came with the Guest Night, an enjoyable evening tinged with sadness. 'A Victorian Evening' was presented, arranged by Mrs Bryant and hosted by Mr Derek Macleod. Mesdames Banister, Caird, Hill, Macgregor and Murray and Messrs Ouston, Bryant, Carleton, Dover, Watt and Scott read extracts from Queen Victoria's 'Letters to King Leopold', and from books by Hardy, Houseman, Browning and Hilaire Belloc, and also articles from the Spectator. Among the songs were 'The Lost Chord', 'The Chorister' and 'The Little Maid of Arcady' rendered by Professor MacFarlane and Mesdames Bugay and Hill, with music by Messrs George Scott, Bryant, and Murray and Simon.

The founder members of the Club would have been delighted that it had fulfilled its aims, 'to give people a right enjoyment of their leisure'. It was, too, 'a medium of expression and aesthetic enjoyment'. Every year a small number of members gave a lot of time to ensure that it ran smoothly. There was an atmosphere of enjoyment and of helpfulness. Hundreds of suggested plays were read and considered by committee members before selections were made. Then there was the back-stage work, for example someone would willingly collect the Piries' Charles Rennie Macintosh chair from West House and transport it to the venue – and take it back again. All sorts of things were collected for 'props'. The casting committee struggled to please all who wished to read ('Oh dear! we simply MUST find a part for Dr Howden'). And there was plenty of fun, at committee meetings, at rehearsals and at readings – I remember in 'London Wall' someone had to light a cigarette and accidently burn Connie Macdonald's arm. Not a smoker, his struggle went on and on, while Connie sat with her arm thrust out and the audience giggled with delight. The standard of reading was high, and Mrs Harrison's advent as a first-class producer made it higher still. Many of us remember rehearsals in Mrs Harrison's flat in Alexandra Place. She was handsome, with smooth dark hair and glowing brown eyes. In her deep voice she would explain what was needed, and patiently see that we attained it.

The selection of plays reflects the character of the membership, the locality, a Scottish University town with a thriving select boarding school for girls, and many retired people who had chosen to live in St Andrews. The great popularity of the plays of J.M. Barrie may have been partly because he was Rector of the University and a close friend of Sir James Irvine. The sentimentality and the whimsy of his writing were suited to the mood of the twenties and thirties. However his plays were selected right up to 1959. Plays by George Bernard Shaw were the most popular, especially in the first two decades, but again in the 1950s, and two were read in the 1960s. Plays by A.A. Milne, J.B. Priestley, John Galsworthy, Oscar Wilde run about level; Chekhov and Galsworthy featured occasionally in the earlier years and a few plays by Bridie. I wonder how 'Look Back in Anger' was received in 1966. 'The committee tried to cater for all tastes.' No doubt that was not so easy as it had been in the 1920s. The John Van Druten plays were really lightweight. Was there some discontent in the fur-lapped bosoms?

Given one wish, an impossible one, I would ask for two videos: one of the reading of *Twelfth Night* in 1922-23, and one of G.B. Shaw's *St Joan* at Guest Night 1925.

The Byre Theatre and Play Club

The Old Byre

It was the end of the twenties and beginning of the thirties, a time when interest in the theatre was reviving and dramatic societies were starting up in the cities and towns. Alex Paterson was a member of Hope Park Church, and once a year the Bible Class used to put on a full-length play, and occasional one-act plays in the Church Hall. One day in the winter of 1933 some members of the Hope Park group were out for a walk along the Kinkell Braes. Alex returned to a favourite topic of his: the need to set up a small theatre in St Andrews. Someone remarked that the old byre of the Abbey Street dairy farm (which had closed some years previously) was lying unused. Alex stopped in his tracks. 'Lets go and see it,' he said. They turned and hurried back to look at the premises. 'This would be the very place for us,' Alex decided. They went into action immediately, and the Town Council agreed to rent the byre and its loft to them at £10 per annum, with the warning that it might have to be demolished before long to make way for the proposed trunk road. Happily they had a clear run until 1969.

In his book *The Byre Theatre Through the Years* Alex describes how they set to work. First there was 'the herculean labour of cleaning out the byre'. Then they tackled various necessary alterations. A stage was put up, the dimensions 12 ft by 12 ft filling the entire end of the building. The loft above was to be the changing room, and to reach this from the stage they put in a perpendicular ladder. Fire regulations meant they had to have a second exit from the loft. An iron ship's ladder was purchased at a scrap yard at Burntisland, and Gibby McMillan, who became the Play Group's technician, fixed it up, George Cowie organised the raking of the floor and the installation of seventy-four tip-up seats kindly donated by Jack Humphries, Manager of the Cinema House. The St Andrews Play Club was formed, went into rehearsal and put on a series of plays, the income helping to meet the costs of establishing the new theatre. A licence having been obtained, the first public performance took place in May 1937. The play chosen was A.B. Paterson's 'The Foreigner'.

It happened that the Dundee Rep. company had asked if it might run its season of six weeks at the Byre, as their own theatre was being reconstructed. This fitted in well. And then came the war, and everybody went off on active service, including Alex. In the spring of 1940 Douglas Storm together with Edith Ruddick, Flora Britton and Pauline Reeves formed the first St Andrews Repertory company, with professional actors and amateurs, and ran a season of weekly plays. Before long they enlisted the help of Charles Marford, a very experienced old trooper. It was due to him and his wife Molly Tapper, together with Millie Paterson and Emma Todd (the only two play club members left) that that the Byre kept going through the war years. Casting problems increased each year. What is so amazing is that among the plays presented were 'Macbeth', 'Twelth Night', 'The Taming of the Shrew', 'The Merry Wives of Windsor', 'As You Like It' and 'The Merchant of Venice'. In each production the actors played several parts on stage, and undertook all other jobs including the cleaning of the theatre.

In 1945 Alex came home and Charles Marford handed over the administration of the Theatre to him. Alex carried on as unpaid Administrator until 1970. Charles Marford produced a summer season of plays in the following two years, and then John Lindsay became the Producer. In 1949 Elliott Playfair returned to run a winter season. He wrote, 'I have played in my beloved Byre many times and the spell of this wonderful theatre gets a deeper hold of me every time. I travel round on tour in Repertory theatres all over the British Isles and almost everywhere people come and ask me about the Byre. Its fame is out of all proportion to its size.' John Lindsay came as Producer for 1947 and 1948. He experimented with running a full professional company during the winters, and this turned out well. One highlight was Jean Forbes Robertson as guest artist taking the title role of Hedda Gabler.

Throughout the next seventy years the Play Club produced plays in the Byre, making in total an enormous sum of money for the support of the Theatre. For instance from Alex's account of 1982: 'A contribution was made by the Play Club to the Theatre from a production of "The Gold Sovereign", a new comedy by David Joy. The Play Club and the Byre Theatre have been seen by some as an indispensable partnership'. It was possible in those years for amateurs to work on stage with professionals for a limited number of weeks a year, and they were often needed at the Byre. One of them, Catherine Ritchie, is still remembered; her death in 1961 was untimely. Alex wrote of her, 'An actress of outstanding ability, she was one of the original members of the Play Club, and for over twenty years she gave her service unstintingly as an actress and as member of the committee.'

Many people remember Michael Elder, Lyon Todd, Damaris Hayward, Roy Boucher and his wife Una McLean (who had first met at the Byre) and John Cairney. Audiences filled the old Byre to see plays by Shakespeare, Shaw, Bridie, Barrie, Ibsen, Sheridan, Synge, Wilde, and Coward. And there were popular contemporary plays: in 1957 'The Glass Menagerie', in 1959 'The Entertainer', in 1961 'The Caretaker'. The first Christmas pantomime was 'Dick Whittington' in 1940; Charles Marford returned many times to produce pantomines and also some Shakespeare plays. From 1973 to 1981 Rex Howard Arundel was welcomed back to produce the annual pantomime. A.B. Paterson's own plays were greatly enjoyed. Over the years there were repeat performances of 'The Open' (this is usually staged when the Open Championship takes place at St Andrews) 'Reunion in St Andrews', 'Witching Women of St Andrews', 'The Man who was Rob Roy', 'The Last Provost' and 'Paw's Awa'. It became a custom to open the Rep season by the Play Club presenting an A.B. Paterson play.

A New Byre Theatre

I quote here from Alex's book:

> In 1966 plans were now being discussed for the erection of a new Byre Theatre, about fifty yards from the original. The Town Council was preparing for the demolition of the houses on the east side of Abbey Street and from the Byre Theatre southwards. We were asked to collaborate with Mr T.P. Rodger in drawing up plans for the new theatre.
>
> In 1967 Mr T.P. Rodger visited the Mermaid Theatre, London, and used it as a model. The total cost was to be £40,000. The Scottish Arts Council gave a grant of

£10,000, Fife Council £10,000 and St Andrews Council £10,000. A limited liability company was set up – 'The Byre Theatre Company Ltd' – and also a new association, 'The Friends of the Byre'. Mr Ian McGavin, a member of this group, was chosen as fund-raiser. That fund reached £13,202. To avoid confusion the Play Club temporarily disbanded and became 'The Andrew Soutar Company', but no longer fulfilled its traditional role in administering the theatre. (It was re-formed in 1977.)

The last performance in the old Byre Theatre was on 3 January 1970. The play was 'Grouse Moor Image' by William Douglas-Home. When it ended the curtain was not drawn; this was to signify there would be continuity in the new Byre Theatre. And so there was: Andrew Cruickshank (Dr Cameron in 'Dr Finlay's Casebook') performed the opening ceremony on 14 March 1970. This was followed by a performance by professionals and amateurs of A.B. Paterson's version of 'Weir of Hermiston' and then a reception in the Town Hall. When the flitting took place it was unfortunate that one special item was lost. It is one of the things which people recall when talking about the Old Byre, a unique notice which had been fixed to the front of the stage: 'Please keep your feet off the stage'. The old doocot was built into a wall of the new Byre.

Patrick Maladhide was Director for the first season. The attendance was 24,000 which was 68% of capacity. The first annual grant from the Scottish Arts Council had been awarded in 1963 and was £300. In 1971 the Arts Council grant was £6000. Other companies used the theatre out of season, among them the Play Club, The University students' Mermaid Society, the University German Department, plays organised for The St Andrews Drama Festival, the Madras College, the Purves Puppets, the Anstruther Guysers, the Mull Little Theatre, and Wild Cats.

It was a great team at the new Byre. Harry and Nan Eagle were appointed caretakers and no two people could have worked harder. For many years Andrew Cowie played a vital role as technical adviser, photographer and Board Member, and his early death in 1980 was a great blow. Joan Ritchie was a member of staff for almost the whole of the first fifty years. Aileen Dow from the Play Club became secretary to Jon Whatson who took over from Alex as Administrator in 1980, and also to Adrian Reynolds (Artistic Director 1981-83). Tom Jarrett, who had begun his career as an amateur actor before the Second World War, became secretary of the Byre Company.

It was a good feeling to walk into this small (but when it was new it seemed really large) smart, comfortable theatre and be greeted by your name, and then shown to your seat by another member of the Friends, to get an ice-cream from Sandra (who was my hairdresser) and to have your interval coffee and biscuits served by yet another volunteer. Coffee? Yes, for in 1980 there was a new appeal for £21,000 to build a cafeteria, and to provide accommodation for the Administrator. Of course it was successful; the new building was named the Paterson suite. At some point a caterer took over and it was open for lunches, but this was not a financial success.

In 1978 the first amateur Drama Festival took place at the Byre. Then in collaboration with The Arts in Fife the company toured and played at schools and Youth Centres. Eventually work with schools and with young people increased, a special post was created and a junior play club was formed. Adrian Reynolds changed the pattern by engaging a company of experienced professional players, almost all of them Scots. There were some excellent productions, but the costs went up. It was no longer possible for amateurs to take parts, and paid posts were created to carry out duties that Play Club members had previously undertaken. Some plays toured; there was a notable success at the Edinburgh Festival: 'Shylock', a rock musical based on 'The Merchant of Venice', won the Scotsman award for for the outstanding event on the Fringe. The plays I remember most clearly were an excellent production of 'Educating Rita' with a Scottish setting, and

'The Entertainer' in which Jimmy Logan played the lead. Adrian Reynolds and his wife Marion had a house at Kingsbarns, and gave a lovely party in the garden with the Logans as the main guests. I felt as if I was in the cast of a very enjoyable play.

Anne Makein has written this account which gives a further insight into Alex Paterson's Byre and the part of the Play Club.

> In 1970 Andrew Soutar put on one of Alex's plays in the Boy's Brigade Hall. It was to raise money to build a cottage in Glen Isla for the Boys' Brigade as a memorial to Andrew Thom. I was asked if I would like to read for a part. The Play was Alex's 'Reunion in St Andrews'. I had never been on the stage before but I got the part of Miss Rawbone. As well as Andy Soutar and myself, David Joy and Jimmy Bone and Margaret Christie were in it. We played for three nights to about 700 people, and made about £200. Alex then asked us to do it at the Byre, and we played to full houses for three weeks. I was so pleased to see the pleasure we seemed to give to everybody, and I was lucky to start with such helpful and kind people. Andrew Cowie did all the stage managing plus lighting, and to this day I have never known a better stage manager. The next play we did was 'Three's Company' with just Andy, David and myself. Then we put on one of Alex's plays every year. David, Andy, Jimmy and I were in them all. Andrew Cowie used to play tricks on the last night, and I remember how difficult it was to keep a straight face when he put a china egg on for David for the breakfast scene, and he had JOY BOY written all around the plate. Carol and Alan Tricker started the Play Club up again and the Quinaults, Peter Fisher, Sandra Skeldon and various others joined. We started out doing one English play and

> one Scots play a year. ... Later Play Club members did David Joy's 'Fit Like' and 'Keep Fit Like' but then we left the Play Club.

The (new) Play Club has performed several plays in the Crawford Centre in recent years.

When A.B. Paterson died in 1989 it was a keen loss to a great number of people. In 1958 he had been awarded the MBE for services to the theatre, and in 1971 the University of St Andrews conferred on him the first honorary degree of Master of Arts. In the same year he was given the STV Oscar for outstanding services to the Scottish theatre. In 1977 he was awarded a Jubilee medal by the Queen. He remained Chairman of the Board of the Byre Theatre until his death. There is a seat in the Cathedral Graveyard to commemorate his life.

Another New Byre Theatre

In 1995 the Board of the Byre Theatre decided to apply for a Lottery award to make additions to the building – offices and a green room. The answer to the application was that the Arts Council National Lottery fund advisers wanted the Byre to be rebuilt. It was a case of 'Think Big'. One difficulty was that only for about a month in the summer season were all the seats filled; an increase in seating was not needed and was not requested. Nevertheless, whatever the discussions, it was decided to put in for the award to rebuild. A competition to design the new theatre was held, and the winner was Nicoll Russell Studios of Broughty Ferry; the two architects were Doug Binnie and Scott Turpie. The grant award was for three million pounds, an additional tenth of the costs was to be raised by the company. The last performance in the 'New Byre' was on January 1996. To many of us, the demolition of the building which had such a happy and comparatively short history was painful.

There were considerable delays in the building programme, and with them increasing costs. These have been met by an increased Arts Council grant amounting to a total of £4.05 million to date; Fife Council has given £625,000 and Scottish Enterprise Fife £249,500. It was planned that, in the gap period after the Byre closed and the new Byre opened, some plays might be staged in other venues ('The Byre on the Move'). For this reason, the Artistic Director, Ken Alexander, and the Managing Director, Tom Gardner, were kept on, together with the Education Officer. There have been a few plays presented in the Crawford Centre and locally, but with the long delays in the completion of the building – which has taken four and a half years – many St Andrews people have sorely missed the repertory company.

The Byre Theatre was opened by Sir Sean Connery on 5 June 2001. The interior of the building was a triumph for Nicoll Russell Studios and the project architect Scott Turpie who won the competition for the design for the Best Small Theatre in Scotland. The opening musical show, *Into the Woods* by Stephen Sondheim and James Lapine, gave scope for the whole team – director Ken Alexander, the cast of seventeen, stage managers, lighting, sound – to show off the new features of the building. It ran for three 'full house' weeks. Eileen McCallum starred in *Parking Lot in Pittsburg*, a new play by Anne Downie. In the play *Neville's Island* by Tom Firth, the stage managers rose to the challenge and created an island in Derwent Water on the stage. The shipwrecked characters did not WALK on – they SWAM on! Sue Glover's *Bondagers* captured the audience. More successes followed: over the Christmas season Charles Dickens' *A Christmas Carol*, the Play Club with Liz Lochhead's *Mary Queen of Scots got her Head Chopped Off*, and then a gripping ghost story, Susan Hill's novel *The Woman In Black*, adapted by Stephen Malatratt. The attendance at each event has reached or surpassed its set target. The 2002 programme from January to May offers 36 plays by many different visiting companies, including four Shakespeare plays (one presented by St Leonards School), A.B. Paterson's *Fit Like* by the Auld Byre Players, *Brigadoon* by the St Andrews Operatic Society.

The Byre is open all day, from 10 a.m. until midnight, and on Sundays from noon. The coffee bar and the restaurant are popular. It is operating as a community theatre, with shows in the A.B. Paterson auditorium and in the Laurence Levy studio theatre with its own productions, visiting professional companies and local amateur companies. There is music (so far two visits by Scottish Opera), jazz evenings, poetry sessions, talks and workshops. Education plays a vital role; the Youth Theatre has two senior groups and a junior group, some of whom had parts in *A Christmas Carol*. There is also a writers' group. The Hay Days Club has flourished; one midday a week it takes over every available space and, in addition to all sorts of activities, has a choir and a bellringers' group.

The news of the Arts Council's 2002 grant is a matter for rejoicing: the Byre has been given funds to ensure that it can develop its building, which cost £5.2 million. The grant was a 90% increase on the 2001 grant.

The St Andrews Dramatic Society

I have a list of plays presented bi-annually in the New Picture House from 1930 to 1952 for three nights March/April and in mid-December. The producer was Mr G. Paterson Whyte, occasionally assisted by Ian Hendry.

1930	*What Every Woman Knows*	*A Song of Sixpence*
1931	–	*The Show*
1932	*Are you a Mason*	*Three one-act plays*
1933	*Tons of Money*	*Bunty Pulls the Strings*
1934	*Passing Brompton Road*	*Pygmalion*
1935	*Kye Amang the Corn*	*Murder on the Second Floor*
1936	*Yellow Sands*	*Fresh Fields*
1937	*A Scrape o' the Pen*	*The First Mrs Fraser*
1938	*Storm In the Manse*	*Winter Sunshine*
1939	*Marigold*	–

1940	*Charity Begins*	–
1946	*Dear Octopus*	*Candied Peel*
1947	*Quiet Weekend*	*Barnet's Folly*
1948	*Aubrey Writes a Book*	*Quiet Wedding*
1949	*Miranda*	*This Happy Breed*
1950	*A Play for Ronnie*	–
1951	*The Chiltern Hundreds*	*Mystery at Greenfingers*
1952	*Bunty Pulls the Strings*	*The Middle Watch*

John Johnson has lent me his collection of programmes. The earliest is that of Winter Sunshine by G.A. Thomas which took place 28 and 29 November 1938 at the New Cinema House; Hunter Scott was the Stage Manager. The action took place on the promenade deck of the Royal Mail Steamer 'Southern Cross', outward bound from London with passengers and mail for Bombay and Australia. Hunter's parents, Mr and Mrs Alfred Scott were in the cast. The Ship's Commander was played by Mr T.T. Fordyce, and John Trench by Mr D.S. Cooper. At the front of the programme (price 2d) is a list of forthcoming films: Clark Gable, Myrna Loy and Spencer Tracy in Test Pilot, Gary Cooper and Claudette Colbert in Bluebeard's Eighth Wife and Ginger Rogers and James Stewart in Vivacious Lady. Have you got the atmosphere of the times?

The rest of the collection are either John Johnson's or those of Sheila Robertson who became his wife. The front of each programme is embroidered with the autographs of all who took part in the production. The programmes are merely printed information, but such collections evoke vivid and happy memories. Great days! The programme for *The Middle Watch* is marked AH FUNG JOHN C. JOHNSON, and below is written 'Love and well done Sheila'. John was also the stage manager.

Those in the cast of *Winter Sunshine* (1938) – Mr and Mrs Alfred Scott, Mr D.S. Cooper, Mr George Scott (a teacher at New Park), and T.T. Fordyce himself, an impressive figure as the Ship's Captain – were for many years the leading lights of the Society.

In this 1938 programme Mr Fordyce's full page advertisement begins:

> WINTER SUNSHINE
> is produced by the St Andrews Dramatic Society after weeks of study but
> XMAS SUNSHINE
> can be produced by a generous distribution of Goodwill at little cost from the wonderful variety of Useful and Acceptable Gift Goods provided by
> THE DRAPERY HOUSE AND T.T. FORDYCE's at 64 South Street.

Among the lists of possible gifts are Bear Brand and Wolsey Hose, Pesco and Viyella slumber wear. This is so typical of the little St Andrews of those days.

Other amateur actors whom I remember from the early fifties and later are Ann Leslie, Ishbel Macauley, J.G. Cooper, Margaret Gilchrist and her husband John Gilchrist, Marianne Bromley who became Mrs Sandy Caird, Peter Fisher, Bert Dawson, Tom Watson, Arthur Taylor (Guard Bridge Paper Mill), George Milligan (New Park School), A.S. Philp, Margaret Bairner, Mrs Childs, Rear-Admiral Barry and Mrs Barry, Dorothy Scott, Eileen Fitzgerald and Norval and Sylvia Lunan – and more. The hard work was not only on the stage but also off-stage. There is a long list of teamwork productions telling of effort, achievement, of fun and friendships. And during all those years the audience filled the Picture House at each of the two performances.

Come to 1950: *The Chiltern Hundreds.* In the sitting room of Lister Castle we find Arthur Taylor as the Earl of Lister; Mrs Barry as the Countess, Sheila Robertson from the American Embassy, Ann Leslie as Bessie, George Milligan as the stately butler, George Scott as Lord Lister's son, T.T. Fordyce as Mr Cleghorn, and myself as Lady Caroline Smith. And 'the telephone was kindly lent by G.P.O.' The sitting room had French windows; the curtain were raised and lowered in those days, and the National Anthem was sung.

Some people left, some people continued to play major parts (not necessarily on the stage). And some new members came along. In the sixties the membership of the Society decreased; the popularity of television may have accounted for smaller audiences. By 1968 the writing was on the wall. At a meeting early in 1969 Bert Dawson, treasurer, reported there was a deficit of £2.40. It was decided that the time had come to wind up the Society, to pull down the curtain.

The Three Masques

Members of the Byre company, the Play Club, the Dramatic Society, the Operatic and various music societies took part in Alex Paterson's three masques which were played in high summer in the Cathedral grounds. In 1954 The Masque of St Andrews was performed with Andrew Common played by Michael Elder. In 1955 The Masque of the Cardinal was presented with Lyon Todd as Cardinal Beaton. In 1956 it was the turn of The Masque of the Legend with Michael Elder as 'The Spirit of St Andrews'. The orchestra was conducted by Miss Macfarlane, dancing directed by Mrs Steele and Mrs Grant, and the very reliable Miss Quigley was prompter. The masques were directed by David Cooper, produced by Ian Hendry, and the stage managers were John Johnson and Michael Cox. Some of these masques were repeated over the years. I remember that at one point in the Masque of St Andrews the entire audience rose, left the Cloisters, and walked to the site of the next scene. John Gilchrist was an elderly man but he moved smartly, scrambled over a low wall or two and went down to the harbour. What a setting, what turbulent scenes from the past came back to life. Were any ghosts stirring?

The St Andrews Film Society

This was a joint venture between Town and Gown promoted in the late 1940s with the agreement of the management of the New Cinema. The committee selected a film for each week in university term-time. These films were shown twice, on Sunday afternoons and Sunday evenings. J.K. Robertson, editor of *The St Andrews Citizen*, was the Secretary. Many of us have happy memories – not only of the splendid selection of classic films, French, Swedish and Greek among them, but also of the social gatherings afterwards at the Thorpe Davies' house in North Street, and at the Woodwards' at 1 Howard Place.

'Fox' and 'King' were two students here around 1950 who belonged to the Society; they remember Ingmar Bergman's *Seventh Seal*, another Swedish film, *Frenzy*, and also *Dr Caligari's Cabinet* and *Brief Encounter*. Others remember *M. Hulot's Holiday*, *Wild Strawberries*, Garbo's *Ninotshka*, *Fan Fan La Tulipe*, *Les Enfants du Paradis* (Jean Loius Barthold), *Smiles of a Summer Night* and Bergman's *Au Revoir les Enfants*. I have vivid memories of cycling home on a winter night when a fierce frost had descended. I had been very moved and distressed by a film about children (perhaps the last one mentioned above), and tears were streaming down my face. I imagined the tears were freezing and was glad I had not far to go behind a cascade of rattling icicles.

The Cinema has no records, but I think the Society may have ceased in the 1970s. The students ran a film society of their own for some years.

Chapter 6

MUSIC: PLAYERS AND SINGERS

From the records that are available and with invaluable help from Dr Christopher Field and Miss Jean McPherson, I now give a brief account of the various societies which have provided a variety of music to Town and Gown audiences, just before and during the twentieth century. It is impossible to give a chronological account; the different groups are University or Town, or both combined, as were the audiences.

The City Bands

The St Andrews Brass Band was formed in 1879; its first bandmaster was Mr Charles Russell. Provost Milton, living at the Roundel (1, South Street), presented the players with uniforms which were blue with yellow facings, the caps blue with yellow bands. The next bandmaster was Mr Charles Auchterlonie who was succeeded by a kinsman, James Auchterlonie; both had trained with the Forfar Light Infantry. James, who played the euphonium, was with the City Band for a total of forty-four years. No less than twelve members of this Auchterlonie family were members of the City Bands. The Band gave weekly concerts in the open space beside the Royal and Ancient clubhouse. Also, as *The Citizen* stated, 'the Band discoursed dance music all the Lammas Market Day at the back o' the Kirk.' Sometimes they played at the pond at Southfield when there was skating in the winter. They were in demand on civic occasions and at private events, and had many engagements. One of the first was to accompany the Guard Bridge Paper Mill workers on their annual outing – on this occasion to Stirling. The Band did not last long after 1914. In the newspaper their demise was put down to 'an invention called wireless which dispensed dance music'. In 1926 through the efforts of T.T. Fordyce, Alfred Auchterlonie and others, a new City Silver Band was formed; it included many of the members of the previous Band. There was a door-to-door collection, and some new instruments and uniforms were bought. Concerts were given in the Town Hall, in Crail, Elie and Dundee. One day several members went out by boat into the bay and gave a concert, but it was not repeated 'as there was no sounding board'. In 1937 the band played in the town on the day of the Coronation of George VI. From 1939 the Band played at popular Sunday evening services in the Picture House. It came to an end on 1 July 1950 'owing to an extreme shortage of experienced players in the town'. Many young men had been called up to National Service. In addition it was without a tutor. Its instruments were returned to the Town Council.

The Freedom of the City was presented to RAF Leuchars on 22 August 1968, the fiftieth anniversary of the founding of the Royal Air Force. A parade of the massed bands of pipes and drums of the City of St Andrews, RAF Leuchars and St Andrews University OTC preceded the ceremony which took place in South Street outside Holy Trinity Church. The scroll ceremony presented by Provost T.T. Fordyce read:

> We, the Provost, Magistrates and Councillors of the Royal Burgh of St Andrews, in grateful recognition of the Services of the Royal Air Force Station Leuchars, in War and Peace and in Honour of the Fiftieth Anniversary of the Royal Air Force, Do hereby confer on the Officer Commanding and on all ranks of the Royal Air Force stationed at Leuchars the privilege, honour and distinction of marching through the City of St Andrews on all ceremonial occasions with bayonets fixed, colours flying and bands playing.

After the ceremony there was a fly-past, a helicopter leading several Chipmunks followed by a flight of sixteen Lightnings. There is a similar parade and fly-past each year to commemorate that great occasion.

The Pipe Bands

The St Andrews Town Band disbursed in 1965. However the Boys Brigade Band remained strong, and a new band was formed in 1971 by a group of Boys Brigade members who were seventeen and eighteen years old. This was called the '1st St Andrews Boys' Brigade Ex-members Pipe Band'. They were joined by other pipers who had not been in the BB, so in 1976 they changed the name to the 'City of St Andrews Pipe Band'.

This Band has had great successes, winning major competitions in Britain and in Europe, and from being Grade 3 in the Royal Scottish Pipe Band Association was promoted to Grade 2. Over the years there were difficulties in finding adequate places for practising. For a time they used the ex-Congregational church in Bell Street (when it was the meeting place of the Eastern Star), and then a garage in South Street. When the schools became community schools, the band had excellent facilities in the use of classrooms in the evening.

Pipe-Majors of the old band were Pipe-Major Kirk and Donald Lassels, and for the new band (1971) Richard Goodman was succeeded by Alex Bayne, Andrew Soutar and, presently, Nick Horn.

For some time the Madras College Pipe Band has excelled, and now has several girl players. It is customary on St Andrew's Day for the bands to hold the ceremony of Beating the Retreat in South Street. On 30 November 2001 I went to watch a very impressive and first-rate performance. There were three bands: the City of St Andrews Pipe Band, the City of St Andrews Junior Pipe Band and the Madras Pipe Band – sixty players in all. In previous years when I had been to the Beating of the Retreat, the bands had assembled at the BB Hall and marched through Greenside Place, up Abbey Street and along South Street. This has been changed recently because of perceived danger in Abbey Street and the resulting expenses incurred. So the ceremony took place in half of Church Square, but there was inadequate space, the lighting was dim, and most of the assembled crowd had a poor view.

However, in 2003 it proved possible for the actual ceremony to take place in South Street in front of Holy Trinity, although the march up Abbey Street was not feasible. The bands are worthy of the outmost support.

Musical Associations

St Andrews Musical Association, 1913-55

There was a St Andrews Choral Society listed in the 1898 St Andrews Directory, with James Cheape President.

The following is taken from *The St Andrews Citizen* of 1 October 1904.

> Why is there no local orchestra and when is the Choral Society to be restored? There are musical societies connected with different churches, but there is no word of the Orchestral Society being revived. Is it not possible to have a high-class orchestral society as well as a Choral Union? There are many instrumentalists living in the town.

It was revived. The St Andrews Musical Association is listed in the 1913 Directory, with Herbert Wiseman as Conductor and Mr Macbeth Robertson Secretary. In March 1914 the orchestra gave a performance of choral works by Elgar and Parry's 'The Choric Song' from The Lotus Eaters. The soprano was Miss Edith Evan from Covent Garden. In the 1932 Directory Mr J.M. Cooper was conductor, Revd

G. Nowell Price Secretary. There is a note to say 'rehearsals take place in the Episcopal Hall on Wednesday evenings 7.15 pm orchestra and 8 p.m. choir'. In March 1936 the Musical Association performed Elgar's The Black Knight, with Mr David McCallum of the Scottish Orchestra as solo violinist. In The Citizen's account are the words 'The St Andrews Musical Association ranks as one of the best orchestras in the east of Scotland'. Each December this orchestra, with guest soloists, gave an annual performance of the Messiah. The Citizen of 11 December 1954 reported: 'A certain anxiety that has been current this year about the future of the venerable Musical Association of the city has been dispelled by the numerically healthy state of the choir at the latest performance of the Messiah.' The report continues with high praise to the soloists Joan Alexander, Ruth Morris, David Scott, to the choir, the orchestra and the conductor, Chester Henderson. However, it seems there was some sad truth in the rumours; there was no performance in December 1955.

St Andrews University Musical Society, 1876-

Although this was a University group, its concerts were open to the public, and were a part of the lives of many people.

Dr Christopher Field did some research on the beginning of this Society and on music in St Andrews between 1880 and 1890 for a talk he gave to the Society in 1982. He has also given me a very useful outline of the Society's further history which I have summarised, with some quotations from the report.

There was a tradition that the Society was founded in 1876 by 'a certain Mr Moody [who] was apparently not a member of the University'; this may have been recorded by Robert Thomson who was President in 1884-5. The first concert reported in the press was on 15 April 1879: 'a body calling itself the University Musical Association gave its first public concert "before a large and fashionable audience" in the United College Hall ..., conducted by Charles Freeman, the organist of St Andrews Episcopal Church. ... The programme had a Victorian drawing-room character to it: it consisted largely of part songs interspersed with vocal solos, duets and trios sung by various student soloists – all male of course.'

During the years 1880-90 the Society was encouraged by Sir Herbert Oakeley, Reid Professor of Music at the University of Edinburgh 1886-91. As a result of communications between Sir Herbert and Principal Shairp, a grand concert was staged in the Town Hall by the St Andrews University Musical Society. Oakeley conducted and Charles Freeman acted as accompanist. A chorus of over fifty students took part, and the Society's orchestra was joined by an orchestra of professionals and amateurs from Edinburgh. The programme included Oakeley's own Festal March *Edinbugh*, his choral song *The Troubadour*, some of his Scots song arrangements, and music by Handel, Weber and Verdi. This was the first of a series of concerts. James McPherson took over from Freeman in 1883, and in the years 1884, 1885 and 1889 Oakeley returned to preside over the concerts. Professors as well as students joined in these concerts. 'A song sung by Sir Peter Scott-Lang, the Regius Professor of Mathematics, came to be a regular feature, usually received with a tremendous encore.' By the late 1880s women began to appear in the Musical Society's annual concerts. *The Citizen* reported on the concert given on 2 March 1893: 'The lady students were a new and important acquisition to the corps of performers, and infused into the chorus singing an exhilarating brightness and sprightliness that was very pleasing.'

In 1903 James McPherson resigned, having rehearsed and conducted the Society for twenty years, and his place was taken for a year by F.H. Sawyer who was here temporarily. 'In 1904 the Society decided to move its practices to the collegiate church of St Salvator, which had just been restored to academic control as a University chapel, and one of its functions became to provide a chapel choir.' But in 1921 it was decided that the Society should concentrate on secular music. F.H. Sawyer returned in 1925 as University organist and conductor of the Musical Society. In 1928 the Society began to collaborate with the St Andrews Orchestral Society, and later absorbed it. Mrs Donald Mills is still remembered as a cellist. Hettie Buchanan, another cellist, has played in many orchestras since 1950.

In 1945 Cedric Thorpe Davie was appointed as Master of Music at the University. Christopher Field writes that, with an increased number of students,

> there was a resurgence of musical activity in the University. A new series of 'annual concerts' in the Younger Hall was established, beginning in April 1949, in which the Musical Society Choir and Orchestra were conducted by Cedric. There were also regular Tuesday evening concerts in Lower College Hall, including an annual 'guest night' which traditionally began with an item from the Madrigal Group.

Cedric was made Honorary President of the Society. His contribution included the revival of 'rarely-heard 18th-century works painstakingly transcribed and edited by Cedric, such as Thomas Augustine Arne's comic opera Thomas and Sally ...' Pieces were chosen to fit the resources available and were sometimes specially composed or adapted. Christopher Field continues:

> A spectacular item in the 1960 annual concert was a performance of Beethoven's 'Battle Symphony', Die Schlacht bei Vittoria, with orchestra, military bands, flags and bins of liquid nitrogen to simulate cannon smoke of the opposed British and French armies. ...
>
> Occasionally there was collaboration with other institutions: a performance of J.S. Bach's St John Passion in the Younger Hall on 8 May 1966 conducted by Cedric brought together the Musical Society choir and

the orchestra of the Royal Scottish Academy of Music and Drama from Glasgow.

Another highlight, remembered because of a lengthy power cut during the dress rehearsal, was the performance of Britten's Cantata St Nicolas on 9 December 1970, 'with the tenor Clifford Hughes as St Nicolas, St Salvator's College Chapel Choir, a girls' choir from St Leonards School, a boys' choir from New Park School, two student pianists, the organist of Holy Trinity, and the Musical Society Orchestra … in a packed Holy Trinity Church …'.

With the introduction of Honours courses in Music in the late 1960s, in order to improve the standards auditions were introduced for sections of the orchestra, and it became possible to put on more frequent large-scale concerts. Christopher Field had now joined Cedric, and the conducting of the orchestra and choir was increasingly shared between them, and later with Elizabeth Ann Reid when she returned to the Department in 1970.

> A significant high point was the 25th annual concert of 24 April 1973, which consisted of Elgar's The Music Makers (conducted by Elizabeth Ann), Czerny's Variations on a Theme of Haydn (with Cedric as pianoforte soloist and me [Field] conducting), and Cedric's Diversions on a Tune by Dr Arne (conducted by the composer). After that, Cedric considered the time had come for a 'graceful bowing-out' on his part.
>
> The culminating event of the Musical Society's 100th anniversary celebrations was the centenary concert in the Younger Hall on 2 March 1976. Oakeley's Carmen Sæculare of 1890 was revived for the occasion, newly orchestrated and arranged for mixed voices by Cedric; Cedric also returned to conduct his own Ode for St Andrews Night… Elizabeth Ann conducted Grieg's Peer

Gynt Suite No. 2 and Brahms Academic Festival Overture; while I [Field] was entrusted with Parry's Ode to Music, and a new work by Kenneth Leighton... Laudes Montium ...'

After Cedric's effective retirement in 1977, the direction of the Musical Society's choir and orchestra was largely entrusted to Elizabeth Ann. The choir continued to take on great choral works such as Brahms's German Requiem, while the orchestra [performed] challenging works such as Martinu's third Symphony and Hindemith's Symphonic Metamorphosis. One concert ... stands out in the memory: a performance in the Younger Hall on 28 November 1978 of Brahms's Quartet in G minor for pianoforte and strings, in which Elizabeth Ann was the pianist, followed by an impressive rendering of the same piece in Schoenberg's orchestral transcription of 1937, which she conducted. Professor David Kimbell, who joined the department of Music in 1979, occasionally directed concerts. [There was a] growth in popularity in the free Friday lunch-time concerts, organized from the Music department but presented under Musical Society auspices ...

University Chamber Orchestra

Elizabeth Ann formed a chamber orchestra in the late 1950s. From 1964 to 1970 Dr Cecil Hill directed a small chamber orchestra under the auspices of the Musical Society. Elizabeth Ann was invited by students to direct a joint Dundee-St Andrews chamber orchestra which flourished for two years. From 1972 to 1988 Christopher Field directed the University Chamber Orchestra which was organised from within the Department of Music. One of the highlights took place on 12 May 1972 in Lower College Hall: a concert of 17th- and 18th-century music for soprano, flutes, trumpet, strings and harpsichord.

The University Chamber Orchestra took part in the St Andrews Festivals of 1973, 1975 and 1979. The 1973 performance featured a new composition by Margaret Wilkins of *Dance Variations* for strings and harpsichord. The composer conducted and Elizabeth Ann played the harpsichord. In 1975 the Orchestra helped to handsel the new organ in St Salvator's chapel with a programme of organ concertos.

(It seems fitting here to refer to Nigel and Margaret Wilkins who founded the St Andrews Music Consort in 1968. The four players were the Wilkins, Hetty Buchanan and Heather Chisholm. They gave concerts in St Andrews, Aberdeen, Dundee, Glasgow and Falkland. In 1980 Warren Edwards replaced Hettie Buchanan and became director when the Wilkins left St Andrews. At some point the group was enlarged and the name was changed to the Scottish Early Music Consort. Christopher Field was one of the players. The group continued until about four years ago, and gave recitals in many places.)

Christopher Field writes, 'My last appearance with the chamber orchestra was a "sennet" in memory of Cedric Thorpe Davie, which took place in Lower College Hall on 18 May 1988. The orchestra played Cedric's *Solemn Music* ... and his cantata *By the River*. After the cessation of the Music department in 1988 the chamber orchestra continued for another two years or so under the direction of Elizabeth Ann, as Master of Music'.

The end of the Music department was a great blow to the music-lovers of St Andrews, many of whom will remember the much-appreciated concerts mentioned above.

Choral Music

The Cloister Singers, c. 1940-82

This choral group was founded by Charles Guild, as The Male Voice Choir, to entertain the troops in the Second World War. The first concert was held in Madras College during War Weapons Week, and £18 was raised for that fund. As members were called up for National Service, ladies joined and a mixed choir sang unaccompanied songs ranging from church music to negro spirituals, folk songs, madrigals, carols and of course Scots songs.

When the founder left for National Service, Robert Foster, Guardbridge, and Mr J.F. Richardson held the fort until Charles Guild's return some years later. The Choir then became known as the Cloister Singers. When Charles Guild was forced to resign through ill health, Robert Taylor became conductor, and in turn he was succeeded by Irene Redford.

From its inception, proceeds from concerts went to charitable causes, and the Choir has raised thousands of pounds for many causes, including the Scottish National Institution for War-blinded, Guide Dogs for the Blind, The 1st St Andrews Company Boys Brigade Building Fund, the Memorial Hall Building Fund for St Andrews British Legion, National Thanksgiving Funds, The Red Cross, Welfare Service in N.A.A.F. hospitals, St Andrews Girl Guides Building Fund, the Infantile Paralysis Fellowship (Fife Branch), Kinloch Eventide Home at Collessie, the Marie Curie Memorial Foundation, Kathleen Ferrier Cancer Research, Alwyn House Ceres, British Red Cross Society, Fife Society for the Blind (St Andrews Branch), Scottish Council for the Care of Spastics, British Empire Research for Cancer, Multiple Sclerosis Society, Mentally Handicapped Children St Andrews Branch, Fife Mission to the Deaf and Dumb, Migraine Trust, Chest and Heart Association, Cystic Fibrosis, Deaf Children, Possum, St Andrews Students' Voluntary Association, Cancer Relief (St Andrews Branch), Age Concern and Scooniehill Riding for the Disabled.

Concerts were given in the Younger Hall, the Buchanan Arts Theatre, the Town Hall, and in church halls and village halls the length and breadth of Fife and Angus. In addition the Choir sang in Dunblane Cathedral and Dunkeld Cathedral. In 1971 the Cloister Singers performed with Leon Goosens at Glamis Castle Musicale.

Each Christmas from 1946 until 1980 they provided the Lessons and Carols at St Leonard's Church, and also at Crail Parish Church from 1965 to 1981. On several occasions the Choir broadcast from Dundee or Edinburgh studios, and from 1949 also participated in Edinburgh and Perth Festivals and carried off first prizes.

Miss Redford has given me the above information. She writes:

> The Choir has given many young artistes their first opportunities of performing to the public. One, for example, was Charles Reedie, a pianist, who was formerly a pupil of Madras College and went on to bigger and better things. A Wind Ensemble from Madras and the Lomond Wind Ensemble also performed with the Choir.

Eventually in the early 80s it became hard to recruit new members, particularly tenors. We realised that unaccompanied part songs were not everyone's cup of tea and so regretfully in March 1982 the Choir ceased to exist.

Their record is a proud one and a host of people must be thankful to the Cloister Singers for the pleasure they gave and for their great generosity.

The St Andrews Madrigal Group, 1946- (current)

This group was founded in 1946 by Mr Evelyn Webb, a student returning from wartime service. In the early days the group confined itself to singing English madrigals – secular songs of the sixteenth and seventeenth centuries. The choir once won a class at the National Eisteddfod in Wales, singing in Welsh! It is entirely student-run, and has a proud record; its concerts in the town are greatly enjoyed. It provides music for advent and Christmas carol services, and a charity carol round. On May morning it gives the traditional dawn performance below the Castle ruins. (This is when some of the students plunge into the icy sea in the Castle Rock pool.)

The Renaissance Group 1956- (current)

In 1955 Douglas Gifford, lecturer in the Department of Spanish, and his wife, Hazel, were living at Mickle Folly at Den Head. It was here that the idea of starting a choral group in the Spanish Department was hatched. It arose from some 17th century Spanish medieval church music which Hazel had heard in Pamplona (Spain) and copied out by hand. The proposal was greeted with enthusiasm by some of the students, among them Lyn Ross, Margaret Rutherford and Derek Fry.

The Renaissance Group has flourished for nearly fifty years. From the start it was not entirely composed of students and university staff. For example, Heather Chisholm came from Aberdeen to St Andrews in 1957 to teach music at St Leonards School; her father had heard from Douglas Lloyd (lecturer in Chemistry and organist) about this group, and Heather made her approach and was welcomed to join it. Rehearsals were held at the next home of the 'Giffs', The Dirdale at Boarhills. There the singers enjoyed singing, and Hazel's famous suppers of sustaining soup and home made bread, together with contributions from everybody. Heather writes, 'I met Ferdy Woodward [Professor of Spanish] and David and Mary Weeks. I went on to sing in the first-ever Renaissance Group tour when we took two mini-buses to Nottingham and Leicester to sing in Hazel's brother's lovely church, and then on to Bristol. Many years later I went north with them, singing in Pluscarden Abbey and en route to Elgin and to sing in St Magnus Cathedral, Orkney.'

A great number of people have vivid and happy memories of these musical pilgrimages. Their repertoire was from 15-17th century church music – Tallis, Byrd, Palestrina – and they sang unaccompanied. Each year in the 70s and 80s, before the January term started, the Renaissance Group regularly sang the daily services for a week in either York or Lincoln Minster, a wonderful choral experience. Every alternate year in the Easter vacation they visited churches and cathedrals from Orkney to Cornwall, including Durham, Norwich, Oxford, Windsor, Bristol, Belfast and Dublin. In other years they toured the continent. A support team accompanied the singers: Ian Joy as photographer and his wife Netta, and bus-owner and driver Tom Niven and his wife Vi. Bob Murray and Stan Robertson went along as singers and treasurers; Douglas and Ferdy were relief drivers of Tom's bus. One of Ferdy's stories was that when he offered to do this he had to take a bus driver's test. All seemed to go well; his last instruction was to back the bus, which he did. 'Have I passed?' he asked the instructor. 'No, you've failed.' 'For what reason?', Ferdy said, surprised. 'Improper Use of Mirrors when you were backing.' But I didn't use the mirror – I turned round and looked through the window.' 'Exactly. That is what is called Improper Use of Mirrors.' 'But how?' Ferdy asked, but no explanation was forthcoming, and he retook the test – with 'proper use of the mirrors'.

The group went abroad to sing in cathedrals and monasteries: to France (they sang in Chartres Cathedral on ten occasions), to Spain (Santiago di Compostella and Madrid), to Italy (St Mark's in Venice), to Portugal (Lisbon), to Austria (Vienna). One year they got as far as Russia and gave concerts in Moscow and Leningrad. It was a triumph of organisation and of the work and zest which went into the many rehearsals. Visits to Poland brought about a welcome exchange visit from the choir of Cracow Cathedral in the difficult and dark days of the early 1980s. Students came into the group and went; new students took their places. There was a hard-core of members based in St Andrews, among them John Hall, Jenny Wallace, Christine and David Gascoigne, and those mentioned above.

Hazel writes: 'When Douglas retired in 1989, David Gascoigne took over the group, and it still flourishes under his leadership.' In 1995 he and Christine, with Hazel, organised a forty-years reunion, and over one hundred former members came back to St Andrews for a gloriously nostalgic weekend. 'We all sang the famous 40-part motets by Byrd and Striggio at a concert in Holy Trinity Church, and thereafter, of course, consumed hearty quantities of food and wine, and renewed cheerful memories.'

St Andrews Chorus and the Heisenberg, 1977- (current)

In 1977 the St Andrews Chorus was born out of the Holy Trinity augmented choir under the leadership of Tom Duncan, organist and choirmaster at Holy Trinity. For the first concert, Bach's *Mass in B minor,* the choir joined the Scottish Chamber Orchestra, and this successful partnership continued for many years. The performances have included Verdi's *Requiem,* Mendelssohn's *Elijah,* Beethoven's *Missa Solemnis* and *Mass in C,* and Handel's *Israel in Egypt,* and more recently Tom has conducted a revived Holy Trinity augmented choir on three occasions. The last, in December 2001, was a magnificent performance of Handel's *Messiah* with the Heisenberg Ensemble.

In 1994 the chorus reconstituted itself more formally as the Choral Society. John Grundy accepted the invitation to be its conductor, and Tom Duncan was elected Honorary President for his distinguished service over the years. John Grundy had studied music at the University of Edinburgh and piano in Rotterdam, and had worked as a pianist and conductor, notably at the 1984 and 1985 Edinburgh Festivals as Director of Music for *Ane Satire of the Thrie Estaitis.* This involved arranging the music composed by Cedric Thorpe Davie. In 1988 John Grundy was appointed Musical Director of the Sydney Philharmonia. For seven years he worked extensively throughout Australia, especially at the Sydney Opera House as Director of the Australian Opera and Ballet Orchestra. In 1994 he returned to Scotland and for one year was Principal Teacher of Music in St Andrews University's Music Centre. In 1996 he was appointed Director of Music at St Mary's School of Music in Edinburgh.

The chorus appears with the Heisenberg Ensemble which was

founded in 1989 by Gillian Craig, its musical director. It was assembled to put on a single concert: 'given the precarious nature of its inception, it seemed fitting to name the ensemble after the eminent physicist, philosopher and pianist, Professor Heisenberg who visited St Andrews in 1969 to give a lecture and was famous for his Uncertainty Principle!' The ensemble brings together local players and visiting professionals.

Among the rare works performed in recent years under John Grundy are the following: two rarely heard Gabrieli anthems, Handel's *Dettingen Te Deum*, Haydn's *St Nicholas Mass*, Rossini's *Petite Messe Solennelle* (which was commissioned by the Choral Society), the world premier of Jeremy Thurlow's *The Queen-like Closet*, Brahms' *Requiem* and Bach's *St Matthew Passion* and *Magnificat*.

Various well-known guest singers have taken the principal roles, among them St Andrews own Angela Bell, well known as a soprano soloist. She was a member of the Renaissance Group and joined the St Andrews Chorus thirteen years ago. She was the co-founder of the contemporary music group the Abacalulli Ensemble, and has performed and directed a wide range of the avant-garde repertoire. She has also appeared with the Legrenzi Consort and the Edinburgh-based early music ensemble Seicento. She teaches recorder, and she founded in St Andrews the very useful shop The Musicmongers.

The Heisenberg has gone from strength to strength. It continues to have the happy role as accompanying orchestra to the St Andrews Chorus. It plays an important part in the community with its concerts for children. It is entirely self-financing, depending on ticket sales and various fund-raising activities, many of them run by the Friends of the Heisenberg Ensemble.

St Andrews Amateur Operatic Society, 1939- (current)

This society was formed in early 1939 at a packed meeting in the old Court Room in the Town Hall. The originator, Mr Alex Maxwell, said he had been rather surprised to find that a city the size of St Andrews was not represented 'in this branch of the theatre art'. In fact it seems that an earlier society had performed annually from 1906 to 1912. On 21 March 1939, with Dr Mair as Chairman, the Society was formally inaugurated, and preparations were made to perform *A Country Girl.* But this was never to take place.

I am indebted to Michael Cox for his help in providing information about the Society. He first performed in *The Mikado* in 1950, and Sheila, later to be his wife, appeared with him in *The Gondoliers* in 1960. These two have surely earned a place in the Guinness Book of Records: they have been active members of the Society for a total between them of 93 years, and continue to take parts in the productions.

After the war the Operatic Society was re-formed in 1946 with Sheriff More as President. In February 1947 the Society performed *The Pirates of Penzance* in the New Picture House. The 'New' at that time had seating for an audience of over nine hundred, and boasted a proper orchestra pit. The orchestra was composed mainly of amateurs; Joyce Cuthbert was accompanist and Adam Cross first violin. The conductor-producer was Mr Andrew Henderson of Perth. And who better to take the part of the Pirate King than Mr T.T. Fordyce? In the 1952 production of *The Gondoliers* Mr Fordyce took the part of Grand Inquisitor, and had encores for all his songs.

In the late forties and early fifties Town Council meetings were cancelled during the Operatic Society's performances as the cast included Neil McKenzie (the Town Clerk), J.Y. Conchie, (the Housing Officer) and T.T. Fordyce. Their respective wives also took leading roles. Other names which appear in early programmes and continued to appear are 'Master James Bone' who made his first appearance in the 1952 *Gondaliers* as the little drummer boy, Roderick McKenzie (University Works Department), John Gilchrist (later to be Provost) and his wife Meg, Mr and Mrs J.L. Mowat (supervisor of the University Botanic Garden), Ishbel Macauley, Kathleen and George Milligan, and later leading lights (and they remain so now) were Grace and Ken Morris, Wendy and Frank Quinault. The pattern was set: a Gilbert and Sullivan opera was performed for three evenings in the last week of February at the New Picture House. In the programme for *Patience* in 1951 the conductor of the orchestra was Miss J.R. Macfarlane (the Honorary Conductor for many years), and the Producer Brigadier Soutar. Running through the Gilbert and Sullivan productions from 1947 to 1963 the titles were: *The Pirates of Penzance* (1947, 1954, 1963, 1978), *Iolanthe* (1948, 1956, 1985), *Trial by Jury* and *HMS Pinafore* (1949, 1959, 1996), *The Mikado* (1950,1958, 1968, 1994), *Patience* (1951, 1962), *The Gondoliers* (1952, 1960, 1967, 1989), *Ruddigore* (1953, 1961), *The Yeomen of the Guard* and *Iolanthe* (1956, 1985), and *Princess Ida* (1957).

In 1964 the New Picture House was no longer available due to film distributors' schedules. The operas for that year and the next were played in the hall of Madras College. In 1969 the Society staged *The White Horse Inn* in the Town Hall, and since then this has been the place for the main production of the year. Expenditure began to exceed income, and so in 1964 Gilbert and Sullivan made way for *Oklahoma.* This has been followed by an amazing variety of shows, with the occasional return of favourite Gilbert and Sullivans. Among the titles were *Brigadoon* (1965, 1982), *The White Horse Inn* (1969), *Guys and Dolls* (1986), *Fiddler on the Roof* (1988, 2000), *My Fair Lady* (1992), *Annie Get Your Gun* (1993), *When the Lights Come On Again* (1989, 1995), *Oliver* (1998), and in 2001 *Can't Stop Singing.* Let's hope they can't stop singing for many years of the 21st century.

Michael Cox writes:

> The membership of the Society comes from all sections of the community, the University, the schools, professional people, artisans, shop workers and school pupils. Some may be members for a short time, others stay many years. The Society has been successful in attracting younger members, having had children in

their casts. The Society usually has 35-40 members acting on stage. A member may be appointed as producer, or musical director, choreographer or accompanist. Many talented local people have taken on these duties. St Andrews has been one of the operatic societies which construct most of their own scenery. The Society has a number of patrons who contribute to Society funds and help to meet the considerable cost of staging each annual production. Some of them help with front of house duties during the performance.

Summer shows and concerts have been performed in many venues, such as the Buchanan Building, the Byre Theatre, and the church halls. Concerts and entertainments have been given for university summer schools, and for bodies all over Fife. The Society had donated much time and money to many local charities and to the Byre Theatre appeal, being a founder member.

Societies which arranged Concerts

St Andrews Chamber Music Society, 1931-52

On 25 May 1931 a meeting was held at Balfour House with the purpose of forming this society. The founder members were Lady Irvine who became President, Mrs Mary Burnet Secretary, Mrs Janet Laing and Mrs Elizabeth Boase (Law Park). Subsequently this Committee co-opted Miss Kitching and Mrs Eva Cunningham, who later became Secretary. The plan was to have a sufficient membership to provide for three concerts of chamber music between October and March, aiming at engaging high-quality London artistes. A circular was prepared and sent out at the beginning of February 1932. One hundred and three people applied for membership. By 1934, with the subscription now 30s., there were 140 members.

This small Committee made all the arrangements. It decided which musicians to invite, and what to request in the programmes, or what might replace some of the musicians' proposals! The booking was done through Messrs Ibbs and Tillett. Concerts were held in Lower College Hall; to fill any spare seats, selected students were invited (tickets at ls.!). The concerts during the first season were given by the London String Quartet, the Isolde Menges Quartet and the Brosa Quartet. These three were to return many times.

This Committee met regularly, usually at University House. Arrangements were made about such matters as spare tickets, and the 'hospitality for the players' which was usually at University House. Small difficulties were overcome. Each year an effort had to be made to collect overdue subscriptions. At one time a fire in College Hall made it necessary to change the venue for the concert to Parliament Hall in South Street. Occasionally there was a cancellation, and negotiations began for a substitute group.

A liaison was made with St Leonards School who regularly took tickets. Lady Irvine went as representative to conferences of the National Federation of Music Societies of which the St Andrews Society was a member for a few years. However, it was not the policy of the Society to book touring companies, although when a quartet was engaged which was performing elsewhere in the area (say Dundee) a reduction to the fee was usual. Lady Irvine worked hard at all aspects, and she missed only one meeting in twenty years.

The war came; concerts were given in 1939 and 1940, and then there was a gap until 1945. The Society rallied; the Arts Committee of St Andrews gave a grant of £50, and a similar sum came from the Walker Trust. Concerts resumed with The Calvet String Quartet, The London Belgian Piano Quartet and The Hirsch Quartet. Then came a sad time. First there was the untimely death of Regula Burnet (daughter of Professor and Mrs Burnet) who had been acting as Secretary. The minutes record the feelings of the Committee in these words: 'she was a member always willing to help, ready to undertake more work. She was enthusiastic, energetic, clear headed, decisive, since when ill health made her burden heavy. In loneliness she was brave, in trouble uncomplaining. We record our gratitude and affection for Regula Burnet.' Then in 1948 the death of Mr Sawyer, University organist and choirmaster, was noted by the Committee as 'the loss of a member of exceptional musical knowledge, great kindness, helpfulness and courtesy'. His place on the Committee was taken by Cedric Thorpe Davie who had been appointed by the University in 1945 when Mr Sawyer retired. It was with foresight that Sir James Irvine selected this distinguished musician, not just as choirmaster, organist and lecturer, but as Master of Music. It was Cedric who built up a Department of Music which was able to offer a single honours degree. He was Professor of Music from 1973 to 1978. He had a great effect on music in St Andrews – Town and Gown.

Over the years concerts were given by the following, some of them returning several times: The London String Quartet, The Brosa String Quartet, The Isolde Menges String Quartet, the Pro Arte Quartet, The Griller Quartet, The Buda Pest Trio, The Trio de la Cour de Belgique, The Kolisch Quartet, The Grinke Trio, The Lener Quartet, and The Scottish Orchestra Octet. After the restart in 1946 there were concerts from The Czech Trio, The London Belgian Piano Quartet, The Calvet Quartet, The Aride Mangeot String Quartet, The Dorian Quartet, The Hirsch Quartet, The Philharmonia String Quartet, The Troiller String Quartet, The Vienna Philharmonic Quartet, The Amadeus String Quartet (1950), The Marjorie Hayward String Sextet, The Quartetto Di Roma, The Aeolian String Quartet, Yfrah Neaman (violin) and Howard Ferguson (pianoforte), and also William Pleeth (cello) with Margaret Good (piano).

This brings us to a meeting of the Committee on 12 February 1952 when the seriousness of the Society's financial position was discussed. In 1946 there had been 182 subscriptions; the numbers were now down to 113. The reserve cash had been used, and the balance was small. Lady Irvine felt it was impossible to continue. She moved that

'The Society should go into abeyance, but keep the standing committee'. This was carried by 3 votes to 2.

The Arts Committee of St Andrews was founded in 1946. It had three sub-committees to arrange activities: musical events (Chairman Cedric Thorp Davie); exhibitions (Annabel Kidston); plays (A.B. Paterson). By 1952 this Committee it was in difficulties and had to decide to wind up its increasingly costly activities. As a result, it looked as though there would be no professional concerts in St Andrews. The Arts Committee wished to investigate alternatives, and Lady Irvine agreed this was the best thing to do. A public meeting was held in the Town Hall on 4 February 1953, and a committee was set up to examine the possibility of the formation of a Musical Society, whose purpose would be to give public concerts of good music in St Andrews. Those elected were Cedric Thorpe Davie, Jack Allen, Jean McPherson, David McCurrach and Roy Wilson.

The St Andrews Music Club, post 1953

This group met several times and drew up a set of recommendations which were issued on 9 March 1953. Briefly, they stated the society should be a music club composed of subscribing members with an executive committee and officers elected from among its members. It should have a written constitution which would qualify it for membership of the National Federation of Music Societies. A more varied programme was suggested, beginning with four concerts in the first season. The costings were worked out, and the formation of a sponsorship scheme was recommended so that enough money might be raised to cover the first year's programme of concerts. All concerts would be open to the public, but from time to time there would be 'members only' events. The venues would be Lower College Hall (offered free of cost), St Leonards School Hall, the Town Hall and the Younger Hall (all chargeable). The policy was that the Club should keep down expenses by combining with other clubs to select artistes.

These proposed plans were circulated, and a public meeting was called early in May 1953 at which it was agreed to go ahead. The sponsorship account already stood at £275. The Committee elected was: Professor Jack Allen, President; Mr Cedric Thorpe Davie, Vice President; Miss Jean McPherson, Secretary; also Mr Ian A.C. Cameron, Mrs Tweedie, Miss Burgess, Mr D.F. McCurrach, Mr Roy Wilson.

On 26 June Cedric reported that the St Andrews Chamber Music Society had finally wound up and a balance of £14-10s. handed over to the Music Club. It was agreed that the subscription for the first season, 1953-54, would be £1 for ordinary members and 10s. for students and juniors. By December there were 350 members (248 ordinary, 100 junior, and 2 honorary members). The Concerts in the first season were: Campoli (violin) with Flora Kent (pianoforte), Cyril Preedy (pianoforte), The Lyra String Quartet, The Saltire Singers, Margaret Fraser and Constance Mullay. The University Chapel Choir's concert became an annual event, held in May in the Chapel, and given twice, the second performance being open to the public.

On 24 May 1954 there was a concert by Myra Hess in the Younger Hall. In a letter to *The Citizen* Mrs Elizabeth Boase commented on Myra Hess's playing of the Beethoven A flat Sonata Opus 110: 'I felt it transcended any reading of the great pianists I have ever heard. The broken adagio was wonderful in its beauty.'

This was the pattern of years to come, each season there was a varied programme. Tickets were obtainable, for many years, at the Information Centre and then at The Music Shop; members had priority booking. There was often a complete sell-out. Chamber music concerts were usually held in Lower College Hall, and other concerts in the Town Hall, in the Buchanan Theatre or in St Leonards School Hall. The Younger Hall was used for the 'big draw' concerts – and there were many of these. Here are some of the names of celebrated soloists: Peter Katin (in 1957 and 1964), Denis Matthews , Julius Katchen, John Ogden (in 1962 and 1969), Peter Frankl, Fou Ts'ong, Lili Kraus,

Vladimir Ashkenazy, Michael Roll, Audrey Innes, Yonty Solomon, Whun Chung, Tamas Vasary, Julian Bream and (in 1960) Jacqueline du Pre. Among solo singers were Joan Alexander accompanied by Cedric Thorpe Davie, Kenneth McKellar, and Janet Baker. There were recitals by The Berlin Philharmonic Quartet, The Jacques Orchestra, The Berlin Philharmonic Soloists, The Beaux Arts Trio (of New York), The Smetena String Quartet, The Prague String Quartet, The Early Music Consort and The Quartetto Esterhazy Orchestra. For some years Opera for All presented a selection of operas.

The 1973-74 season was especially splendid, with almost all the concerts taking place in the Younger Hall. It began with the Smetena String Quartet, a piano recital by Peter Frankl and then, on the occasion of the Club's hundredth concert, the celebrities Szymon Goldberg and Radu Lupu. In January 1974 we had The King's Singers, in February Yehudi Menuhin, followed in March by Peter Williams (harpsichord).

Selecting from the programmes up to 1980, the artists included The Slovak String Quartet; The Northern Sinfonia, The Scottish Piano Quintet, The Berlin Philharmonic Octet, The Allegri Quartet, The Janacek Quartet, Philomusica of London, and The Philadelphia String Quartet. Recitals were given by Peter Katin, Julian Bream, Fou T'song, Whun Chung, Tamas Vasary, Andre Tchaikovsky, Peter Frankl, and violinist Ruggiero Ricci.

The last decade

About 1980 a noticeable change was experienced in many music clubs. A number of factors seemed to bring this about. Competition increased; the Scottish Chamber Orchestra gave an annual series of concerts in the Younger Hall, and many people subscribed each season, so The Music Club was no longer the sole provider. Television at that time screened some good programmes, an easy alternative for some of the ageing concert-goers. CDs of first-class performances became available. Also there was a general cultural change in younger people towards popular music and, for many, chamber music became a minority taste. It is hard to say how much effect the reduction of the Music Department had. Cedric Thorpe Davie retired, and Professor Kimbell was appointed in 1979. With cuts and restructuring came the decision that the professor and lecturers of the Music Department would join those in the Department at Edinburgh University. Elizabeth Ann Frame remained in St Andrews to run a one-year course.

In any event, there was a sharp decline in the number of Music Club members. It was now not possible to use the Younger Hall, although the prices for Lower College Hall and the Buchanan Building were reasonable. But then came a real blow. Mrs Arnott, the wife of Principal Struther Arnott, undertook to supervise the renovation of Lower College Hall so that it might be hired for wedding receptions and other functions and thus bring in an income. The platform was removed, the stone fireplace revealed, and an enormous carpet was laid over the entire floor. The kitchen was renovated and could be used only if specified caterers were called in (which put an end to its venue for the Ladies' Club meetings). And of course the fees went up. When the first concert took place the sounds were muffled; some of the performers were in tears. Jack Allen tested the acoustics by firing a starting pistol, and declared the hall 'acoustically dead'. The Town Hall was used for a short time, but the piano was not good enough. Jeff Ashcroft records that there were often difficulties with pianos, and occasions when the guest artist declared it impossible to play on the instrument provided. Myra Hess actually brought her own piano. For some time the firm of Largs shipped pianos from Dundee, and then eventually a good piano was bought for the Younger Hall.

To return to the Music Club – often when one door shuts another door opens. St Leonards School Hall, built in 1986, was offered free for Music Club concerts. An anonymous donor presented a first-class piano. The splendid hall accommodates one hundred people. And this was just right, as the Music Club numbers had stabilised to between

80 and 100. Jeff Ashcroft has been a prominent committee member and office-bearer since 1977 and takes over from Heather Chisholm as President in the 2001/2 season.

Six concerts are given each season. Lady Irvine would have been delighted, for chamber music is performed by top players. One of the most successful concerts was given by The Kyrsia Osostowic; others were by The Domus Ensemble, The Amati String Quartet (from Switzerland), The Raphael Ensemble, The Stamic Quartet (of Prague), The Endellion String Quartet, The Schubert Ensemble, The Schubert Ensemble, The Skampa String Quartet (Czech), and a memorable recital by Lorraine McAstan, a Scottish violinist.

It is heartening to know that the Music Club is 'stable and successful in its scope'.

The St Andrews Festival, 1971-93

The first festival of a series of twelve, staged every alternate year, took place in February 1971. It was the brainchild of two students, Peter White and Michael Dale, and went from strength to strength to become a miniature Edinburgh Festival in mid-winter. The structure of organisation developed. Patrons included the Chancellor (Lord Ballantrae) and the Vice-Chancellor and Principal of the University, the Professors of Fine Arts (Art History) Professor John Steer and his successor Martin Kemp, and Rectors Frank Muir and John Cleese. Financial assistance was given by firms, businesses and by individuals, and there were grants from the Scottish Arts Council, Local Government and from Trusts.

The Directors were Dr Ian Gilchrist 1971-1979, Mrs June Baxter 1979-1989, and Colin Brown 1989-1993. The Directors appointed the student convenors for Drama, Classical Music, Modern Music, Films, Poetry, Exhibitions, Finance, Publicity, Bookings, Festival Café and Hospitality (many of the performers were given hospitality by local families). Later this team of conveners numbered twenty-four.

After the event each convener wrote a full account, with advisory notes for his/her successor. The executive committee was composed of local residents; Mrs Joyce Pirie, Dr C.D.S. Fields and Mrs June Baxter were constants on this committee, which offered advice and guidance to the conveners.

In 1975 Andrew Wright, chartered accountant, was appointed Financial Convener and was an enormous help. Also in 1975 The Festival Society was founded; in 1980 it became a limited company. In 1983 over one hundred events were staged, but for the first time there was a deficit in the accounts. This happened again in 1987, but at the end of the final Festival there was a balance – which says a lot for the good management.

A mainstream programme and a fringe programme took place, and there was a Festival Café with late-night events (in the Town Hall, and in later festivals on the top floor of the Students' Union) and a Festival Ballet to end the programme. The content of the programmes is very impressive. Over the years notable orchestras returned: The Scottish Chamber Orchestra, The BBC Symphony Orchestra, The Fife Youth Orchestra, as well as distinguished quartets – the Moscow String Quartet and The Gabrieli among many. Famous soloists such as Peter Katin, Darryl Rosenberg and Julian Lloyd Webber delighted large audiences. Scottish Opera and Scottish Ballet came several times. In the earlier years the Rector Frank Muir (Rector of the University) put on 'Frank Muir and Friends' at three Festivals. Later Nicholas Parsons (Rector in 1989) performed in 'A Celebration of Nonsense'. The acclaimed 'Scotland the What' was advertised with the words 'THEY'RE BACK'!

Poetry readings included contributions by Norman McCaig, Alistair Reid, Sorley McLean, Iain Crichton-Smith, Edward Morgan, Tony Harrison, and Douglas Dunn. Films were shown at the New Picture House. As many as ten exhibitions at a Festival were mounted all over the town. The Naismith Exhibition and the Barlinnie Special Unit Exhibition were memorable. The Byre Theatre was host to Winged

Horse Company; 'Lumière and Son Theatre' played in the Students' Union (which had, through Festival Committee, acquired stacked seating), and The Medieval Players were engaged for several Festivals.

In addition, local and student groups performed: those recorded in the section above on music, organ recitals by Tom Duncan and by John Kitchen, plays by the student Mermaid Society, and exhibitions by the St Andrews Art Club.

The 1993 Festival was to be the last. Various factors made this inevitable, the foremost being the change in the students' year from three-term to two-term. This meant the Festival could not be held in February, and no other time in the year suited. There were also misgivings about the future of the financial position; an analysis of a survey of attendances carried out by Andrew Wright showed declining bookings. The Festival lit up the dark winters – literally, on the first night when a torchlight procession took place, and throughout ten days of a splendid variety of choices, and a high standard of performances.

Chapter 7

PAINTBRUSH, CAMERA AND EXHIBITIONS

The St Andrews Photographic Society

Early photographers

St Andrews is noted for its early developments in photography. From 1848 to1865 Dr John Adamson lived in the house in South Street which is now the Post Office. He was a physician in the town, and a pioneer photographer. In 1841 he made the first calotype portrait. Dr Adamson taught the brothers Robert and Thomas Rodger the art of photography, and persuaded Thomas to set up as the first professional photographer in St Andrews. His home and studio were at 6 St Mary's Place. He has left a large collection of fine photographs, a record of the town and its people up to 1883. His photographs of eminent visitors brought him fame, and he received commissions to go to London to take photographs of members of the royal family.

In G. Wilson's *St Andrews Directories* for 1909 and 1913, a St Andrews Photographic Society is listed. Office bearers for 1909 were: Hon. President Fred Thomson; Hon. Vice President W.E. Fairlie; President Dr Sidney Kay; Sec. E. Balfour. Other office bearers were Andrew Haxton, James Haxton, and W. Anderson. In 1913 the Hon. President was Professor Purdie and the Hon Vice President Professor Musgrove; the President was Professor Scott Lang and the Vice President, J. Caldwell. Edward Balfour was secretary from 1907 to 1913. Unfortunately there do not seem to be any other records of this society. Presumably it ceased during the War.

The Second St Andrews Photographic Society

Sam Taylor, Professor in the Department of French, and well known as an outstanding photographer, has written a summary of this society from 1958 to date, on which the following is based.

The St Andrews Photographic Society was founded by Dr David Thirkell of the University Bio-chemistry Department and Ian Kinghorn, a technician of the same department. The first president was Dr David Jack (Physics department), the secretary Colin Brown of Wilson's ironmongers, the treasurer Ned Hunter (Inland Revenue). 'Soon there was a strong membership of around sixty composed of Town and Gown. Some of the early members besides Dr Thirkell were Eric Carstairs (Bute Medical), teachers George Kinghorn and Norman Macleod, the well-known David Niven (later to become Provost), a Polish soldier Ernest Makrenko, farmers Peter Lucas and Jim Weir, Flt-Lt Peter Williams, RAF, and John Evans. The professional photographer Ian Joy became a member, but not George Cowie and his son Andrew, who felt it would be unfair to compete against non-professionals. They nonetheless helped the Club considerably. Sam Taylor gives names of others who joined in the sixties 'to show the wide social and professional scatter of members, and the different expertises they brought to the society': from the early sixties University Professors Mike Laverack (Gatty Marine), Bob Crawford (Botany), Sam Taylor (French) Gus Serafini-Fracassini (Bio-chemistry), Dr Gordon Woolley (Chemistry), Dr Alan Robertson (Modern History), Ron Hilditch (Astronomy), Sandy Edwards and Dave Ogden (Bute Medical), Jan Mulder (Linguistics), and Richard Cormack (Statistics). Teachers who were members from the early sixties were Donald Chisholm, Anne Cantley, George Scott, Brian Johnstone and Anne Young; civil servants Robin Russell and Cathie Lawrie and Drs Anne and Duncan Davidson (Ninewells Hospital).

Few women had joined in the early years, given the primitive premises and the predominantly male membership. After Anne Cantley, Heather Walshaw was one of the earliest in the 70s, followed by the first female president Sylvia Cairns, writer Cathie Forrest, and five other ladies. Now the membership is well balanced.

Meetings were initially held in the main ground-floor rooms of Kinburn House, moving after two or three years into the attic, and three years later to the damp basement. Membership fell from the forties to the teens when the society was confined to the basement. It later moved for comfort to the public rooms in Rusacks Hotel, then to the Scores Hotel, the Buchanan Building in Union Street, and the Art Club premises in Loudens Close. The friendly umbrella of the Art Club then continued, and the Society moved with the artists to their new premises off Argyle Street. Later premises have not had dark-room facilities, though the swing to digital processing is making everyman's computer a dark room.

Local photographers George Cowie and Ian Joy gave talks in those early days. Eric Carstairs trained the club in developing and printing. John Evans gave talks on printing techniques. Albert Gregory, the famous Everest expedition photographer, gave a memorable lecture in the Town Hall. George Kinghorn demonstrated making silhouettes of members against an illuminated screen. At that time the Cupar Club specialised in ciné work and those like Peter Lucas, who did ciné work, moved over. However, he demonstrated to the Society his 16-mm ciné filming of work on the Forth Bridge. St Andrews mostly engaged in black and white art-work, colour processing being too difficult or expensive for most people. In later years the Scottish Photographic Federation was created as an umbrella and information base for clubs, listing lectures and judges and instituting competitive Scottish portfolios.

The Society was well organised according to *Amateur Photographer* guidelines which appeared in the 70s. It still has members regularly competing in national and international exhibitions, and its membership is steady at forty each year, with members from the East Neuk, Cupar and Tayside. It has played a significant role in promoting a major improvement in local postcards and supporting local charities. Local churches have benefited, as have the Botanic Gardens, Scottish Wildlife Trust, harbour maintenance, university publicity material, Preservation Trust activities, and St Andrews' week programmes. The promotion of St Andrews' role in the history of photography and the development of local tourism have all been helped. Club members have seriously supported St Andrews cultural exchanges with Upper Arlington (USA) and Loches (Touraine, France) through photographic portfolios and travelling exhibitions. This is one of the societies which has maintained its numbers, increased its range of activities.

The St Andrews Art Club

A public meeting was held in the Town Hall on 29 October 1959 with Mr Ronald Todd (in the absence of Michael Scott) in the chair. It was decided to form an Art Club, and there were forty signatures. The following people were elected to the committee: Michael Scott, Mrs M.A. Ardach, Mrs E. Edwards, Mr John Duncan, Mr T.W. Cubitt, Miss M.R. Darling, Mr Ronald Todd, Mr L. Firth. The committee met immediately and elected the officials. The aims of the Club were recorded: 'To encourage the appreciation and practice of the visual arts and to provide facilities for such practice'.

The question of accommodation was discussed, and was to prove a recurrent and difficult problem for the next twenty-five years. Four possible places were suggested and investigated with no result, as were many others in the years to come. The new Club had temporary use of the Dramatic Society's rooms in Church Square at a low annual rent. Meantime the search continued. In those early days the Club was greatly helped by the advice and practical help of several professional artist members; this continued to be the case.

In 1966 the Town Council accepted the Art Club's offer to rent a condemned cottage in Fleming Place at £10 per annum. A team for cleaning-up operations went into action. Over the years the Art Club has specialised in such teams! Permission was given to remove a partition to make a larger room. Although it was not suitable for art sessions or lectures, it was useful as a store. In 1976 the Fleming Place building was sold; the Club removed its property accumulated there and Rev Peter Douglas gave it a home at Dunino.

In 1969 the owner of 140 South Street, which was listed as

condemned, agreed to rent it to the Art Club for £26 per annum with an option to buy. It was opened as the Art Club rooms on 19 September 1969. In 1971 the Club was able to rent the large room (the L-shaped room) in the Step Rock Swimming Club's rented premises at Loudens Close. The Club then rented the old sewing room in the Craft Centre at St Leonards School for two evenings a week. By 1979 there were ninety members, and the accommodation situation was serious.

In 1982 the Club got a two-year lease of The Preservation Trust's Loudens Close rooms at a rent of £300 per annum. This included the large room. At last members could use the clubrooms at times other than the fixed sessions. Lectures could be held there, and small exhibitions mounted. But it was not the answer, and it was costly. For a short time the Club was held at the Bridge Club in Queens Terrace. Before long the committee was considering (longingly) the purchase of the former Argyle Street golf club factory premises, but the price was beyond its means. Now comes the happy ending to flittings, and the beginning of a new era. At a committee meeting on 20 May 1985 it was announced that Mrs Agnes Campbell, 3 Middleshade Road, a Club member for many years, had offered to purchase the premises of the golf club factory at 14 Argyle Street as a gift to St Andrews Art Club. The price was £12,000 and, in addition, legal fees and surveyor's fees would be paid. What a wonderful gift it proved to be.

In its early years the Art Club managed to get a programme going which was to be the pattern for the future. The first exhibition (of local art) was held 12-15 May in the Victory Memorial Hall in aid of the World Fund for Refugees. The amount given to the Fund was £254. After this the Club held a major exhibition annually in July, for many years in the Volunteer Hall in City Road, and for a few years in the Students' Union. Members became experienced organisers of screen shifting (and painting the screens), of hanging, of volunteer rotas, of advertising and of financial management. Throughout the years, smaller exhibitions have been mounted, some at the Students'

Festivals in the 1970s and 1980s. Paintings have also been displayed (and available for sale), first at the Picture House, then at the Byre Theatre and currently at the Health Centre.

In the early years of the Club, members attended two classes a week at Madras College until it became possible to hold them in Art Club premises. Monthly lectures – sometimes in the form of demonstrations – were given by professionals. 'Sunday summer painting days' were part of the pattern: a local site was chosen. There was also on offer a week's summer course with a tutor. Playing the professional part in these activities were some well-known artists such as McIntosh Patrick, Alberto Morocco, David McLure, Roddy Braggins, Elaine Lambie, Rory McLeod, Calder Jamieson, Elaine Renton, Irene Duncan, Ruth Walker, Winifred and Alison McKenzie and Anne Dick. There were also visits to exhibitions elsewhere and art galleries. A competition was organised for paintings by schoolchildren. An arrangement was made for the Photographic Society to use the Club rooms one evening a week, and the custom began of having a joint evening meeting with paintings and photos of the same subjects.

It is not possible to mention the many leading names over so long a period, but the following is a list of those who held the post of Chairman, and were also on the committees at other times.

1959–61	Mr M. Scott	1984–86	Mrs S. Mackintosh
1962–68	Mr P. Todd	1986–88	Mrs Helen Firth
1968–70	Miss Darling	1988–90	Mrs Esme Chapman
1970–73	Miss A. Robertson	1990–92	Mr Ian Gilroy
1973–75	Mrs J Michie	1992–94	Dr Ronald Emslie
1975–76	Mr I. Liddell	1994–96	Miss Ruth Walker
1977–79	Miss Mackintosh	1996–99	Dr Roy MacGregor
1979–81	Miss A. Cassells	1999–01	Mrs Morag Harrison
1981–82	Miss Terry	2001–	Mr John Johnson
1982–84	Miss E. Thom		

There are others whose work is not forgotten. For the Club's first fourteen years Leslie Firth was Secretary or Treasurer, and on his death in 1973 he was described as 'the power that built and held the Club together'. Other names to add are: James Duncan, Jean Le Maitre, Anne d'Espremenil and Bob Warren.

At present the Club has a waiting list for membership. It holds two tutored classes and one untutored over the autumn and winter terms. There are fund-raising coffee mornings, mini-exhibitions, competitions, and packed audiences at the monthly lectures.

To me, 14 Argyle Street means sitting comfortably in a warm cheerful room in a peaceful contented silence, each person absorbed in effort. And then the coffee break, a time of friendship, of people walking about to see what the canvases show, of encouragement. There is also the scene of the two-week summer exhibition. More than a thousand visitors stream in and make their way round, their faces lit up with interest and pleasure. Difficult decisions are made, and a red dot signifies that yet another successful painting has found a home. Happiness!

Crawford Centre for the Arts, and the Friends of the Crawford Centre

The story of St Andrews for both the nineteenth and the twentieth centuries is one of building and rebuilding, of conservation, and of changes in the use of larger and of smaller properties. Certain buildings in North Street, some of which became the Crawford Centre, illustrate this well. When we came to St Andrews in 1950 my daughters went St Katharines, the junior school of St Leonards, at that time in North Street in a handsome villa built in 1812 for the Lindsays of Wormiston. The grounds behind ran back to the Scores where there were two boarding houses. In 1969 the University bought the school buildings and grounds, and the pupils of St Katharine's moved to premises on the site of the senior school. The boarding houses on the Scores became University departments. The school building was earmarked for the development of a University Arts Centre. By 1971 the architect, James Stirling, had drawn ambitious plans, but these had to be abandoned in 1976 for the sake of economy, and a more modest plan adopted which made greater use of the villa; the first floor was part of the Department of Art History and housed its library. The school's gymnasium was made into a drama studio with a workshop off it. The basement was designed to hold the University photographic unit, but is now History postgraduate offices. The cottages on the street became the Arts Centre office and a store-room; the latter is now the Museum and Gallery Studies study room. A large gallery was built to the east, and upstairs a studio was created for a guest artist. In the old St Katharine's grounds a much-needed new University library was built and was opened in 1976. John Gifford describes it as 'three tiers of ribbed concrete shelves boldly projecting on heavy beam ends from the curtain glazing behind. Almost but not quite elegant.' Mercifully it is set back from both the Scores and North Street.

In 1967 John Steer had been appointed first Professor of Fine Arts at the University. This was the start of an increasingly well-known department of excellence. He had not been here long when he put forward the proposal for a University Arts Centre. This was approved, and the building was ready when Jennifer Wilson, the first Director of the Crawford Arts Centre, was appointed and took over in November 1977. Later Jenny acknowledged the help of a splendid Management Committee, among them John Steer, Louise Hood, John Smith, David Dorward and Charlotte Carstairs. The programme was partly arranged; Jenny set to work to fill in the gaps. She wrote of that time: 'Student interest was already high, and demand from the drama and musical groups was queuing on the doorstep.' Before long the staff complement was completed – an excellent team with Alex McHardy the Technical Manager, and the helpful and efficient Angela Keys. Before long Vera Prunty took over the post of Secretary.

The opening play in the Drama Studio took place in November 1977, when Malcolm Edwards produced 'The White Devil' with a student cast. It was to be the first of many plays enjoyed there, despite the rather uncomfortable and black-draped setting. Preparations for a Becket season were afoot, and Leonid Pasternak's paintings and Eduardo Paolozzi's screen prints were mounted on the gallery walls. Lady Crawford officially opened the Crawford Centre for the Arts on 27 January 1978. The aim of the University's Arts Centre was to foster standards in the appreciation and performance of the Arts, comparable to those which it had long been achieved in other academic fields. But it also aimed at providing for St Andrews and East Fife a range of artistic events. Accordingly, The Scottish Arts Council agreed to give a grant on the basis of equal funding by the University.

How young and shining Jenny looks in a 1983 photograph – rosy cheeks, smooth dark hair, brown eyes and a radiant smile. In retrospect I think she was the ideal person to tackle this arduous and exciting job. She worked with enthusiasm and conviction. She liaised with the Art History department, the students and the Management Committee. She was very much in charge, but thoughtfully open to ideas. There was a private view once a month for the opening of each new exhibition. Jenny wrote, 'I tend to recall the openings themselves through a haze of recollected anxiety – apart from the first test of the burglar alarm in use. For Mr McHardy and myself it was a matter of agreeing how, in future, such five a.m. calls should be met – the road from Crail looked unappealing then.'

Jenny was Director of the Centre from 1977 to 1983, and its course was shaped by many of her ideas. She was adamant that the Centre should be open all the year round, and that the programme would include events for children. Children's holiday workshops and visits to schools by resident artists have been an important and integral part of the work and influence of the Centre. Jenny also worked unceasingly in arranging a broad range of exhibitions – as she put it, 'from photographic to craft exhibitions, clowns to contemporary drama. It was a period of learning, endlessly refining the programme content and defining the audience to whom it might appeal.'

So for those involved, and for visitors, there began in 1978 a period of excitement, of enthusiasm, progress and enjoyment, all made possible through the untiring work of the small team. The first exhibition devised by the Centre was the result of Jenny's meeting with Annabel Kidston, a leading member of The Preservation Trust. Annabel and a few others co-operated with Jenny in the staging of an exhibition called 'Reminders'. Jenny wrote, 'My time spent in a small house in North Street (the Preservation Trust Museum) researching and selecting from the Trust's photographic collection, was rich – in stories, fun and history.' (Would that there was a tape of some of the conversations and discussions!)

Next, Jenny established the Residency programme; for many young artists and writers it has been a welcome step on the road to success. The studio is upstairs to the south of the big gallery. The first of a long succession of artists in residence was Seona Mason who took up her post in November 1978. I remember many exhibitions mounted as a result of the experiences and work of these artists. Some of their names are: Margaret Milne, who came from Methil and whose skill in portrait painting brought her a commission to paint the portrait of Principal Steven Watson; Peter Howson, who was the first of many of the resident artists to work with children in local primary schools; George Wylie, famed for his 'Straw Locomotive over the Clyde' and other such startling works of art; Reinhard Behrens; Ruth Saxon; Ruth Stirling; Matthew Inglis; and craft workers Andy Lang, Christine Haliburton, Sheila Wishart, Lorna Miller and John Yellowlees.

The artist in residence best known to me was Cherry Pickles. She came to stay with me for a term, and was an inspiration. In bitter winter weather she was up early, getting ready to be at the castle as soon as it was daylight, to put in as many hours of painting as possible. She was dressed from top to toe in layers of clothing – she did admit that her fingers 'got a bit cold'. Just before she left St Andrews in the spring she mounted an exciting exhibition, and gave a remarkable barbecue party on the Castle beach one evening.

There were also theatre directors Alistair Cording, Paul Godfrey and John Moulton Reid. Alistair Cording produced Calderon's 'Doctor of Honour' with a student cast; this play had not been staged for 300 years and was a great success. John Clifford wrote, 'It meant for me, the translator, a very crucial step forward in my career as a playwright. It epitomised very much what the Centre was about.'

I was on the steering committee for the founding of the Friends of the Crawford Centre and on the Friends' Committee for some years. It was part of the policy to have such a society, and their participation in 'gallery sitting' and fund-raising was at the time both useful and supportive. It was a good mix of Town and Gown, and we soon set the ball rolling.

Martin Kemp succeeded John Steer as Professor of Fine Arts, and he and Jenny Wilson collaborated to establish what is now a long tradition of exhibitions researched by staff and students of the Department. Some of the early ones were: J.D. Ferguson (1982); Sir David Wilkie – 'Sketches and Studies'; Muirhead Bone – 'Portrait of the Artist'; 'Building for a New Age' and 'Scottish Furniture'. Many of the exhibitions went on tour. It was fun 'gallery sitting' during Barbara and Murray Grigor's exhibition 'Scotch Myths' (February 1981); the progress of streams of visitors was punctuated by laughter and lively chatter. Quoting from Grigor (1988): 'Jenny Wilson and Alex McHardy worked like MacTrojans to bring about this nightmare of kitsch into a midden of mawkish reality, which became the talk of the Edinburgh Festival and is still on the agenda today.' The exhibition 'The Lorimers – a family of the arts in Fife' was staged as part of the February 1983 St Andrews Festival. It was splendid. Hew Lorimer was a good friend of the Crawford Centre.

The Centre has been an important place for many students. Emma Dewhurst wrote in 1988, 'The Crawford was the Centre of my University universe. I spent more time there than anywhere else, living, breathing, absorbing theatre. Both as an actress and a director, its invaluable gift was the time and space it gave me to learn. It was a unique springboard to a professional theatrical career.' Once the only student dramatic society was The Mermaid; the 'Crawford' has given incentive, and now there are several student drama groups under the umbrella of the Mermaid Society.

The Crawford Centre continues to be an important place for children. Visits by parties of school children have always been part of the programme. In the summer of 1984 the first of a regular series of children's workshops was held, and in May 1985 a club was formed for children aged 5–12 years old: the CC Juniors. The Friends of the CC soon achieved a good membership, and there were enough volunteers for 'gallery sitting'. Some reliable regulars covered the weekends when small payments were given for their services; this lightened the heavy load of the small staff. Sometimes, sitting in the gallery, one would hear a cry from a visitor, 'Oh LOOK! This was the cloakrooms' or 'This was Miss Ludgate's room'. From my diary: 'gallery sitting is made arduous by the arrival of a complex cash box. I thought today that I had mastered it and when someone handed me nine postcards of equal price I tried multiplying the amount. The figures kept appearing until there was no room left on the screen. I summoned Alex, who looked stunned. "How on *earth* did you manage to do that?" he asked.' It took a lot of experimenting to unravel my venture.

The fundraising role became increasingly vital. In February 1982 'Lady Crawford's lunch' was held, an effort which involved a lot of work but was very satisfying. The drama studio was given a completely new look: the black drapes were removed and light poured in through the windows. Tables were covered with embroidered cloths, and flower arrangements adorned every surface. In my diary (January 1990): '150 tickets sold for the Crawford lunch; we filled 300 rolls and prepared much else in the morning. We were appealing for more people to join the Friends. After the lunch I was seated at a table, hopefully waiting for people to sign up. Lord Cayzer was one of the lunch guests; he came and said he would like to join the Friends; I asked for £5 and gave him his membership ticket. He had just left when I noticed that on the cheque he had forgotten to put a dot after the 5, so that it read £500. Then I saw the words "five hundred pounds". I was electrified and got Joyce Pirie to sprint after him and thank him profusely.' Such generosity was most heartening.

We raised money in other ways: at an annual Christmas Fair; at a Christmas party when readings from Pepys were given; at the usual coffee mornings; and more recently at an annual Summer Fair held out of doors, and at wine-tasting parties.

A sideline of our activities was the Record Library, which was started in early 1980, and soon had its own sub-committee. It was set up with a grant of £200 from the Management Committee, plus a lot of work and worry. I agreed to take charge, but my diary entries are not happy ones. Initially we were greatly helped by Peter Branscombe; he gave us invaluable advice and also a large and generous gift of many records and boxed sets. We had cupboards made in one of the smaller galleries, and drew up a record order to place with a Dundee firm. Noted from my diary: 'Jan. 1980. The sliding doors have stuck. Also the boxed sets won't fit into the cupboard, but must be kept locked up.' 'Two horrible days processing records. The Dundee firm did not get the rest of the records on the bus as promised.' Sept. (by which time the Record Library had a separate committee): 'The Student Fair; two stalls adjacent were booked for "Friends of the CC" and "Record Library". They were not adjacent and this made for truly awful day.' 'March 1982. 82 new records to be processed. Came home exhausted.' 'Oct.10th. It seems essential to hold library sessions on Wednesday afternoons and Saturday mornings, we must stick to it. But crises must be met. Someone has forgotten to turn up and can't be contacted; someone rings at the last minute – can't make it. And the work is continuous. Records have to be checked for scratches; the book has to be checked for late returns and notes sent.' Soon there were the difficulties of the divergence into CDs, and worn records needing replacement. We were steadily getting new members. Eventually, to my great relief, Tony Thorpe Davie took over the Record Library. Finally, it was moved out of the Crawford Centre to the University Music Centre in the Younger Hall.

For some years there were lectures which the Friends attended; these were sometimes connected with the current exhibitions. A talk on 'Paisley shawls' is unforgettable. Rows of elderly ladies sat with their heirloom shawls wrapped in rolls of tissue paper. The paper made a gentle rustling background to the speaker's voice. Then the owners filed up to display their shawls, and some were valued. The owners' expressions of pleasure and surprise were like those in the Antiques Road Show. On 20 March 1983 we had a lecture by Timothy Clifford, newly appointed Director of the National Gallery of Scotland. In it he revealed his hopes and plans. They seemed ambitious – on the verge of revolutionary. Question time was opened with the query, 'Could you explain how you intend to carry along your Board with these new ideas?' Looking back he seems to have managed to do this.

A difficult period

In the October of 1983 Jenny Wilson handed over to a new Director, Robert Livingston. Robert and his wife Judith settled in Pittenweem and soon had a host of friends. Robert was to steer the Centre through the worst of its stormy seas. Trouble had first come in the Summer of 1982 when the Centre lost one full-time post and a substantial University programme grant because of cuts in UGC funding. In 1984 came the bombshell announcement that the Arts Council had decided to withdraw all its funding from the Centre. Robert, the Management Committee and others inaugurated a strenuous public campaign, which led the Arts Council to overturn its decision; they agreed to restore £29,000 funding and to match grants for individual exhibitions, with the proviso that some cuts were unavoidable. The show went on.

But in spite of a thriving programme and the support of an

increasingly large number of Friends, there was further trouble. Principal Steven Watson, who had been very supportive of the Centre, was replaced by Principal Struther Arnott in November 1985, and one of his first recommendations was that the Crawford Centre and the University Botanic Gardens should be jettisoned. The District Council took over the Botanic Gardens, but the situation looked very ominous with regard to the Crawford Centre. For over two and a half years it was under threat of losing its University funding. From my diary: 'Feb. 13 1986: there was a meeting [of the Committee of the Friends] in the Drama Studio with Douglas Haldane in the chair and Robert attending. The dark curtains made a gloomy background.' Robert made it clear that there was no doubt that the Centre would close in March unless something vital was done. He said that various people were concerned and being as helpful as possible, but he felt it was inevitable that all would be lost. Douglas Haldane was of the same opinion. It seemed unreal. The Exhibitions programme was booked for a year ahead. And how did the Arts Council feel about it? Those concerned fought on.

In July 1986 the play *The Emperor of the Moon* was a sell-out success; it was the first of a series of professionally directed plays staged in the Byre Theatre. In April 1987 special Scottish Arts Council funding enabled the appointment of a Touring Exhibitions Administrator, Susan Davies, and in July and August 'Maisie Comes to Town' proved to be the biggest draw of all exhibitions to date. We continued to try to gain support to prevent the closure. We requested that we might send out an appeal to Alumini. It took a long time to get agreement from the University; but when it came we set to work and were cheered by an excellent response. There were some important people on our side: Martin Kemp; Douglas Haldane, who was Chairman of the Friends' Committee; Clive Sneddon who became Chairman of the District Council in 1988, and as such a member of the (University) Court; and our MP Menzies Campbell. It would be tedious to go through the whole process; instead here are a few extracts from my diary.

4 June 1987: 'At a meeting of the Management Committee of the Crawford Centre a letter from the Principal was read. The gist was that the University could no longer support the Centre.'

27 June: 'The General Council meeting. Sir Kenneth Dover was in the chair. I felt rather nervous, but got up and asked my questions about the closure of the Centre. I asked whether the money contributed to the appeal by the Alumni, an appeal sanctioned by the University, would be returned to the donors. I questioned the figure of £67,000 given as the University's annual cost of the Centre. The Principal promised a break-down of that figure.'

20 July: 'Various people have written letters to the Principal. From his replies the situation looks hopeless.'

To cut this story short, there was a Management Committee meeting at the beginning of October, and the Principal sent David Dorward to inform the members that from the end of the present term the University would withdraw all funding from the Crawford Centre. This would be ratified at the Court meeting the following day. However, as a result of telephone calls with regard to the effect of cancelling booked programmes, the matter was not brought up at the Court meeting. The University continued to pay its share for a year, and an agreement was made with the Arts Council. Clive Sneddon called a public meeting in the Town Hall, and a new company was formed with an elected board to administer the Crawford Centre. Agreement was reached with the University; the premises would be rented to the company annually at a low figure. The District Council promised a grant, and the Arts Council to increase its funding.

The Crawford Arts Centre since 1988

You will note that there was a slight change in the name. Diana Sykes was appointed Director when Robert left in September 1988. Her links with the Centre had started soon after it opened. She had been the first 'guinea pig' student to create an exhibition in the galleries – the Fergusson show; she then made her name as the stalwart who toured the Arts Council mobile exhibitions caravan to the Islands and remote parts of Scotland. She was to need all her strength and ingenuity at the Crawford. Two of the staff went: Alex McHardy was given a technician's job in United College, and Vera was offered a secretarial post at St Mary's. The Arts Council continued its funding; annual grants were given by the North East Fife District Council and Fife Regional Council. When Fife Council took over, a single grant came from the Department of Community Services, which covers Sports, Leisure and the Arts. Money was also donated by business trusts, fund-raising and sales of art and craft work. The smaller galleries usually have outstanding exhibitions of work (which is on sale) by artists in a variety of crafts. Somehow Diana and Susan have managed to keep up the high standard of revolving exhibitions throughout the whole year, various workshops, and Adult Life classes. The flow of artists in residence continues, with painters and craft workers now awarded a four-month fellowship rather than the earlier six-month stay. Some have found fame, such as Nathan Coley and Tracey McKennar.

The exhibitions are mainly of contemporary art by professionals, but there is the occasional historical exhibition, with the involvement of the Department of Art History. Students from this department, when taking the Museum and Gallery Studies course, assist by gallery-sitting and other involvements. School parties regularly visit the Centre, and in the holidays there are children's workshops. For the last four years the Drama Studio has been booked for productions of plays, mainly by the student groups (who this summer are giving a series of Greek dramas), and also by the Play Club, and for such occasions as the annual poetry festival, Stanza.

From Diana I have the following information.

> A main trend with diminishing financial resources has been collaboration with other organisations locally (e.g.

Fife Museums Forum, Kingdom of Fife Tourist Board, Byre Theatre) and nationally (Scottish Touring Exhibitions Consortium which we helped fund to pool resources to organise such exhibitions as Monumental Miniatures). With the Byre we co-manage the local Youth Theatre. Fife Council has worked with us on outreach projects and in running film and video workshops at the Centre.

Although the Centre is no longer part of the University we still work together on projects such as the annual exhibition organised with students on the vocational Museum and Gallery Studies course. They have produced many other exhibitions such as on international artist Richard Long, on Scottish rugs and on University architecture. Varied departments have provided expertise for artists working with the Centre who were interested in, for example, science or geology.

Historical exhibitions continue to be mounted occasionally as part of the programme where local research or a local connection exists – not always through the University. Some examples are June Baxter's exhibitions on Hugh Waller Paton and on Sam Bough, the Lucy Brown researched exhibition on Anstruther born Scottish portraitist David Martin, and the bringing over of the 19th century French paintings of Emmanuel Lansyer from Loches.

The National Lottery has brought lots of paperwork, but opportunities to organise major projects. The Straw Bales project allowed us to celebrate the Centre's 20th birthday outwith the Centre in the rich Fife landscape. Appalling weather (we chose the worst harvest in thirteen years) made it quite a challenge. Just as a freak storm shipwrecked Charlie Hooker's sand sculptures off the west sands several years before during our previous outdoor foray! The Calendar Project enabled adults right across Fife who have learning difficulties to take part in art workshops and produce a colourful exhibition which cheered up many a visitor. Following on from this the Friends of the Crawford have obtained lottery funding for Adinda van't Kloostere's residency which worked with people at Rymonth House (St Andrews). A lightbox incorporation of their work is now installed at the house to be enjoyed by all who live, work or visit there.

Residencies and educational work as well as touring exhibitions have allowed the Centre to work outwith St Andrews. Jim Buchanan's work with local schools, for example, resulted in a labyrinth being built at Buckhaven School.

So, thirty years from its opening the Crawford Centre is still alive and doing well.

Chapter 8

TALKING POINTS

The St Andrews Literary and Philosophical Society

In early March 1838 thirty-seven gentlemen met in the University Library to discuss the founding of a society. 'The general aim is that of promoting literary and philosophical research, and the Society would especially have in view the founding of a Museum.' Some of those who signed the document were John Adamson, Walter Glass, Robert Haldane, David Brewster, John Bain, Thomas Duncan, M. Tennant, George Buist, Charles Lyon, W.D. Playfair, H.L. Playfair, Thomas Aitken, Cathcart Dempster, and others mentioned below who were elected as officials.

What has this got to do with societies of the twentieth century in St Andrews? Well, it did continue into that century; also, there are certain achievements of this Society which had later effects. It was a splendid mixture of 'respectable gentlemen of the Town and neighbourhood' and staff of the University. It was the first body to take an active interest in the preservation of the ancient ruins. The Museum which it founded, built up, and kept in good order was an innovation in St Andrews. It eventually became the Bell Pettigrew Museum allied with the Department of Biology.

The first meeting of the new Society took place in the Library on 16 March 1838. The officials elected were as follows: President, Rt. Hon. Lord W. Douglas (he was replaced by the Duke of Argyll in 1851), and Vice-Presidents, Sir David Brewster, The Rev Principal Haldane and the Rev. G. Cook. Councillors were Provost Patrick Wallace, Major H.L. Playfair, Rev C.L. Lyon, Rev William Lothian, Lt. Col. Playfair, and Mr John Adamson, who became the Curator of the Museum. Mr Stuart Grace was Treasurer for very many years and was succeeded by his son, Charles Grace. As well as the councillors, there were ordinary members, who were proposed and elected; there were sixty-eight of these within the first year. Other groups were 'correspondence members' (very many Museum artefacts were sent from abroad), and a large body of 150 honorary members. Also there were associate members who could attend the part of the monthly meeting when the papers were presented; after 1889 this included ladies. The meetings took place once a month except in the summer. At every meeting a long list of donations to the Museum was read; in the first years gifts poured in from local donors and from abroad, and continued to come for the next seventy years.

In November 1838 various pieces which had been in the University Library were transferred to the Museum. This was first housed in a classroom in United College and then moved to Upper College Hall. In 1840 a meeting was held with the purpose of considering the connection between the Society's Museum and the University, and for making a report for the information of the Royal Commission which was about to visit. The agreement made with the Senatus was to the effect that:

1. The Museum could be considered the joint property of the University and the Society, but subject alone to the direction of the ordinary members of the Society, so long as there exists no class requiring the immediate use of the Museum room.
2. If difficulties should arise a Museum Committee of equal numbers should be appointed, those from the Society to be from the ordinary members and being no part of the University.
3. If the Society should fall into abeyance, the Museum would belong to the University, but previous Society members would be admitted free of charge.
4. The Society shall not be considered to be dissolved if it has ten members and has held four meetings in the year.

Dr George Buist exhibited and discussed a stone he had found in the ruins of the Cathedral. This led to the election of a committee of six and a secretary, whose purpose was to look after the antiquities in the Cathedral and Abbey grounds, and to find means for their preservation. Members were to keep a watching brief on the antiquities in the city. Two years later Dr George Cook gave the report of the Antiquities Committee on the clearing up of St Leonard's Chapel. In December 1839 the Society heard that the Abbey walls with their towers and gateways were under threat. The Society sent a petition to the Commissioners of Her Majesty's Woods and Forests, having found that the lands of the Abbey were to be up for sale. 'The minds of the petitioners have been filled with alarm and consternation, as, in the sale of the former lands, it is intended to include the walls, gateways and towers. We earnestly implore your honours to rescue these relics of Antiquity from destruction.' A reply was received from the Lord Lieutenant of the County, Mr Ferguson of Raith, to say that the lands had become the property of the University. 'With the help of the university and the Government the Society was successful in this matter. The wall was likely to remain a monument of the piety and the magnificence of our ancestors'. Much later the Society helped to settle some difficulties about the erection of, and payment for, a shelter to protect the carved stones of the Cathedral graveyard. The Society also took part in the archaeological excavations at Dura Den in 1862 which led to the discovery of the famous Dura Den fossil fish. This find included the new species *Glyptopomus kinnairdi*, which caused a stir. The Rev Dr Anderson of Newburgh had many years earlier been shown a slab of stone, split by workmen when building a lade to the mill and had recognised the importance of the specimen. The Dura Den fossil collection was held in the Museum, together with excellent drawings by Professor Huxley.

In 1875 Provost Milton reported that members had investigated two underground tunnels beside his house (1 South Street, The Roundel). They found a stone coffin with a skeleton carved on the lid. The Rev Lyon gave an account of a well which had been discovered in (North) Bell Street near the foundations of Greyfriars. He also gave a paper on the degradation of the rocks and the inroads of the sea below the north wall of the Cathedral, and read the translation of a Latin paper on this subject written in 1330! Dr George Buist began his plan to carry out meteorological observations in the county, and periodically reported on this. Dr Adamson gave findings from his ongoing study on mortality in the city, with statistical charts. Dr Adamson died in March 1870 and was praised for 'his zealous and efficient services as curator to the Museum'. The new curator was Dr Trail.

It was some time before the Museum was open regularly. Robert Walker was appointed as part-time assistant curator to the Museum, at a fee of £10 annually, paid jointly by the Society and the University. The Government gave the Society a large grant for fitments. It was decided it would be open on Wednesday and Saturday afternoons: admittance 2d, children 1d, and students free. It was also noted that 'the services of a Stuffer are available and it should be possible to make a complete collection representing local ornithology'.

Presentation of Papers

Two or three papers were given at each meeting, and were almost all of a scientific nature: geology, geography, natural philosophy (physics) or archaeology, but later the pattern changed and one long paper was presented. I have selected some titles which are interesting in subject matter or were given by eminent people (or both). Sir David Brewster, Principal of St Salvator's and St Leonards Colleges, spoke on a great number of topics – the solar spectrum, photogenic drawings by Fox Talbot, and demonstrations of his kaleidoscope and stereoscope. He played a central role in the Society until he left in 1859 on his appointment as Principal of Edinburgh University. A distinguished physicist, his work on optics and polarised light led to the use the flat Fresnel lens in lighthouses. The Society paid homage to him on his death in 1868.

Some of the old members went, but new ones came: John Purvis of Kinaldy, Dr Buddo, and Mr John Paterson among others. The majority of the papers were still on scientific subjects, for example Principal Shairp on 'Cinerary urns: the excavation at Kirkheugh' and the Rev Tuttieth on 'Coal and causes of explosions in mines'. He advocated the use of peat as having no sulphurous exhalations. After 1860 there were some useful contributions from new members: Sir Lambert Playfair, 'The era of piracy and Christian slavery in the Barbary States'; Professor Lewis Campbell, 'The idea of immortality among the Ancient Greeks', and Dr Heddle on 'The 409 hills in Scotland over 2700 feet high'. Was he the pioneer of the Munro bashers? He also gave a talk on 'Climbing in the Grampians' (1875). Alex Brown's subject was 'The eclipse of the sun in 1874' and Dr Hay Fleming's 'The Baxters of St Andrews'. Dr Cleghorn, showing amazing foresight, lectured on 'The benefits of maintaining a dense population of forest land in the countries of the world'; Dr W.A. Lonie spoke on 'The great circular storm of 1874', and Dr Robert Chambers on 'An object at Denino [*sic*]'. Other contributors were A.K. Lindesay, Sir Charles Auchterlony and Dr A.H.K. Boyd.

There were various demonstrations of new apparatus; Professor Swan showed 'A metallic thermometer' and later (1860) 'A new regulator for the electric light'. Members were amazed by a presentation of the phonograph, which 'not only repeated spoken words, but portions of songs and even a bugle call were recorded with remarkable clarity'.

The Secretary had a heavy load, but the minutes are immaculate and detailed. Dr Alexander Thoms, as the Secretary over the last decades of the Society, gave outlines of hundreds of papers; in addition, there must have been many letters to write.

The Museum and the John Knox Pulpit

In 1876 the Society received notice that the Senatus proposed to make new Museum regulations. A committee examined the Museum, and a new joint committee was formed, with an equal number of representatives from the University and from the Society. The insurance of the Museum was covered by the University. One of the most treasured possessions of the Museum was the John Knox Pulpit. We learn from Christine Wolfe's *A New Guide to Holy Trinity* (1998) that this old wooden pulpit was removed from Holy Trinity in 1798. One wonders whether it was in the safe-keeping of the Town Council until the Museum accepted it. It was placed at the top of the staircase outside the door into Upper College Hall and was obviously considered a fine acquisition.

At the March 1890 meeting Dr Anderson proposed that the pulpit should be returned to the heritors of the Town Church, but Professor McIntosh moved a counter-motion, which was carried. In 1904 Dr Playfair wrote asking for the John Knox pulpit for Holy Trinity. The reply stated that 'it was a difficult time and no decision could be made'. However, the minutes record that in the discussion it was said that there was no proof that the John Knox pulpit had been in Holy Trinity, that 'it was possible it came out of St Leonards, but some said out of St Salvator's Chapel'. I have found no information as to when it was set up in St Salvator's Chapel, but it must have been after 1905.

The Society meets Difficulties

In 1874 the Society was described as 'being in a deplorable state'. There were only thirty-three members and a dearth of speakers on philosophy and literature. In 1879 came the resignations of Dr Heddle, Dr Pettigrew and Mr Andrew Aikman, all of whom had made big contributions. No reasons were given in the minutes. Sir Lambert Playfair died in February 1899. Those who were involved in the

Society latterly were the Rev Sloan, General Moncrieff, Captain John Allen Allen, Mr (later Dr) Alexander Thoms, J. Whyte Melville, Mr Alexander Bethune, Dr Robert Chambers, Provost Milton, Mr John Paterson, Professor Purdie, Dr Bayne Meldrum, Professor McIntosh, Dr D. Hay Fleming, Dr Cleghorn, Provost Milton, Mr Browning, Mr Birrell, Professor Swan, Dr (later Professor) Musgrove, Sir Archibald Geikie, Mr Charles Grace (Treasurer), Mr David Thoms.

In 1888-9 there was a crisis; the number of members had gone down and it was felt there were too many scientific papers. Dr M. Anderson suggested the society should continue on a broader basis. A committee was formed to re-invigorate the Society, to increase the membership and to find speakers.

Dr Heddle, Vice-President and for many years curator of the Museum, was on the brink of giving his large collection of minerals to the Museum – it was thought to be worth over £2000. His offer was that he would ask £1000 for the first thousand artefacts and present the remainder as a gift. This was held up by a unique contretemps. Principal Donaldson was the President and Mr Alexander Thoms the Secretary. Alexander Thoms reported to the committee at a special meeting (recorded in the front of the minute book) that he had met Principal Donaldson in the street on 9th or 10th [of October 1891]. The Principal asked him what was the number of members in the Society. Mr Thoms gave an estimated number of forty. The Principal asked him if he had seen the Government Ordinance which had made over the Museum to the University Court. Mr Thoms expressed amazement and said the contents of the Museum were the property of the Society and the University. The Principal said he would send a copy of the Ordinance; that if the society had an interest, why had no representative appeared before the University Court when the matter was discussed? He said that there would be insuperable difficulties if the Society wished to maintain an interest. If they persisted they would have to find new premises and the University would start a museum of its own. He suggested that Thoms might resign and persuade friends to do likewise, in which case Thoms might like to be elected by the Court to the new museum committee. He requested a reply before the Court Meeting on 14 November.

A copy of the Ordinance dated 3 April 1891 was received and studied by the committee. The Secretary referred to an earlier agreement with the University in 1840 between the Society and the University (quoted above). Dr Bayne Meldrum proposed a motion that there was no reason why the Society, which had forty members, should relinquish its proprietary right. This was carried, and Dr Thoms (as he was now) wrote to the Principal giving the view of the Society: 'the Ordinance conveys certain rights and principles which had previously belonged to the Society and the college, and *nothing else*'. The Secretary would call a meeting if the Principal would give some definite statement and proposal. The reply to this was a note from Principal Dondaldson giving notice of his resignation from the Society.

The whole matter was discussed at a meeting of the Council and Museum committee. After studying the interpretation of the University of Scotland Act Ordinance no. 8, they came to the conclusion that 'there is no reason why the Society should relinquish its rights of proprietorship and management of the Museum which in the last fifty-three years it had done so much to create'. The result was that a compromise was reached, and a larger Museum committee was formed.

The Settlement

The minutes show no indication of what was to happen next. On 2 March 1903 an agreement was registered between the Society and the University. On 2 April 1903 in a letter to the Court:

The Society now beg to convey to the University its share in the proprietorship and control of the Museum under certain conditions as follows.

1. The Museum must remain at St Andrews and be available free to members of the Society, and open to the public.
2. The Museum should maintain its integrity, i.e. the whole collection must be kept together.
3. The University Court would see that the windows of St Leonards chapel be glazed and a roof put on; this should then be handed over to the Crown for placing the objects as they are at present.

The legal agreement in toto is recorded by Alexander Thoms in a large handsomely bound volume in the archives of the University Library. The agreement was signed on 17 December 1904 and registered on 29 December 1904. The signatories were as follows: for the Society David Bayne Meldrum, David Hay Fleming, Rev D.A. Storm, Alexander Thoms, James Musgrove (Professor of Anatomy), Robert Robertson (Botany); and for the University Principal Donaldson, Principal Stewart (St Mary's), Andrew Bennett (Secretary). The history of the previous events, including the agreement of 11 July 1840, is given, and then the words 'owing to the altered position of the partners the position can no longer be conveniently maintained. It is desirable that the second party become the sole proprietor and director of the Museum.'

The conditions listed in this volume are fuller than those in the letter above. There is a clause that certain items 'listed in a schedule to follow' should go to the Town Council to preserve. (In fact most of these artefacts went to the Cathedral Museum, being tombstones or fragments, etc., unearthed in digs at Kirkhill or in the Cathedral grounds.) Conditions 4-7 were:

> *Condition 4.* If another Museum should be set up in St Andrews to house archaeological objects which belong to St Andrews and neighbourhood, they should be handed over. (These objects were kept in a museum in The Swallowgate which became the Department of Ancient History. Added to them was the splendid collection of

Terence Bruce Mitford. In the early seventies part of this collection was donated to the new Kinburn Museum and part to Edinburgh).

Condition 5. There should be secure and accessible accommodation for the artefacts. (It seems the University was not willing to accept the St Leonards Chapel suggestion.)

Condition 6. This stresses that the collection must be kept in St Andrews in its integrity.

Condition 7. In the case of any dissension the matter should go to the Sheriff of the County for arbitration.

There follows a handwritten inventory of the thousands of items in the collection. Each is properly classified with source and with name of donor. There are over a hundred cinerary urns or fragments of such, and about 150 artefacts of pottery, brass, bronze, etc. There is collection of coins from foreign countries and Britain, which must be very valuable. Casts of 59 seals and medals of the bishops are identified and listed.

Reading this amazing inventory one feels it was surely an enormous feat that this small Society had built up such a fine collection. The list itself is witness to the amount of work involved by the curators and the secretaries of the Society. I am told that Upper College Hall was 'bulging', and the overspill extended down the stairs. A plan was evolved that an extension to College Hall on the west side and running across to Butts Wynd should be built. Professor and Mrs Bell Pettigrew occupied The Swallowgate, and she made very strong objections to the plan. (This lady, whose maiden name was Gray, had been born and brought up in West Hartlepool, married an Irishman and gone to live in Ireland; when her husband died she married again, and once more became a widow.) Professor Bell Pettigrew was her third husband, but not the last. She married Professor Musgrove – and they continued to enjoy an uninterrupted view from The Swallowgate.

(I was told by an old lady that there was much comment at her last wedding because she wore a white gown.)

The Society continued, dispirited, with the monthly meetings and presentations of papers until the end of 1909. The subjects seem to have widened. Dr John Wilson, who was elected as a member of the Society, used lamplight illustrations when presenting papers on 'Some New Garden Plants', 'The Arum Family', and also 'The Teaching of Nature Knowledge'. There is a gap in the minutes from 1910 to 1916. The final meeting is recorded in 1916 with the words, 'This Society having been moribund for some years has decided to come to a stop'. In the ensuing arrangements it was agreed that the balance of funds would be used to have the Minute Books and papers bound, and to request that the University Library accept them for safe-keeping and future consultation.

The Bell Pettigrew Museum

When Professor Bell Pettigrew died in 1908 his widow gave a large sum for the erection of a Museum which adjoins the Bute building. The Bell Pettigrew Museum was a splendid setting for the treasures which were transferred in 1912. There was a large foyer with a mosaic floor. Here stood the skeleton of a whale. The Great Hall and its galleries were flanked by rows of neo-classical pillars. Professor D'Arcy Thompson purchased more specimens for the collection, from the British Museum. In the years that followed, some geological and anthropological specimens were removed for display elsewhere. But it was in 1958 that the Society's agreement with the University was ruthlessly broken. Major alterations were started, and 60% of the Museum space was taken over for teaching and research. The Museum was reduced to the lower half of the main hall. Many thousands of specimens were disposed of; many of them were given to other museums. The collection of Dura Den fossil fishes was broken up; in 1966 fifteen specimens were gifted to what is now the National

Museums of Scotland, but several other similar specimens had already been passed to them at the end of the nineteenth century, and also to other museums.

In 1964 Dr David Burt, having just retired from twenty years as Acting Head of the Zoology Department, embarked on the challenge of restoring the Museum and its remaining specimens 'which were in a dilapidated and ramshackle state'. He made a fine job of it. It is open to the public once a year on St Andrews Day, but also to schools and visitors by appointment.

Today I have been to the Bell Pettigrew Museum. Once you have navigated the maze of cell-like rooms in the Bute, you reach an enchanting oasis. Students work there in the zany and delightful company of silent motionless flying lizards, Ethiopian wart hogs, cockatoos and a King Lory. A duck-billed platypus stares at two-toed and a three-toed sloths hanging upside down. A painted snipe pirouettes, and a ruff and a reeve look pensive. The skeleton of an eighteenth-century racehorse stands alongside that of a camel. And much, much more. It is an 'Alice in Wonderland' setting and story.

The Discussion Club

Dr Colin Muir, a member of this club for the last thirty years, has sent me information on its history and has most kindly made a list of all the speakers and titles of papers presented for discussion since it began. Quoting from his letter:

> Inside the flyleaf of the first minute book, Dr John Mulligan, Lecturer in Anatomy and for many years the Secretary of the Club, has written: 'In a conversation with Mrs Waterston at 5, Windmill Road on the 15th February 1951 I learned that the Discussion Club was formed in 1916 by Professor and Mrs Waterston, Professor and Mrs Stout, and Mrs Janet Laing the writer.

The first meeting was led by Professor Stout.'Below this Mr Mulligan adds 'In a conversation with Mrs Waterston at 2, Howard Place today 8th December, the above statement was ratified and in addition I learned from Mrs Waterston that the idea of a discussion club was originally hers. Professor Waterston had been a member of a discussion group in Northwood London which was for men only, and Mrs Waterston desired to have a similar club founded in St Andrews, but with the membership open to Ladies.'

The first membership book runs:

Professor and Mrs Stout	Professor of Logic and Metaphysics
Professor and Mrs Waterston	Professor of Anatomy
Mr Morrison	subsequently Professor of Moral Philosophy
Mrs Laing	pianist and writer (pupil of Clara Schumann)
Mr C.D. Broad	subsequently Professor of Philosophy, Cambridge
Miss Bentinck Smith	Head Mistress of St Leonards School.

Further members invited to join were:

Dr Paton	Medical officer to St Leonards School
Principal and Mrs Galloway	St Mary's
Mr and Mrs Williams	he was subsequently Professor of History
Mr Myers	
Mr and Mrs J.N. Wright	he was subsequently Professor of Logic
Mr Box	Lecturer in History
Dr Bryce	

Mr and Mrs Mace	he became Professor of Philosophy in London
Miss Ker	
Miss Ketelby	teacher at St Leonards, subsequently became lecturer in the Department of History.

The names of many other well-known people appear in the minutes, including those of Rex Knight and Edwin Muir. Edwin and Willa Muir lived in St Andrews in the late thirties and early forties, first in the Scores, and then at 18 Queen's Gardens. He led the discussion in May 1939 on King Lear, and Mrs Muir spoke on 'Looking into language' in December 1939.

Originally the meetings were held about four times a year in the homes of the members. This meant that there was a limited membership of about twelve to fifteen, but the numbers increased, and meetings came to be held in hotels. Then, because hospitality was offered by Miss Murray and later Miss Walker, Wardens of University Hall, the numbers increased to as many as twenty-five. Dr Muir writes, 'One cannot overstress the hospitality these ladies showered on the meetings that made them a gustatory as well as an intellectual delight. In the minutes are also recorded more formal dinners or even a summer afternoon garden party.'

It may be interesting to look at the topics and speakers during the first years of the Club, much over-shadowed by the War.

Nov. 1916	Life After Death Prof. Stout
Feb. 1917	The Ultimate Belief Miss Bentinck Smith
Feb. 1917	Newspapers Mr Broad

March 1917	The State of the Church and Science Mrs Waterston
Oct. 1917	Temperance Reform Dr Paton
Dec. 1917	Conscientious Objectors Mrs Waterston
March 1918	The National Debt Mr Broad
March 1918	What is Genius? Mrs Laing
Oct. 1918	Peace Proposals Mr Broad
Nov. 1919	Immortality Mr Broad.

War continued to be a theme of discussion, as in the following:

1928	Night Thoughts of a Pacifist Mr Sellon (Department of French)
1934	Is War Ever Morally Justifiable? Professor Porteous
1935	Changes in the Sentiment of Patriotism as Reflected in Post War Poetry Mrs Oesar
1937	War and Peace Professor Turnbull
1940	Italy's War Aims Mr Simpson
1941	The Inevitability of War Professor Rose
1945	The Atomic Bomb Professor Turnbull.

Regarding the speakers, even if one counts the wives of University members of Staff as 'Town', University greatly exceeded non-university until recent decades, as shown in the figures below (though this may not be true of the total membership).

Period	*Gown*	*Town*
1916-29	35	20
1930-39	36	9
1940-49	40	5
1950-59	35	7
1960-69	39	9
1970-79	31	14
1980-89	26	16
1990-99	13	16

The following list indicates the interest in psychology in the twenties and thirties.

April 1922	Rivers on *Instinct and the Unconscious*
	Professor Stout
Nov. 1923	Psycho-analysis
	Dr Bryce
Nov. 1924	Psycho-analysis and Moral Methods
	Mr Wright
Nov. 1924	The Systematic Structure of Rivers' *Instinct and the*
Unconscious	Mr Morrison
Mar. 1925	Criticism of Dr Bryce's paper on Psycho-analysis
	Professor Stout.

(The full title of W.H.R. Rivers' book is *Instinct and the Unconscious, a Contribution to a Biological Theory of Psycho-neuroses*; it was published in Cambridge in 1920. In the early 1930s The University set up courses in psychology which included an honours course. Dr Oesar was appointed as Lecturer in Experimental Psychology with Mr Babington Smith, Dr Pierce and Mrs Pallister assisting him.)

Dec. 1933	Intuitions; How Did You Guess?
	Mr Babington Smith
Mar. 1934	Laissez Faire in Education
	Mr Oesar
Feb. 1937	Road Accidents
	Mr Babington Smith
Feb. 1938	Some Social Conditions in America
	Dr Oesar.

The introduction of the teaching of Astronomy at the University was marked by these contributions to the Club:

1942	The Existence of Man is not Necessarily Restricted to the Earth Dr Freundlich
1943	The Importance of Newton in the Modern World
	Dr Freundlich
1955	Modern Ideas on the Structure of Stars
	Professor Freundlich
1954	Astrology: Is it Any Use?
	Dr Cizar
1960	Is There Life on Mars?
	Dr Cizar
1960	Astronomy and Primitive Cosmologies
	Dr Cizar
1961	The Age of the Universe
	Dr Cizar
1962	The Moon
	Dr Cizar

Professor Rose, the well-known classicist, gave a number of papers between 1923 and 1960, which indicate the range of his interests and knowledge.

The titles were:

Ghosts (the title of Mrs Waterston's 1929 paper was 'It Is Reasonable to Believe in Ghosts')
The Origins of Magic
The Future of Religion
Sherlock Holmes – Saviour of Literature?
The Collapse of Democracy
Should Small Nations Be Tolerated?
Why Is Art?
The Future of Religion in Western Europe
Is this Age Exceptionally Irreligious?
Headlines – Why?
Universal Education is Neither Practicable nor Desirable
Are the Vulgar Irremediable?
Heaven, Hell and Purgatory
Classical Ideas Concerning the Course of Historical Events.

Mr Williams (brother of Lady Irvine) and his wife lived in the Roundel; he was Lecturer in History and later became Professor. The titles of their few papers to the Discussion Club are unusual:

1928 Family Endowment
Mrs Williams

1923 Essay on Spiritual Regeneration as a Basis for Reconstruction
Mr Williams

1925 Pseudo-Ingulf
Mr Williams

(*The Croyland History*, printed by Savile in 1596 was for long erroneously attributed to Ingulf, Abbot of Croyland [d. 1109]. It was shown by Sir Francis Palgrave to be a forgery of the 15th century.)

1933 Some Thoughts on My Present Discontent
Prof. Williams

1939 *Apologia Pro Mea Whigismo Mea*
Prof. Williams.
(How I wish I knew the context of his last two papers!)

Some topics seem to relate to events of the times, such as these:

1919 The Dogmatic Instruction of the Young
Mr Morrison
1922 The Sex Disqualification (Removal) Act
Mrs Stout & Mrs Waterston
1924 Birth Control
Dr Bryce
1935 The Group Movement
Prof. Turnbull (Mathematics)
(The Oxford Group was a religious group founded by Frank Buchman who visited Oxford in 1921. 'In the main its principles are Christian fellowship, public confession of sins, group "sharings" of spiritual experiences, and dependence on divine guidance in every day affairs of life.' (*Brewer's Dictionary*) I remember that it had a powerful effect in the 1930s. Mrs Copson, whose husband Edwin was then a lecturer in the Department of Mathematics, recalls attending a meeting in the Athol. She said, 'When it came to confessing, I held Edwin firmly down.')
1943 Can Germany be Re-educated?
Mr Lederman
1975 Can Ecology Save Our Environment?
Dr Crawford

Many of those whose papers introduced the discussion kept to their own academic or professional subject. Aspects of religion were considered by Professor Black, Professor Dickie and Professor Baillie of St Mary's, and by Dr Rankin, First Charge of Holy Trinity, and The

Rev Moffat. Papers on medical topics were presented by Professor Waterston, Dr Mulligan, and ('Town') Dr Somerville, Dr Buchanan, and Dr Ward, who was a graduate of this university and returned in the 1960s as M.O.H.

Many aspects of education were discussed from papers given not only by members of the University, but also by Miss Bentinck Smith, and later Miss Macauley, of St Leonards School, by Rectors of Madras College, Dr John Thompson and (later) Dr Gilroy, and by Mr David Wallace of the Burgh School (who was also a famous teacher of chess and an adjudicator at world chess championships). Economists and historians led the discussions away from philosophical and scientific topics to considerations of the United States, of South America, of Europe and the East. Others spoke on the Arts.

Dr Colin Muir has played an important role in the Club since the late sixties. His subjects have covered a wide spectrum. From these examples, can you guess in which department he was a lecturer?

1968 A Defence of Chemical and Biological Warfare
1971 Virtue: the Gap between Intention and Achievement
1972 Are There Only Two Cultures?
1975 Biology of Politics
1977 Could I Become a Devil?
1980 Ambition and the Work Ethic.

The list continues right up until the present and gives no clues. In fact, he was Lecturer in the Department of Biology.

Another member was Douglas Gifford (eventually to get a personal chair in Spanish in 1978) who joined Professor Woodward (Ferdy) in the Department of Spanish in 1950. It was a lively, joyful department. Douglas's contribution to the Club was through his special interests: The Basques, witchcraft, and the Incas. He and his wife Hazel, who taught English at St Leonards School, gave a joint paper on 'Impressions of Argentina' in November 1990 not long before

Douglas died. Hazel has continued to contribute, with such subjects as 'The Role of Public Television' and 'Ageing'.

I hope I have given a flavour of the complete list with a range of topics which I find impressive and often intriguing. This Club illustrates the enormous effect of the University on St Andrews, and the long partnership of Town and Gown in very civilised discussion and friendship, not only within this Club but on innumerable other occasions through the twentieth century.

The St Andrews Ladies' Debating Club

In 1918 a bill gave the right to a parliamentary vote to certain categories of women. In 1928 women were given full rights. A St Andrews Ladies' Debating Society was set up on 26 February 1922, it is said with the funds from the Suffrage. The connection may have been the part the Edinburgh Ladies' Debating Society played in the Suffrage cause. Unfortunately the early minutes have not survived. I was told that one of the objectives of the Club was that 'College and School might mix' – that is, the wives of the professors and the Mistresses of St Leonards School! However, at all times the membership has been a good mix of University, Town and St Leonards School. Honorary Members are listed in the Minutes as Mrs Forrester, Mrs Read, Mrs Hawes, Mrs Donald Mills, Miss Doris Wilson, Mrs Ritchie, Miss Ketelbey and Mrs Williams.

The meetings were to be held in the drawing rooms of members, and the hostess was to be Chairman. Each member was required to attend at least half the meetings during the season. The proposer of a motion and the opposer were each allowed to speak for fifteen minutes and their seconders for five minutes. An early ruling was brought in at some time that topics relating to religion and politics were banned; it was remarked later that this was 'a custom more honour'd in the breach than in the observance'. At first it was laid down that Members should wear evening dress at the debates, and on 'Hat Night' hats, but of course this was changed. The Hat Nights have continued: copies of various motions (often amusing) are placed in one hat, members names in another; names are drawn for each short debate, so a member must be able to speak impromptu 'wearing any hat'.

When I joined in the mid 1950s, Mrs Woodward and her mother Mrs Bradshaw, the two lady doctors Dr Orr and Dr Cochrane, the Rev Dr Helen Woods and Mrs Nan Macdonald made for some very lively debating and quite a lot of laughter. The topics for the debates, the speakers and the results are listed in the minutes from 1972. In November of that year, the motion 'That the Permissive Society is Moral' was defeated by two votes. As early as November 1971 the house was split on the motion 'Car Ownership is now Immoral'. In 1982 the motion 'That to Preserve Life at all Costs is Immoral' was passed 10-7. In 1978 'This House approves of the Ordination of Women to the Ministry of the Church' was proposed by Dr Helen Woods and was passed 9-5.

On one occasion 'This House Believes in Ghosts' was debated, and on another 'This House Believes in the Supernatural'; on both occasions the motion won. I remember Mrs Williams describing dire and mysterious events in the Roundel (where she lived), and three speakers talked about ghostly experiences in the Pends. Dean of Guild Linskill had written a book *The Ghosts of St Andrews.* No one had seen Archbishop Sharp's coach rumble down South street on the anniversary of his murder at Magis Muir, but two Dutch ladies staying in Gregory Place witnessed, at midnight in midsummer, a nun who chanted in plainsong as she walked slowly through the graveyard, and went into Dean's Court. On enquiries there next day, no nun had been seen.

St Andrews Speakers Club

This Club was founded in January 1953 as St Andrews Toastmasters Club. It was the only club of its kind in Fife, with both men and women members. The name was changed to the Speakers Club, and its reputation grew. Several current members had gained the Advanced Speakers Certificate. Sadly, the last meeting of the Club, which had continued for almost fifty years, was held in December 2001. Margaret Murray presided over the meeting and spoke of the skills and confidence which members had achieved, as well as the friendships made through the Association of Speakers Clubs.

Chapter 9

A MISCELLANY OF INTERESTS

Scottish Interests

The St Andrews Burns Club

From the first minute book:

> Royal Hotel St Andrews on the twenty-fifth day of January in the year eighteen hundred and sixty-nine, which day being the hundred and tenth anniversary of the day of the Birth of Robert Burns, the Illustrious Scottish Bard
>
> *A few good souls with fervent wish and blythsome mind,*
> *Re-kindled by the grateful rays of memories kind,*
> *There met to celebrate the fame of Scotland's Bard,*
> *And Anniversary of his birth, with due regard.*

The company consisted of the following Gentlemen:

Mr Walter Thomas Milton, Residenter and ex-Provost of the City, the Chairman
Mr David Archibald, M.D. and City Treasurer
Mr John McPherson, Ironmonger and Bailie
Mr Robert Bonthron, Clothier and ex-Bailie
Mr John Laverock, Saddler and Town Councillor
Mr James Duncan, Farmer and Town Councillor
Mr Archibald Downie, Calotypist and ex-Councillor
Mr James Campbell, Road Surveyer
Mr William Davison, Hotel-keeper

Mr William Russell, Tailor and Clothier
Mr William Brown, Baker
Mr James McRobbie, Draper
Mr Robert Milne, Architect
Mr John Sorley, Registrar of Births etc.

The minutes continue:

> Eight o'clock in the evening was the hour appointed for the company to assemble, and sup together within the Royal Hotel. A few of the gentlemen seemed to 'Take no note of Time' and arrived late, and those who had to wait relieved the tedious interval by indulging in a 'Spark o' Spirits'. Very soon all put in an appearance and, supper having been duly announced, ex-Provost Milton was unanimously called upon to occupy the chair and Dr Archibald to act as croupier. The Chairman then said Grace and 'All around the table sat'. The act of uncovering the dishes having been performed with all due ceremony, the usual harmony of Steel and earthenware mingled with the savoury fragrance of the steaming viands resounded in clashing and peculiarly inviting strains. While the Chairman was dealing off slices of a really delicious roast of beef, and those who shared it were sounding high its tenderness and excellence, the Landlord of the Royal took occasion to inform his guests that the Identical roast of beef under discussion was intended for that very day's dinner for the Earl of Breadalbane, but that his Lordship had to leave St Andrews sooner than he had previously intended and did not require it in consequence. This piece of pleasant information was received with shouts of joyful exultation by the Company, who wreathed the Noble Earl with laurels of good wishes for the benefit he had unconsciously conferred on them by his very seasonable departure from this Ancient City.

The Croupier distributed an excellent Scotch Haggis, of which everyone had to partake or else be subjected to swallow a tumbler full of water well seasoned with salt. Needless to say all professed themselves to be in love with Haggis. ... As no particular history was given regarding the numerous other viands which graced the table, no special record can be made of them. Suffice it to say that the Supper passed off amidst much pleasant talk and jesting, and not a few of Wit's piercing shafts were cast about and as quickly picked up by the swift hand of the 'Repartee'.

Soon as the 'King o' grain
Inspiring bold John Barleycorn'
adorned the festive board and flavoured
'The smoking bowl before us'
for the company believed with our National Poet that
'Freedom and whisky gang thegither'
everyone therefore
'Heaved care o'er side
And large before enjoyment's gale
Did tak the tide.'

The Chairman, ex-Provost Milton, to become President, having called upon all to fill their glasses, then stated the how and why he found himself at the head of such a jovial band, and concluded by proposing the toast of Her Majesty 'The Queen'. He then gave 'The Prince and Princess of Wales', 'The other Members of the Royal Family', 'Her Majesty's Ministers', 'Both Houses of Parliament', 'The Army Navy and Volunteers'. All which having been disposed of in the most loyal and patriotic manner, the Chairman demanded a special bumper, and then proposed the Toast of the Evening – 'The Birth of Robert Burns, the

Immortal Poet and Bard of Scotland'. The Toast was received and responded to

'With honour due Bend loyalty true
And rounds of deafening cheers' – which
'Re-echoed from each mouth' 'And Willie was'
Shook 'wi' a thunder of applause'.

Mr Sorley was called upon to sing and sang the Birthday song of Robert Burns, 'Rantin' Rovin' Robin'.

The Croupier proposed the following resolution which was seconded by Bailie McPherson and unanimously agreed to: 'That all the Gentlemen here assembled now resolve themselves into a Club to be called the St Andrews Burns Club having for its special object the annual celebration of the Anniversary Day (January 25th) of the Birth of Robert Burns with becoming honour and dignity'. A committee was elected to prepare a code of Rules and Regulations.

The rest of the evening was spent in songs by various members of the company interspersed with toasts. And so each year this enjoyable and moving celebration took place. Annually a few new members were admitted, not just from St Andrews but from the wider area. It was a mixed company of tradesmen and professional gentlemen – the two Masters of the Madras College, Reverend Laurence Tuttieth, the Rev Dr Matthew Rogers, the Rev R.W. Wallace. But of the University, in these early years, only Professor M.J.D Meiklejohn and Professor John Birrell (St Mary's) became members. Within ten years many of the hotel keepers had joined. The Burns supper was held at the Royal for as long that hotel was with us; and Mr Davison the proprieter was a founder member. His praises were sung each year, for example, 'The supper was served in Mr Davison's recherché style…'. In 1883 Mr William Rusack 'of the Marine' was welcomed as a member. Familiar St Andrews names are Mr Charles Grubb, Mr W.R Kermath (chemist), Mr A.C. Aikman (Rathelpie), Mr Thomas Rodger, Mr Andrew Haxton.

In 1895 Mr William Rusack as President gave the loyal and patriotic toasts. Quoting from the minutes:

> At the outset of his address Mr Rusack said he felt highly honoured that he, of German birth, should be chosen as the President of the St Andrews Burns Club. The Poet presented to him Scottish life and scenery in a rare picture, which he had learned to appreciate and love with his whole heart. 'True genius like that of Burns was above the limits of nationality and demanded the homage of any-one to whatever country he belonged – who had a brain to think, and a heart to feel.' Mr Rusack compares Burns with Goethe, and found a bond of connection with Scotland's national bard. He concluded by saying that [the countryside of] Burns possessed many similarities to that of Northern Germany, where was his birthplace, and dwelt on the veneration with which Burns is held there. 'Burns was naturally a religious man; he had done more in a few simple lines for the sanctity of the home, and of womanhood, than any other writer in prose or verse.'

At each Burns supper, greetings from other Clubs were read. The St Andrews Club was the thirtieth to be formed in the list of member clubs of the World Federation. Poems by the Bard were recited, and the Reverend Canon Tuttieth composed a new poem for many of the occasions.

So we come to the 132nd year of this club's existence. I learned from the current Secretary that 'normally the only event of the year is the supper, held on the Friday nearest to 25th January. However, we have, in the past, had a concert in the Byre Theatre on St Andrews Day (and may do so in the future), and in 1996 we sponsored a production about Burns' life at the Edinburgh Festival by an Edinburgh amateur theatrical group. We sponsor and give book prizes for the annual School Competition for Burns recitations and singing. Also each year we give the George Cowie Class award for Citizenship.'

I quote again from the immaculate minutes of the first secretary, Mr Sorley. These words end his lengthy account of the evening on 25 January 1969, and seem to me to stand for what this venerable Club helps to promote.

> This gathering was in all respects pre-eminently fitted and worthy to shadow forth the great event they had met to celebrate, – Viz: to revive and re-animate in the hearts of every lover and admirer of Robert Burns ... the spirit of brotherly love, kindness, sympathy, and social friendship which he so prominently and strikingly manifested in his whole life and character, and to express in action as well as in desire, what he in language almost prophetic, has expressed in these words:
>
> *'Then let us pray that come it may,*
> *As come it will for a' that,*
> *That sense and worth o'er all the earth*
> *May bear the gree and a' that,*
> *For a' that and a' that,*
> *Its coming yet for a' that,*
> *That man to man the warld o'er*
> *Shall brothers be for a' that.'*

St Andrew Society of St Andrews

Soon after its foundation, this Society was re-formed as the St Andrews Society. On 13 January 1981 a meeting was called in the Burgh Court room of the Town Hall with the purpose of founding a St Andrews Society. Nick Halpin, student counsellor, had put forward to Gordon Christie the idea of making oral records which would contribute to the archives of St Andrews. Those who assembled approved of the formation of a society, to be named The St Andrew Society of St Andrews. A committee was elected as follows: President Mr David Niven, Vice-Presidents Dr Ronald Cant and Mr Gordon Christie, and committee members William Craig, Dale Duncan, Kenneth Fraser, Nick Halpin, Jurek Putter, Tom Sutherland, Mrs Jaques, Miss Jessie Robertson and Miss Vickers.

The objectives were to encourage the meeting together of Scots and of others interested in Scotland and Scottish culture; to celebrate St Andrew's Day and such other Scottish occasions; and to make contact with Scots visiting St Andrews.

At the next meeting Nick Halpin reported that already eight tapes had been made with the assistance of Jurek Putter who had registered the intention of the Society with the Oral Archive History Society. These sound recordings continued over the years, first by Nick Halpin and Jurek Putter, and then – when the Society purchased a tape recorder – by Gibby McMillan and A.B. Paterson. Many of the talks given to the Society were also taped. With a view to producing a booklet for making historical tours of the city, Jessie Robertson undertook to research the various possible routes, and Ruby Reid to write it.

The St Andrew's Day Celebrations

For nearly twenty years the Society co-ordinated the events and published the programmes. This was done with the co-operation of the Community Council who took on the responsibility for the Church Service and parade, and for items connected with the University. The Society introduced a St Andrew's Day lunch for 30 November, for a time at the Four Woods and later in the St Andrews Golf Hotel. By 1990 up to a hundred people were attending. It is the custom to invite some special guests, and the chosen speakers have been excellent. For some years there was also a free breakfast at the Byre Theatre on 30 November. The big event run by the Society, with co-operation from the St Andrews Golf Club, is the annual Tri-Am Golf Tournament which is played on the Jubilee and Eden courses. Alex Smith and Miss Vickers were the first organisers of this popular competition for which the Society donated prizes. In 1997 the date of the Tri-Am was moved to 1 March.

An early innovative and exciting contribution from the Society was a demonstration of an air-sea rescue given by an RAF helicopter and the Broughty Ferry lifeboat, but this was discontinued. For many years the Society also arranged a popular concert in the Town Hall. St Andrew's Day Competitions were organised for school children, first in the form of quizzes run by Ann Robertson and Derek Barrie, and later in a variety of competitions.

Publications

The Merchants' Association had produced a map of St Andrews in 1936. A new map brought out by the Society was based on this, together with a historical chart and later an illustrated map (researched by Ken Fraser); 16,000 had been sold by April 1983, and since then there has been a steady stream of reprints. It has been a most useful contribution and has also brought funds to the Society. In 1984 a golf map of the Old Course and historical golfing events was produced by Nick Halpin, Laurie Auchterlonie and Gordon Christie.

In 1985 Ruby Reid's booklet *Discovering Old St Andrews*, written for the Society, was published. It was very popular; a second edition of 1000 copies came out in 1991, with regular reprints since then (6th edition is dated 1995). Using the book, school parties have been taken round the city. On Gordon Christie's suggestion and on behalf of the Society, Ruby Reid wrote a booklet for the bicentenary of Sir Hugh Lyon Playfair in 1986.

Events

The Society programmes for each year have included local speakers on a variety of topics, mainly to do with St Andrews. As a start, Jurek

Putter gave a historical series. Others presented film and slide shows of many facets of St Andrews. There have been tours of St Andrews – including the Lang Riggs, the Cathedral Graveyard, the East Cemetery, Madras College and St Leonards School Library. Expeditions have also been made further afield to museums and places of interest, and annual summer outings were greatly enjoyed. Visits to May Island have been popular.

Contacts

There has been communication between the Society and the Community Council, The Preservation Trust and the Burns Club. A close liaison was built up with Madras College. In recent years, events with song, dance and music have taken place at Madras in an effort to attract young members. From the beginning, contact has been made with American students at the University, inviting them to the Society functions. Gordon Christie has been responsible for involving visiting Americans, and is in touch with many St Andrews societies in the USA and elsewhere. He has made trips to visit some of these and has handled a large correspondence.

Officials

David Niven was re-elected President from 1981 to 1993 with a gap of one year in 1991 when Jessie Robertson took over. Douglas Hamilton was President from September 1994 to April 1999 when Alex Sinclair took his place. As for the job of Secretary, two valiant members covered the years 1984-2000. The first was Nina Vickers and the second Cathy Lawrence, until her sudden death in August 2000. Both were highly esteemed. So were many others who have done so much to the success of the Society.

In 1997 there was a succession of meetings with members of the Tourist Board which proposed making the St Andrew's Day celebrations last for a week. With regret, the Society had to hand over the organisation of the programme to the Tourist Board.

In common with many societies there were difficulties in finding officials, and the membership fell, although the financial position was healthy (the Society has been able to contribute to various local causes over the years). In March 1999 a notice was sent out: 'The long-established St Andrew Society of St Andrews is at present in an ailing, but not we hope moribund, condition having lost the energetic leadership which enabled the Society to thrive in past years. We are in need of new blood – new members who could contribute to its revival'. Now, in 2003, it is struggling to survive.

Scotland Alba The Saltire Society

The Saltire Society was founded in Edinburgh in 1936 'to encourage everything that might improve the quality of life in Scotland and to restore the country to it proper place. It seeks to preserve all that is best in Scottish tradition and to encourage new developments which can strengthen and enrich the country's cultural life. It has wide-ranging interests including history, literature, music, drama, architecture and planning – and promotes excellence in many fields through a series of national awards.' There are now ten annual awards in different fields.

The Saltire Society St Andrews Branch was inaugurated in 1987 by Lillias Forbes. The first Chairman was Christopher Maclachlan. Early members included Margaret and Michael Welch and Mary Gatheral. The first meeting was held on 29 September 1987 when Douglas Gray of 'Scottish Records' spoke on 'Tourism in Scotland'. The Society met monthly, and its programmes covered a wide range of topics including musical and poetry evenings. Sadly, this Branch has now ceased.

The St Andrews Forty Club

The minutes are held at by the North East Fife Museums. The first official meeting of this Club was held on 9 January 1933, when it was decided that the motto would be 'SERVICE', and the rules were agreed. The Club should not exceed forty members. The enrolment fee was set at 2s., and a cost to be paid for each dancing night of 3d. In the winter months there was (and still is) dancing: Scottish dancing, ballroom, etc. There were also paper games, recipe nights, hat nights, etc. Activities in the summer months were three outings, putting, and a visit to the Royal College of Dancing Summer School. Committee members were Mrs Methven, Mrs Ganson, Miss A. Nicholson, Miss J. Smith, Mrs E. Johnstone.

Dancing classes were held in 1936 in the Imperial Hotel, 1938 in MacArthurs Café, 1942 in the All Saints Guide Hut, 1943 in the Cross Keys, then from 1952 in the Victoria Café. Miss Quigley was the Treasurer for a long stretch of years. The dancing teachers were, first, Miss Baptie, then Miss Jean Smith, Mrs Irene Caithness, Mrs I. Bennett. Special occasions have been a Hallowe'en fancy dress party in 1958 and dinner dances. By 1999 the annual subscription was £22.50.

The Royal Scottish Country Dance Society St Andrews Branch

Miss Jean Milligan founded the Scottish Country Dance Society in 1923, and is a legendary figure in Scotland. She was nominated as Scotswoman of the Year in 1973, and she died in 1978. Such was the success of the Society she started that there are now 100 branches and 260 affiliated groups. The St Andrews Branch is still going strong. During the winter months there are three classes a week; the Beginners Class and the Intermediate Class meet in St Andrew's Church Hall, and the Advanced Class at the Victory Memorial Hall. The Club also holds two dances each year. Some of the members of this (and perhaps of the Forty Club) attend the Scottish Country Dance School which has been held in St Andrews for many decades. For three weeks in July the town is filled with elegantly dressed dancers (in kilts of course) who are making their way to various rendezvous. The climax is the Saturday Night Ball held in the Younger Hall. It is well worth buying a viewing ticket and watching a fine show from the gallery.

St Andrews and District Franco-Scottish Society

This Society was started as a national one in the (late) nineteenth century at a time when relationships with the French were not good. The Society saw itself at having an ambassadorial function, and aimed to improve relationships over a period. The St Andrews branch was originally a University society which ran for many years, but eventually closed. It was revived as a 'Town and Gown' Society in 1996. The instigator was Joy Steel whose son married the daughter of an Aberdeen couple: Albert Craig was the National Treasurer to the Franco-Scottish Society and his wife was French.

Joy was successful in the venture, and last year there were over forty members. Jimmy and Mary Freeborn were among the founder members, and he was the first President. The monthly meetings usually take place at St Rule's Club. Speakers – official and others – are invited to the regular monthly meetings when either French or English is spoken. Members attend the National AGM which is held in rotation at the branch centres.

The Loches Alliance

Soon after the Franco-Scottish Society was revived, Mary Freeborn started a successful alliance with Loches in France, and within a few years many contacts have been made. Members make yearly trips to Loches and vice versa. Pupils from St Leonards School and Madras College have exchanged visits with French schoolchildren. The Renaissance Group have visited Loches, and also football teams. There have been exchanges of paintings and photos. Altogether a thousand people have been involved. Mary Freeborn was President, but recently Donald McGregor took over the office.

Such is the success of the links formed between the two towns in the last six years that the Community Council is considering giving its support to an official twinning.

The St Andrews Branch of the Edinburgh League of Prehistorians

This Society was instigated by Professor David Waterston, Mr I.C. Campbell and Lord David Douglas Hamilton. The first committee meeting was held on 8 January 1932 and officials were elected: President Professor Waterston; Vice Presidents Professor Rose and Professor D'Arcy Thompson; Secretary J.C. Gordon Campbell; Professor Baxter, 'Town members' Miss E.M. Hutchinson, Dr Mears of Leuchars, J. Tennant (Chief Constable of Fife), Mr Macbeth Robertson, Mrs Maitland. The objects were the furtherance and study of research in pre-history. Expeditions were to be entirely practical, and local excavations would be carried out. The Society would hold lectures concerned only with recent excavations, and planned to make an archaeological map of Fife. Members immediately set about collecting specimens. Dr Mears offered his collection. A request was made to the University Court 'that they might reconstitute Upper College Hall into a general ethnological and archaeological museum'. Not surprisingly this was turned down, but the Court offered a grant towards some display cases, with the suggestion that additional space might be created in the Bell Pettigrew Museum. Douglas Young and Terence Bruce Mitford came onto the committee in 1933, and the latter at once got to work on making the map which was eventually completed.

It seems that Professor Childe was very interested in this Society. He came occasionally to examine a site, and each year to give a lecture. In 1933 the title was 'Aryan Nonsense', and it dealt with the absurdity of Nazi claims. Other well-known lecturers were Sir Leonard Woolley, who described his excavations in North Syria, and Professor Talbot Rice. Professor Baxter spoke on 'The Amber Trading Route', and in 1936 he described, with illustrations, his important discoveries in the excavations at Istanbul (begun in 1922) on the site of the ruined palace of the Emperors at Constantinople. He described the wonderful forty-foot mosaic passageway of the palace with effigies of birds, a deer, a griffin, a dog, a mother and child, and a man playing a mandolin.

Expeditions were made to Tentsmuir where Dr Mears and others excavated cists at Morton Loch. A dig at Brackmont Hill, Leuchars, yielded Bronze Age articles – an incense cup, nine urns and a food vessel – and another dig at Kinshaldy found medieval pottery. An exhibition of the Morton Loch collection was held. The Society made a very active and enthusiastic start.

The minute book entries are from 1931 to 1936. A second book gives only a few entries up to 1938, but there follows a more detailed and chatty account of various quests. In 1934 a Mr A. Wilson of Tayport offered his collection to the Society, but when the Secretary went to visit him he found him dead. The collection duly came to join the artefacts in the Bute.

Another report was this (it is not clear who wrote this account):

> Mrs Boothby (Balnacarron) wishes to sell her jet necklace and asked Mrs Maitland to find out if the University would buy it for £30. The University can't afford it. Of course the Society would like to have it. One had sold in London at £130. An offer of £5 might be raised to £20. It seems unusual to swindle the woman, but I hold it justifiable; it shouldn't be in private hands. We have the rest of the Balnacarron material – she ought to give it to us.

Sadly this curious entry has no follow-up, but the necklace did reach the University collection which went from the Bute to a small archaeological museum in the Swallowgate, when that house became the University Departments of Classics and Ancient and Modern History. Subsequently the necklace was given to the Kinburn Museum.

This jet necklace is 4000 years old. It is known as 'the Balnacarron or Lawhead jet spaces bead necklace'. It was found in a cist in a field near Balnacarron House, and 'gives information about the activities and connections of Early Bronze Age Fifers'. Before being exhibited at Kinburn House in summer 1993, it was sent to Edinburgh for conservation and restringing by Will Murray, the Scottish Museums conservator. It had been very old when buried and had been cobbled together from parts of four necklaces and one bracelet, which had been made of three different materials: the original jet (from Whitby), lignite and cannel coal. A book published by the National Museums of Scotland in 1989 (edited by J. Calder) reports, 'The necklace would have been a very prestigious and valuable article – there are only about seventy others from the whole of Britain and Ireland.' It is made up of a triangular fastener, six 'spacer plates' and 79 oval-shaped beads, very few of which are the original jet beads. The report says it would have had 30-40 more beads and would have been strung together in a crescent shape.

Professor Rose was President of the Society in 1938. There seems to be a gap during the war years, but then the Society restarted; there is a membership card for 1946-7 giving Professor Rose as President, G.P. Henderson and T. Bruce Mitford Joint Secretaries, committee members Miss Wilson, Rev. A. Cant. Speakers were to be F.T. Wainwright, Prof. Stuart Piggot, R.B.K. Stephenson, W.D. Simpson.

The Society re-formed as 'The St Andrews University Archaeological Society', but the members are a mixture of Town and Gown. For a long time Terence Bruce Mitford was the guiding light. He was active in excavations in Cyprus. The Society continues with a regular lecture programme. It was strange that archaeology never found favour with the University, even in the 1960s when there was such interest and activity. Under the guidance of Mrs E.V.W. Proudfoot, members of the Student Archaeology Society have recently done a recording of all the Cathedral graveyard monuments.

The St Andrews Angling Club

The formation of an Angling Club at St Andrews was discussed at a meeting in the Town Hall on 25 May 1898. Mr J.L. MacPherson (solicitor) was called to the Chair. The objects of the Club were stated by Mr D. Blyth as 'improving the fishing facilities in our immediate neighbourhood, and as a club to gain the sympathy and sanction of the Town Council for improvements in this, and even in extensions – in having the water storage ponds stocked with trout.' The Chairman said he had 'every sympathy with the Gentle Art of Angling' and would do what he could to make the Club a success. Those present were elected as the first committee, and were the founder members of the Club: Mr James Gillespie (architect) who consented to become President, J.L. MacPherson to be Vice-President, D. Blyth (who was Secretary until 1910), John C. Lyell, Wm. Foulis, Jas. R. McCormack, David Lyell, John Spence and Andrew Haxton.

By obtaining sets of rules from Cupar and other angling clubs, a set suitable to the new club at St Andrews was drawn up and was submitted and approved at the next meeting.

I will list the Presidents throughout the years.

1898-1915 James Gillespie
(a minute of 21 March 1917 states Mr Boase proposed 'that it be recorded in the minutes the great loss the Club had sustained in the death of Mr James Gillespie who died fighting for King and Country in France'. Out of a membership of 36, ten were serving with His Majesty's forces.)

1916-1924 Philip M. Boase
(the three Boase brothers and their wives were prominent in the activities of the town.)

1925-1927 Harold G. Wilson

1928-1931 Capt W.F. Low

1932-1936 David Pirie
1937-1940 Dr G Matthew Fyfe
1941-1950 Dr G.A. Cumming
1951-1959 Robert Leonard (who was Provost 1958-61)
1960-1961 Professor R.D. Craig
For shorter spells of 2-3 years between 1962 and 1979: D.T. Lowe, William Thomson, E.V.K Brill, Charles Lyall, R. Malvenan, Peter Malcolm, William Campbell.
1980-1999 Keith R. Neilson
Keith is also well known as a Fife Regional councillor and as the founder of the successful movement to establish Rymonth housing for the handicapped in St Andrews. It is from him that I have an excellent summary of the Angling Club's history.
2000- Andrew Robertson

Competitions

The first competition was on 10 June 1898. 'We leave by the 6.10 a.m. train, fishing any part of the river Eden between Springfield and the sea; the competitors pay a 1/- Sweep towards the prizes, the first two to be for the heaviest baskets ...the third prize to the Competitor having the heaviest fish .... We return by the 10 p.m Train, Contents of the Baskets to be weighed at the Railway Station on the arrival of said Train.' On the 14 and 16 July there were half-day competitions on the Kenly, 'fishing on any part between Cameron and the Sea and legal lures to be used. Baskets to be weighed on the arrival of the 7.44 p.m train from the Coast.'

In August Mr Mudie gave the Club permission for a day competition on Montrave Loch. An entry for 1 October runs, 'On Saturday there was a good turn out all [*sic*] on the Kenly and the weather and water was all that could be desired, ... fish taking either the Fly or Worm freely and the few hours fishing was fast and furious ... one member having a nice fish of 4 lbs 2 ozs.' In October by invitation of the Cupar Club the members of the St Andrews Angling Club joined them on Lindores Loch for a day's pike fishing. An entry of 10 April 1899: 'The turnout for the Carhurlie Competition was very disappointing. The morning being wet, only five members being loyal to their colours, started from the Royal Stables at 7.40 a.m. in Brake and reaching the water about 9.30.' (Keith Neilson commented that the turnout 'has not changed over the years'.) 'The stables behind the Royal Hotel were a popular source of transport. In June the competition was at Ballo, and the competitors took the 6 a.m. train to Leslie and hired a conveyance in the evening to drive them to the Markinch railway station, thereby getting an hour's extra fishing.' Another interesting record: '20th April 1890. The first of the Club Competitions for the season took place yesterday at Carhurlie .... There were ten members took part, the day was the most unfavourable that could be had for Angling, a frosty morning and a bright Sunshine, the whole day with a hard westerly breeze scarcely a fish was to be seen. But not withstanding, those present enjoyed the day's outing very much, a perfect Picnic party. The Drive was enjoyed both to and from the water, the conversation pleasant, everything passed off harmoniously, and Mr Andrew Carstairs, Joiner, was duly proposed and seconded and admitted into the membership of the Club.' Keith Neilson, referring to the weather, writes 'How many Competition Days have we had similar to the above stated?'

The first Prizes donated in 1899 were: a six-pound leg of mutton for the best aggregate over the season, and a pocket-knife for the best aggregate among junior members (i.e. under eighteen years of age). Next year Mr J.B. Scott of the Royal stables gave a prize of a Fly Book, and in 1926 Captain How gave a cup known as 'The Cameron Cup' and Mr David Pirie gave the Loch Leven Cup.

Other business

At the ABM in March 1989 it was agreed to become affiliated with the Scottish Trout Anglers Association whose objectives were to secure a close time for trout, and to put down all illegal practices of taking fish from the Streams. In the event of any lawsuit the Club would get all the assistance possible from the Association. In February 1901 the Club sent a petition to the Secretary for Scotland, Lord Balfour, and to the local MP Mr H.T. Anstruther, also to Mr H.H. Asquith, to have a Close Time for fishing in Scotland (as there was in England). The Club later sent petitions in favour of the proposed 'Fresh Water Fish (Scotland) Bill', which was duly passed. The Club later gave support and a financial contribution to the Cupar Club's 'Policing the Eden against illegal practices'. There was also a Watcher at the Kinness Burn. In 1910 Cllr Norman Boase represented the Town Council at a meeting of the Club to discuss the construction of proposed weirs on the Kinness Burn for the better protection of trout. (My Nursery School children thought the 'waterfalls' were put there for racing the paper boats they made!). A committee was appointed to arrange about the erection of the weirs. The restocking of the Burn was discussed and Mr David Louden stated that '1,000 Three Months Old Fry, also 300 Yearlings had been ordered from the Howieton Fishery and that enough money had been subscribed to pay for these'.

Cameron Reservoir

On 9 March 1911 an event took place which was to be of great importance to The Club. 'There was a large gathering of the St Andrews Town Council and others at the new water works at Cameron to witness the Ceremony of the cutting of the first sod on the site of the new reservoir. Mr James Kinniburgh, the contractor for the reservoir, presented Provost Wilson with a silver spade to cut the sod. In the course of his speech the Provost said the extent of the reservoir would be 100 acres with a capacity of 180 million gallons of water.' In 1938 a cup was donated by Dr Matthew G. Fyfe for competition from boats at Cameron. Cameron Reservoir became the main local fishing waters of the Club. An entry for 9 March 1938 is the first of many on this subject: 'the Secretary was instructed to write to the Town Council stressing the serious view the Club took on the matter of weed growth on Cameron Reservoir, not only from a fishing point of view but also as it affected the purity of the water supply'. At a committee meeting on 5 December 1965 a long discussion took place on the possible implications of the 'take over' of Cameron by the Regional Water Board. A year later the Secretary was able to announce that the negotiations had at last been successful, and that as a result of enquiries with the Fife and Kinross Water Board the Club would continue to enjoy the facilities of Cameron Reservoir.

Cairnsmill Pond

In April 1917 the Club received an agreement from the Town Council to lease the fishing at Cairnsmill Pond, with the proviso that the Club should undertake to keep down the rabbits and safeguard the condition of the banks. 'Mr Boase lost no time in ordering 1,000 yearling trout from the Howieson Fishing Coy which arrived in splendid condition.' A set of rules was drawn up, including: that the pond would be open from 15 April to 30 September; only fly fishing would be allowed; and for season 1918, members limit themselves to killing four fish per day. In June 1928 new filters at Pipeland were working, and the town's water supply no longer came from Cairnsmill Pond. The Club had it cleaned out and restocked. The Club fished here until 1953 when, after the summer, they had to give up the rental and the fishing rights because the water was polluted.

The Club after 1930

There was a large increase in membership in 1930, and it was agreed to make each competition at Cameron a two-day event and The Cameron Cup to be competed for in bank fishing only. During the 1939-1945 war, each year money was sent from the funds of the Club to the

Recreation Funds of the 'A' Squadron 2nd Battalion Fife and Forfar Yeomanry. All those who joined the Forces were made honorary members for the duration of the war. In 1944 Mr James Haddow, Mr H.L. Kidd and Mr David Pirie died. (In January 1957 his son Burton Pirie was elected Hon. Vice-President and was made a Life Member.) In 1945 four keen anglers, members of the Club, died: David Blyth, J. Cuthbert, James Whyte and D.B Tulleth. In 1946 the membership of the Club was restricted to 100, and a waiting list was kept. In 1953 the limit was raised to 120. On 31 March 1947 a presentation of a rod and reel was made to Mr A.P. Aikman as a token of appreciation for his valued services as Secretary over ten years. Another form of appreciation was the award of Life Membership to Ted Brill (Lecturer in the German Department) and J.A. Macdonald (later Professor of Botany).

The annual competitions on Loch Leven (established in 1959) between the three angling clubs, Cupar, St Andrews and Leven, caused some difficulties in the 1960s in regard to the fair booking of boats. Treasurer David Dorward sorted that one out, as he did any problems with the Club finances. When reading the minutes, I enjoyed one item from 9 December 1959 about competitions, suggested by Mr Law: 'A Novelty Competition from the bank on Cameron, the competitor to state before he commences that he has entered ... cast of 51b B.S. consisting of Bob-Kingfisher Butcher, Woodcock and Yellow and Tail-Greenwell, all size 12 single hook'.

The Club continues to flourish with the same good fellowship, and with the same loyalty of members in office. In the early days George Baird was Secretary for twenty years; that record has now been overtaken by Peter Malcolm, Secretary from 1977 to the present day.

Bridge Clubs

There are three bridge clubs in the town. The St Andrews Bridge Club was probably started in the winter of 1938/9. The places of meeting were various, but the Club currently meets in the New Golf Club and is flourishing, with a membership of over ninety and an average attendance at the Tuesday evening meeting of over seventy.

The St Andrews New Bridge Club is an offshoot of the above. It was started after the AGM 1948/9, when there was a difference of opinion on some policies, and a number of members split off. The first meeting place for some long time was the Tudor Café; presently it is in the Town Hall. Iris Buchowski tells me that her mother, the wife of Jimmy Alexander who was the famous starter at the Old Course, was a member of this Club and used to say that she preferred bridge to going to the cinema, 'as you didn't meet friends at the Cinema'. Some of the founder members were Bill Langlands President, Ann Brown Secretary, J.K. Robertson, David Anderson (Kinburn Hotel) and Charlie Mudie. Nowadays there are some people who play in more than one of the clubs.

I have been unable to find out when *The St Andrews Ladies Bridge Club* was formed. There were various venues until Alison Patisson, daughter of Professor Rose, bought the large house at the west end of Queens Terrace (the house in which the first St James' Roman Catholic School was held). Alison was a keen member of this Bridge Club and she offered it the use of the basement rent-free, but on certain terms. Eventually – some time after Alison's death – the Club had the chance of buying their Club rooms; they raised the money and did so. This puts it in a unique and advantageous position. This Club is so flourishing, and the list of ladies waiting to be admitted is so long, that an Associate Membership was instituted, and the Club rooms are much used.

Other Societies

Cage Bird Society

This Society is listed in the 1934 St Andrews Directory, its Honorary President being Professor D'Arcy Thompson and its President Mr T.

Auchterlonie. The Society held its 15th annual show on 10 December 1955 (presumably there were no shows in the war years). D. Grieve was winner with his budgerigars, and R. Cation was owner of the champion bird of the show. This Society was in action until three years ago, but no longer appears in the library's list of societies.

There used to be a fine selection of birds in a large caged area in Kinburn Park. This was a highlight when we took my nursery school children there for a walk. The birds were moved to Mercat Wynd, the small indoor shopping mall in Market Street, but this was recently changed into new premises for Boots chemists, and there are no longer any birds for children to admire.

I do not remember ever meeting Professor D'Arcy Thompson in the street with his parrot on his shoulder, but many have recorded this colourful sight. A rather sad thing happened some time after his death. His daughter, Barbara, who was a mistress at St Leonards School, inherited her father's parrot; she was friendly with Miss Mabel McCall, the scripture mistress, who had a dachsund. One day my daughters came rushing home with the latest news: 'A terrible thing has happened – D'Arcy T's parrot has been *killed* by Holy Mabel's dog.'

St Andrews Philatelic Society

On 26 November 1946 a small group of enthusiastic collectors met at John Carstairs' home to see a display given by Mr Frank Fairweather of Newport. At the meeting it was decided to form a Society and draft a constitution. The object of the Society was 'to study all matters pertaining to philately in general or any particular branch; to promote and encourage such matters in the U.K. or elsewhere.' Some of those present were Messrs J. Carstairs, D. Ritchie, T. Robertson, J. Lea, J. Gourlay, C.K. Karsten and Dr Cummings. At a later meeting it was decided to join the Association of Scottish Philatelic Societies with J. Carstairs as delegate.

There was a break during the war; in 1955 the Society was restarted and it is still going. Meetings were held once a month between October and April, at first in the Torch Club rooms and later at Madras, Kilrymont School. The members were so keen that, for a few years, meetings were held twice a month, but then reverted to the monthly meetings. The Society has seen some very interesting and exceptional displays given by prominent Scottish philatelists, and many of its own members have given displays to other societies. Three members of the Society, Michael Scott, J. Gourlay and C.K. Karsten, have been awarded the Association of Scottish Philatelic Societies Award of Merit for their service to the promotion of Philately. I have this information from C.K. Karsten; he and J. Gourlay are the only surviving founder members.

The St Andrews Railway and Transport Society

This Society started in 1961, its aim being to provide talks and excursions for all interested in this subject. Until 1988 it met fortnightly from October to May, then switched to monthly meetings. The membership is steady at about thirty-five.

Ramblers Association

The St Andrews Branch of the Scottish Ramblers Association was started in 1991, two of the founder members being Sandra Knight and Ann Killean. The membership is steady.

* * * * * * * * * * * *

Other clubs to suit other tastes include a jazz club, a chess club and a skateboarding club. There was also an ornithology club which was founded in 1909 by the Rev Peter Whittet; there is no record of how long it continued, but there is now a Fife club.

Chapter 10

GARDENS AND PLANTS

The St Andrews and District Horticultural Association, 1833-1914

This society, one of the oldest, was formed at a meeting in the Town Hall on 16 September 1833. It was named the St Andrews and District Horticultural and Floricultural Association. The minutes deposited in the University archives are from 1867-1893, 1906-1913, 1925-1937, 1950-1978. Since then the Society has continued without a break.

1867-93

The founders are not known, but the officials at the 1867 A.G.M. were: Patron Provost Walter Milne, President Dr George Lees, Vice President Mr Alex Reid, secretary Mr David Fletcher (bookseller). Committee members who continued to do a lot of work for the Association were Mr J. Malcolm, Mr J. Wilson (florist), Mr Melville, Major Chiene, Lt-Col Hunter, Mr W. Kidston, and Mr Dicks. The business at the first meeting and subsequent ones was mainly the drawing up of rules, revisions of rules, classes for entries, prizes and other arrangements for the annual show which was held in August. There were three classes of membership: professionals, amateurs and cottagers. (If a cottager had a greenhouse he was not allowed to compete as a cottager.) This classification set the varying rates of subscription (professional and amateur 3s., cottager ls.), and for entries to the show and for exhibiting. Each year a list of possible judges was drawn up. They were professional gardeners from as far away as Errol Park, Falkland Palace and Birkhill, and from nearby houses with large grounds. After the three judges had done their work in the morning, they were taken to lunch by the officials and the committee; the changes were rung – to The Royal, The Cross Keys, The Golf Hotel, The Star, until it was found to be more economical (or less trouble?) to have a caterer provide a meal at the site of the show.

The sites for these years were as follows: (1868 is entered as the fourth show: what were the dates of the earlier ones?) 1868 to 1873 The 'New' Town Hall; 1877 to 1882 The Rink (this was in the Scores on the site where St James Church was built); 1883 and 1884 The Town Hall; 1885 to 1892 The Recreation Hall. (This useful building in City Road was built by a private company as a recreation hall, and was later also called the 'Volunteer Hall' or 'Drill Hall' or 'Badminton Hall'. It was demolished in the 1980s and a large block of flats, after the style of the Alexandra Place houses, was built.)

Each year the committee spent time and trouble deciding which band should be engaged. These were the choices: 1867 to 1873 The Volunteer Association Band; 1874 The Band of the Training Ship Mars (a training ship on the Tay for delinquent boys); 1875 and 1876 The Largoward Brass Band; 1877 The Fife Light Horse Band; 1878 The Rifle Brigade Band; 1879 The Cupar Rifle Volunteer Band; and then each year from 1880 to 1892 The St Andrews City Brass Band (apart from 1883 when they had the Dunnikier Brass Band). There was usually dancing in the evening of the first day of the show from eight to ten o'clock. Supporters were generous in giving prizes, trophies, cups and money prizes; for instance, *The St Andrews Citizen* gifted a cup, and in 1885 a children's award for the best vase of wild flowers was announced. The committee also had to choose someone to open the show and someone to present the prizes. In 1869 the MP Edward Ellice, and subsequently General and Mrs Moncrieff of The Priory, then Provost Milton, and other prominent local people.

Those who were active in the Association in the second part of this period were R.E. Curwen of Westerlee, Mr Purdoe of Castlecliff, Captain Randle Jackson (of North Cliff, The Scores), Mr C. Grubb (merchant), John Macgregor (73 Market Street), Provost Paterson and Mr John Balsillie. (I am told by the son of a Mrs Balsillie, who was the niece of John Balsillie, that he lived in Melbourne Brae, and was a very keen gardener. There are several families of this name in Fife, descended from two brothers Balsillie who came over with Mary Queen of Scots, and were given lands in Fife.) In 1879 on the committee, which aimed to be of twelve working members plus officials, there were five gardeners, three joiners, a wright, a grocer, and a book-seller. Periodically there was difficulty with funds, as was the case with many other societies. When there was a deficit in the accounts, the committee would decide who might be approached to become a patron. This usually brought an acceptance and the odd guinea. From time to time the proceeds from a concert were more than welcome. At a committee meeting in 1888, Mr Milton in the chair, the bad news was that the balance was only 5s. 4d. After discussion the Secretary recorded 'in spite of the present languid condition it was decided that the show was to continue'. The committee had been meeting in the Town Hall, but now changed to the Good Templars Hall (part of the present St John's in South Street). This saved a small amount of money. In 1891 the date of the show had to be altered 'due to the backward state of the weather'. In the minutes of the pre-show committee meeting in 1892 there is the item 'The Pigeon and Canary committee will make their own arrangements'. The Secretary recorded, 'There was a better display of flowers than usual', and 'the Judges and the committee dined in a side room of the Hall'.

In 1892 Mr Balsillie, the Treasurer, stated the balance was £1.19.2½d. The minutes come to an end at the beginning of 1893 because, in spite of the efforts of a good number of loyal supporters, the Association was about to be wound up – for the time being.

1906-14

A meeting was held in the Town Hall, Mr W. Greig in the chair. It was proposed by Mr John Balsillie that a horticultural association be established and named the St Andrews and District Horticultural Association. This was agreed; also that the rules from 'the other society in 1893 be used as a standpoint'. The membership fee would be 1-6d.

New life began: Principal Sir James Donaldson became the President and agreed to open the show. Bailie Greig was the Chairman and Dr John Wilson the Secretary. Committee meetings were held in the Royal Hotel (the charge was 2-6d.). It was agreed that there would be an annual prize for the best-kept cottager's garden. Mr J. Pirie, china merchant, offered a prize of a pipe and a pound of tobacco, or gloves if a lady won, for the best-kept window box. The University consented to the show being held at the (Carnegie) Sports Park. This 1907 show took a lot of planning. The gates opened at 7 a.m. on 24 August. A programme of sports was arranged; this was an added attraction, and a sum of £53 was taken at the gate. The Mars Training Ship Band had been chosen to play.

A series of lectures was arranged, to be held in the Science Room of the Madras. Dr John Wilson gave a lecture on 'Flowers', illustrated by the lime-light slides of Mr G.B. Rogers of St Mary's Studio. The 1907 show was the pattern for the shows from then until 1914. In 1911 The Kirkcaldy Trades Prize Band was engaged; an added feature came from Dunfermline: 'The Royal Allandane Troupe', a team of girl dancers with a piper. There was a large industrial section in one of the marquees with new prizes for knitting and sewing, beside the jelly and jam and baking classes. The show was opened by Annie S. Swann, the novelist (Mrs Burnett Smith). The Sports Programme offered Clock Golf, Approach Shots, a Farm Servants' Race and a Tug of War; a 220 yards Race, Putting the Stone, a One Mile Cycle Race, a Sack Race, Throwing the Hammer, an Obstacle Race, an Egg and Spoon race, a Blindfold Barrow Race, and a Pillow Fight! And at the end of all that hard work by relatively few people there was a deficit of £20.

Messrs James Wilson, Basillie, Robb, J.R. Wilson (ironmonger), Greig, Mentiply (Brownhills) and D.B. Stevenson continued to work hard. The name of Wilson comes into the minutes of the Association so often that it merits a special note. James Wilson married Margaret Hardie; their family house was at 12 Greenside Place. He was gardener at Sir Hugh Lyon Playfair's fantastic garden at St Leonards, and he later remodelled this garden for St Leonards School. He started a market garden business in the rented grounds of St Leonards Church Glebe, south of Greenside Place. The site of the greenhouses is still to be seen. He opened a florist's shop at 96 Market Street. At each show for decades James Wilson's display was a centre of attraction. One year he was put in charge of the Sports at the show. He was a leading horticulturalist in St Andrews. He laid out the Carnegie Park for the University and he planted the lime trees in South Street.

James and Margaret had one daughter and three sons, Alexander, John and James who had their training from him. Alexander and his family settled in America. In 1880 John Hardie Wilson went to the Edinburgh Botanic Gardens and after two years was put in charge of the rock garden. In 1884 he went to classes in biology and geology at Edinburgh University and was medallist in both subjects in theory and practice. He returned to St Andrews and graduated there as BSc in 1887. He was employed as assistant to Professor McIntosh at the Gatty Marine, and his first papers were published. He gave a thirty-lecture course on Botany followed by a fifty-lecture course, part of his qualification for a St Andrews MD and his DSc. He was university extension lecturer in 1889. In that year he was invited to lay out the Botanic Gardens with the assistance of Thomas Berwick. It seems he was working very hard, but not earning much. He then resigned from the University.

The original Botanic Gardens had to be altered to accommodate the building of the Bute Medical in 1897, the Bell Pettigrew in 1909, and then the Carnegie extension to the University Library. In 1900 John Wilson had been appointed Lecturer in Agriculture and Rural Economy, but with no salary. He coped with the alterations to the Botanic Gardens and continued his hybridisation work using the West Garden for his research on potatoes. He was successful in producing three varieties of blight-free potatoes, and also experimented with disease-resistant oats and turnips. He travelled widely and never spared himself. He and his father James were always ready to help the Horticultural Association. The death of the distinguished Dr John Wilson in 1920 must have been a blow to the members.

To go back to the minutes of Autumn 1912. There was a suggestion that the Association might plant shrubs and plants in vacant corners of the city, and a start was made with a shrub beside the West Port. Major Morris became the new President of the Association. Major and Mrs Morris of Dyer's Brae had 'made a beautiful garden out of wilderness'.

In 1913 an open competition for all of Scotland for sweet peas was established. The 1914 and 1915 shows were held at Madras College with a limited sports programme. The Right Rev Bishop Plumb in opening the 1914 show said he recalled shows in the earlier days of the Society. In 1914 a concert was given by the Choral Society in aid of funds, and it was said that 'The Society had had its ups and downs but was still struggling bravely'. The records end here. St Andrews was involved in a worldwide struggle.

The St Andrews and District Allotment Association

In the boxes of records of the Horticultural Association is one marked as above. The first entry begins: 'On 30th of March 1918 a public meeting was held in the Town Hall. The convener was J. Spence of Abbey Street, Dr Sloan was in the chair'. The proposal was to form an allotment association, and this was agreed. The aims were to encourage the growing of more and better garden produce among allotment holders. Those elected to the committee were Cllr J. Spence (who became the Chairman), David B. Stevenson (who became Secretary), John Balsillie, Alex Bayne, William Robb of the Gibson Hospital and others.

At its first meeting in The Royal Hotel, where subsequent meetings were also held, the committee adopted rules and bye-laws. A letter from Miss Moir, 5 Hope Street wished the Association good luck. This was the start of her enthusiastic involvement. Other supporters were Mr David Rusack, and Mr Norman Boase who was elected President. A ladies' committee was formed. There were to be two shows – a 'spring vegetable' show and a chrysanthemum show in the Autumn.

This new association started with zest. Among the patrons were Sir John and Lady Herkless, Mrs Boase, Dr and Mrs Paton, and Col Anstruther Gray. Monthly meetings were arranged. Lady Griselda Cheape gave a paper on 'The Rearing and Keeping of Rabbits'; Dr John Wilson gave a lantern lecture on 'Troublesome Weeds'. Mrs Boase presented a potato spraying machine, and a demonstration was given on its use. By the end of 1918 there were 118 members!

The committee had great difficulty in getting land for allotments. Mr Cheape offered some in his grounds, and land at Windmill Park was rented. There was a long battle with the Council over obtaining land at St Mary's Street (Conyngyard?), which was eventually settled and a start made. Each year improvement was reported. The committee was active in lobbying the Ministry of Agriculture and the Secretary of State for Scotland over the necessity of granting security of tenure to allotment holders, and making more land available for allotments. A bill was passed to this effect in 1922.

The first annual show was held in October 1919 in the Christian Institute, and was opened by Mrs William Robb. Each year there was a good profit from the sale of flowers and vegetables, and this was donated to the War Funds, and in the following years mainly to the Cottage Hospital.

Miss Loveday of St Katharine's School became a committee member. The allotments were inspected regularly and reports made annually. At one meeting it was said that Miss Loveday's allotment had weeds in it. She apologised, and said her time had been 'too much taken up with school duties, but in the holidays she intended to get it straight'. It was fortunate having her as a member; the 1920 and 1921 flower shows were held in St Katharine's School. The Boy Scouts' Pipe Band livened the proceedings, also Pipe Major Kirk and his girl dancers. Shows were held each Autumn and 'Chrysanthemum Day was held and passed off without complaints'. For a short time a spring bulb show was held.

Inevitably, with the war over and the Horticultural Association wishing to resume its activities, the question of the amalgamation of these two bodies arose. At the committee meeting of 18 February 1921 Miss Loveday proposed a Motion that the St Andrews and District Allotment Association does not amalgamate with any other society at the present time'; this was carried. In 1921 there were 150 members. However, the amalgamation must have taken place in 1922. Mr Stevenson died in January 1923, and in his obituary in *The Citizen* of 13 January it was stated 'he was instrumental in bringing about the union of the Allotment and the Horticultural associations'. He was Secretary in 1922, but there is nothing in the minutes of the Allotment Association to report this event, apart from the fact that the minutes of 26 August 1922 are headed 'St Andrews Allotment and Horticultural Association'. I believe that this is the only instance of an amalgamation of two clubs, and that fact is a significant characteristic of St Andreans.

The Horticultural Association, 1922–

The annual August flower shows were held: 1922 to 1925 at the University Sports Grounds; 1926-1931 The Volunteer Hall; 1932 The Madras; 1933-1937 The Volunteer Hall (sometimes now called the Drill/Recreation Hall). The bands were as follows: 1922 United Services Pipe Band and the Kirkcaldy Girl Dancers; 1923 and 1924 The Tullis Russell Band; also in 1924 The Royal Victorian Troup of Comical Scots; 1925 to 1927 'La Scala Orchestra' (this little orchestra played during silent films in La Scala); 1928 The St Andrews Boys Brigade Band. After this the town bands were engaged – the St Andrews Brass Band and the St Andrews Silver Band.

The 1932 show at Madras College was the Centenary anniversary and was opened by Sir Ralph Anstruther. There were marquees in the quad and stands in the classrooms. Over the years the Association had asked several times for the use of Madras, but it was only granted for special occasions. In 1935 when Lady Erskine opened the show there were 10,000 blooms. What a vast amount of organisation it must have taken. One note states that Mr Pirie (china merchant) provided plates and Mr Mercer (china merchant) vases. This adequate supply was ensured after a terrible crisis one year when there was a shortage of vases!

Mr McDonald was Chairman until Mr Mowat, Curator of the Botanic Gardens, took over in 1936, holding the post at various times until 1973. George Simpson was a keen member; he was the gardener at Mount Melville, and in 1936 was appointed by the King as head gardener at Windsor. The Association presented him with an inscribed wallet.

1950-1978

The war over, here were the old stalwarts and some new ones back at work. Officials were Chairman, Mr Mowat, with Mr Greig and Mr Antequil, and as the years went by Chairman Mr R.J. Mitchell, and Chairman Mr R Rutherford. The first show after war took place in the Boys Brigade Hall, and was opened by Miss Low, with Captain H.B. Pirie as Chairman. Bailie Miss Moir presented the prizes for the municipal gardens competition. Although there had been minor complaints at previous shows, they had been easily settled. This year there was some trouble when the parents of one young exhibitor 'created a disturbance'. Those in charge gave way to stop the commotion, but decided later to ban future entries by the family. The show was the biggest since the Centenary one, and the profit on the year amounted to £162-18s. They were off with a good start, leading to a long series of successful two-day shows.

1951 was the Festival of Britain, and Miss Cox, Blebo, gave two large

Union Jacks to the Association. There were 800 exhibits. The Volunteer Hall continued to be the venue and remained so for the next twenty or more years. The shows were opened by well-known local people, among them Mrs Purvis, Major H.B. Pirie, Miss Moir, Miss Low, Mr Henderson Stewart, M.P., and in 1957 Mrs Henderson Stewart, then Lady Victoria Wemyss, Lady Carmichael, Mrs Cheape, Mrs Macdonald (wife of the Professor J.A. Macdonald), Sir John and Lady Gilmour.

Lectures were arranged by the committee which at this stage was composed of less than twenty-three members! Dr McKerrow Senior (who became President) gave a talk on 'Culture of the Rose', and Mrs Uprichard on 'Modern Cut Flowers'. There was a visit to Edinburgh Botanic Gardens. Evening meetings with Brains Trusts and Quizzes proved popular. Then there was a run of bad weather: *The St Andrews Citizen* reported in 1957 'Bad weather for Annual Show', 1958 'A grand display of sweet peas but shocking weather', 1960 'Show Beats the Storm', 1961 'the weather was adverse', 1962 'difficult weather', 1965 'Show despite poor conditions', 1966 'battery of rain and wind, atrocious conditions'. Mrs Beatrice Copson won the City Challenge Trophy that year; she was a regular competitor and supporter of the Association. In 1970 she was invited to open the show, and did so again in 1972. *The Citizen* quotes her opening words: 'When I came into the Hall a familiar smell came to me, and I realised it was the scent of pleasant memories'.

That is an experience shared by many gardeners. Those words may bring memories of many enjoyable shows: the sight of more than one thousand blooms, of perfect specimens of fruit and vegetables, of jams and jellies and cakes, of the beat of the band and the fun at the dancing.

The Botanic Gardens

The Botanic Gardens were set out by Dr John Wilson in 1889 onwards; there were seventy-eight beds containing eight hundred and twenty-eight specimens of plants in the quarter of an acre. The small, secluded walled garden to the west of the Long Walk was once beautiful, until it became a wilderness in the 1990s. Over the years, rare plants had been sent by previous students of botany.

In 1960 a decision was made to transfer the Botanic Gardens, over a period of three years, to eighteen acres of land which the University owned in the Canongate. This was adjacent to Bassaguard and the railway line to the East Neuk towns, and separated from Cockshaugh Park by the Kinnessburn. Mr Bob Mitchell and J.A. Macdonald, the Professor of Botany, were the leading lights in this enterprise. Valuable specimens were moved from the old site. Now the gardens look so established and mature that it is hard to believe that I can remember the site as fields. The Botanic Gardens were an integral part of the botany courses, but the University decided that it could no longer afford the upkeep involved. Fortunately the North East Fife District Council took them over on 1 October 1987 and has made continuing improvements, so that they are a great asset.

Friends of the Botanic Gardens

This group was formed by Bob Mitchell in 1980. It is a flourishing society whose membership reached 1210 by the year 2000. Its aims are to support the Gardens financially, to increase the numbers of visitors through raising interest and through publicity, and to assist the Council-employed staff. Until this year members went on voluntary duty on three shifts on Saturdays and Sundays, but now the Council employs a gatekeeper throughout the week. The 'Wednesday group' is responsible for potting up plants which are on sale at the gate. The sales for 2000-1 amounted to £11,000. All money raised is donated to the Gardens and this has been a help when finances have been stretched. In the two decades up to the year 2000, the Friends donated £80,000. Volunteers also act as guides – this service is often requested. A good monthly newsletter, an excellent series of lectures, a monthly tour round the Gardens for members, and organised visits to other gardens (day or evening visits) all help to increase the membership and to raise interest. Local Honorary Life Members are Mrs Molly Pirie, Professor R.M. Crawford and Mr Maurice Wilson who was Chairman for 15 years, and Mr Bob Mitchell, who has recently retired after 20 years as secretary to the Friends, and his wife Felicity. Bob continues to be honorary curator and consultant.

The St Andrews and District Amateur Rose Society

The St Andrews Rose Society was founded on 21 October 1926 by Dr A.R.C McKerrow; the co-founders were Brigadier George Fellowes, Dr Maitland Ramsay and Captain Warren Wynne. The first committee was: Mrs How President, Mr A. Tailyour, who was Secretary for the next thirteen years, Mrs Boothby, Mrs Christie Aitken, Dr McKerrow, Mrs Guillemarde, Captain Warren Wynne, Mr A.J. Stewart and Mr Orr. The Society was affiliated to the Horticultural and Allotment Society, to which it paid 1/6 from each subscription of 3/6d. This arrangement came to an end in 1928: the Society could not afford the fees, and the Horticultural show in August was too late for roses.

Dr McKerrow was President in 1934. Speaking on the occasion of its fiftieth anniversary Dr McKerrow recalled its beginnings: 'Soon folks stopped to say, "Now you have set something going." I replied, "I sincerely hope so. Do come and join us."' Which they did – in 1928 the membership had risen to ninety, and for years the numbers were stable.

It was decided that the Rose Show would be held on the second Saturday in August in the Town Hall, which suited well. Occasionally the show had to be held in the Volunteer Hall because the Town Hall was not available. In a few years the show had to be cancelled (1932, 1944, 1994) because of adverse weather, always a source of anxiety. One report begins 'despite the gloomy forebodings the show was a success'. There was always a welcome to visitors to the show, a stall, teas, and a raffle. The members of the committee and others worked hard on the day before the show and the day itself. ('Mrs Tatton and

Mrs Uprichard worked with unflagging energy.'), Brigadier Fellowes was Secretary and Mr Phimister was Treasurer for many years. Mr Childs of the Botanic Gardens and his assistants were indispensable in the preparations for the show, and year after year Mr Childs staged a much admired display, varying the type of roses. He was elected to the committee and later became Vice-president.

In 1938 Mrs John Reid succeeded Dr McKerrow as President. Lady Irvine opening the 1940 show said, 'In this lovely land of ours there is still room for gardens as well as concrete blockades, wire entanglement, and gun emplacements. Ground for vegetables has first claim but there is always a little plot where we can grow our beloved flowers.'

Every three years President succeeded President; The Rev Dr Rankin, Captain Warren Wynne, and in 1953 Dr McKerrow again. That year it was reported, 'The roses rushed into bloom and then collapsed even faster.' Such difficulties cut down the number of entries.

Unfortunately there are no minutes between 1955 and 1971. However, from reports each year in *The Citizen* we can read of successful shows. From 1955 the shows were held in the Recreation Hall. The Judge was Mr A. Russell of Dundee. Dr McKerrow, whose enthusiasm and work had been a mainstay, died in 1970. Gradually support had dwindled; there were only seventeen members present at the 1971 A.G.M. Mr Keith McKenzie was President, Mr R. Murray Vice-president, Miss B. Watt Secretary. Prominent members were Professor and Mrs Copson, Mr and Mrs Pirie (West House), Mr and Mrs John Simon, Professor and Mrs Cameron. A great effort was made at this time to arrange lectures and outings; there was little support – the result was described as 'disastrous' . However, the shows continued. Mrs Buchanan was the new President, and there was an increase in membership and in the number of entries to the show. Mrs Jane Blyth became President and was followed by Mr John Simon. Over the years many trophies had been given: the McKerrow Cup, the Rose Society Trophy, the Elizabeth Cup, the Alexander Trophy, the Cameron Cup, the McPetrie Cup, and the Bell Cup (renewed in

1994) and others. Mr Shaw from Forfar judged the Rose Show for many years, and said it was a splendid day's outing for him and his family. He obviously enjoyed the event.

In 1988 the Society began to struggle. That year rain spoiled the roses. The Society had always been financially sound, but now the membership fee had to be put up to £3. In 1990 there was great difficulty in getting new members. Worse, there were not enough volunteers for the committee. Mr Keith McKenzie had served in various offices for many years; he now retired and was made an honorary member. Mr Douglas Hamilton made a great effort to involve schoolchildren in an art competition, the painting to be displayed and the prizes given at the show. Only The Canongate School responded and later Greyfriars; the competition was a success in its third year, 1991, but interest and entries dwindled and it had to be given up. Mrs Nancy Alexander was both President and Treasurer. Adverse weather meant that the 1994 show had to be cancelled.

A disaster came with the sudden death of Mrs Alexander in 1995. Professor Tom Blyth took over with Mrs Blyth as Secretary and Professor Cameron Treasurer. The Society struggled on – the show of 1997 had poor attendance and a low number of entries. Next year the show was cancelled; there were simply not enough committee members to run it. At a small and sad meeting on June 29 it was voted that the Society be dissolved. The cups – twenty in all – were returned to their donors. Half of the funds were donated to the National Rose Society's Millenium Fund and half to the St Andrews Horticultural Society. But how worthwhile all the work had been. Many people remember that lovely annual event with pleasure and admiration.

Chapter 11

SPORTS CLUBS

Archery

Archery is first recorded as a sport in St Andrews when Queen Mary held private competitions in the garden of the house that is now St Leonards School Library. Butts Wynd, the lane west of United College quadrangle, retains its old name; it leads to the Scores. The Bow Butts were in the hollow, north of where the Martyrs' Monument now stands, and where the Bandstand is.

The University has a fine collection of silver medals, trophies won by students in annual competitions between 1618 and 1751, though there are long gaps in the dates. Each is a work of art; on one side are carvings of the armorial bearings of the winner's family and on the other the name and date and varied designs. Strangely, the winner of the competition had to supply the medal: it seems to have been an aristocratic sport. The medals are suspended on three silver arrows. On one arrow there are 39 medals, on the small arrow three and on the third 30 medals. The sport was superseded by the increasing popularity of golf, but was revived in 1833 by Rev Dr Thomas Jackson, Professor of Natural Philosophy. Members of the Archery Club (Town and Gown), and the St Andrews Society of Golfers, shared a clubhouse known as the Union Parlour. This stood on the site where the Grand Hotel was built. Competitions were held on the second Wednesday in August, the day after the Lammas Fair finished.

The St Andrews Archery Club

This Club was instituted in 1866, promoted by Dr H.G. Bell. He was a committee member for several years. An undated set of rules is contained in the papers of the Club which are held in the University Library archives. The committee members printed in this booklet were Mrs Henderson, Mrs Wolfe Murray, Mrs Robert Mitchell, Miss Berwick. The Club Field Days were held on alternate Thursdays during the months May to October at 'the Park adjacent to the Railway Station, entering from the Strathtyrum Road'. In 1866 the joint Presidents were Sir Charles and Lady Ochterlony. On 29 and 30 October of that year '21 ladies shot'. So it was obviously a ladies' club, although there were men on the Committee, and occasionally a man is listed in the careful entries of the scoring. In August 1867 the Club was host to the Scottish National Archery Meeting. The following year there were forty-nine members. This led to the purchase of a gold medal which was 'to be shot for annually in September'. The 1871 committee comprised of eleven ladies and six men. Sir Charles Ochterlony remained President until his resignation in 1884, when his place was taken by Major-General Cockburn. In these first years the top-scoring players were Miss Tribe and Mrs R. Mitchell. Full records were kept of the individual scores, and in one column the weather conditions were entered.

By 1877 Miss Wordsworth, Miss Gray and Miss Hume Macleod were prominent scorers. An entry for that year states 'the wooden spoon fell to Captain Herbert who had 10 whites'. In 1879 the Club numbers had fallen, making it necessary to reduce the quorum to four committee members. In the 1880s Miss Cockburn, Miss Tribe, Miss Berwick, Miss Wolfe Murray and Mrs Robert Mitchell were the high scorers. In 1886 Principal Donaldson granted the Club 'the use of the College grounds' (I take it that this was the lawn north of College Hall where in later years tennis and croquet were played.)

In 1886 Miss Hume Macleod died. Major Bell was on the committee in 1890; the records end in 1893. But that was not the end of the Club. In 1901 Mrs Robert Mitchell was Secretary. Mrs Bell Pettigrew was President and held the same office in 1913 (now as Mrs Musgrove). I am told that she was remembered for a long time for her excellence at archery. Professor Bell Pettigrew was interested in a different sport – that of flying. He constructed his own flying machine out of sheet iron and wood; it had an oil engine and wings that flapped. He piloted it himself for about 60 feet down the slope where the Memorial Hospital stands. After his death it was moved out of the Bute's experimental physiology room and put into a shed. What an excellent museum piece it would have made in St Andrews – but Mrs Bell Pettigrew sold it off for scrap.

There is a handsome monument to the three of them in the Cathedral East Cemetery: to Professor Bell Pettigrew (died 1908), Professor Musgrove (died 1935) and Eliza Jane Musgrove who died in February 1937. If emblems had been carved on the stone, they might have been an aeroplane, a skeleton, and bow and arrow.

Golf in St Andrews

So much has been written about golf in St Andrews that even to summarise its long history could be a lengthy and unnecessary task. I will give only an outline of the beginnings of the main golf clubs.

We know that golf came from the Low Countries where it was played on ice or on sandy stretches of land. In 1457 the Scottish Estates issued an edict in which 'Futeball and golfe were utterly cryit down and nocht usit'. The reason for this was that it was taking men away from the practice of archery, so essential to defence. Legislation in 1471 and 1491 was not effective. James IV himself played the game, and it is likely that Mary Queen of Scots did so when she stayed in St Andrews. It remained a favoured game with royalty.

The Royal and Ancient Golf Club of St Andrews

The R & A, as it is popularly known, will celebrate its 250th anniversary in 2004. In May 1754 twenty-two "Noblemen and Gentlemen" formed the Society of St Andrews Golfers. This was the modest beginning of what was to become the club which increasingly influenced the game of golf. In 1835, the Union Parlour was opened on Golf Place, one hundred yards from the site of the present clubhouse. The 1850s saw the first steps towards national golf events. In 1847 the R & A arranged the Grand National Tournament. In 1860 the Open Championship was inaugurated by Prestwick Golf Club, and twelve years later an agreement was reached between the R&A, the Honourable Company and Prestwick to co-host The Open. They were later joined by Royal St George's, Royal Liverpool and Royal Cinque Ports Golf Clubs. In 1894 the United States Golf Association was formed. It became apparent that there was a need for a governing body to set up the rules of golf, and in 1897 the R&A formed the Rules of Golf Committee, which held its first formal meeting with the USGA in 1920. In 1930 this R&A Committee began to consult golfing bodies at home and abroad over changes in the Rules of Golf. In 1951 there was a conference with USGA; this led to a unified code of the Rules. The R&A/USGA Joint Decisions Binder on the Rules of Golf was then issued to subscribing clubs, and was published as a book from 1988.

In every country where golf is played, apart from the USA, Mexico and Canada, the rules are those set by three committees of The Royal and Ancient Golf Club. These consist of members of the R&A and advisory members (men and women) from all parts of the world. The Rules of Golf Committee reviews, interprets and makes decisions on the playing rules. These rules are published worldwide in 30 languages, along with supplement volumes with over 1,100 biennial decisions. Overseas Rules Schools are held on a regular basis. The Amateur Status Committee reviews, interprets and amends the Rules of Amateur Status. A third committee makes decisions on Rules which deal with specifications for the form and make of clubs and balls. The first Referee School was held in St Andrews in 1991, and Referee Schools are held abroad regularly. In 2001 the sixth International Golf Conference was held in St Andrews, and delegates from 69 golfing organisations attended it.

The R&A Championship Committee was formed in 1920. It promotes, organises and controls a number of championships and matches at both national and international level. The most prestigious is the Open Championship. Together with the United States Golf Association, it runs the Walker Cup. The Championship Committee organises various other international amateur matches. Team selection for the Walker Cup and other international events is the responsibility of the R&A Selection Committee. The St Andrews Trophy was inaugurated by the R & A in 1956. An event for boys is the Jacques Leglise Trophy which, since 1966, has been played independently of the Boys Amateur and Boys Home Internationals.

Most of the R&A's funding comes from the Open Championship: television rights, spectators' admission money, corporate hospitality, rents for tented village sites, etc. During the next Open, the potential household reach in transmitting coverage over 43 channels will be in the region of 380 million!!

The R&A makes use of this surplus, and of income from other activities, to provide financial assistance for the development of golf throughout the world, including in many developing countries. We have also benefited locally on many occasions. The R&A runs a University Bursary scheme, junior golf is encouraged by coaching sessions, and regular donations have been made to appeals connected with St Andrews.

In 1864 the R&A began collecting historical objects, and by 1987 the collection was so large that a charitable trust was set up to create and run the British Golf Museum. This unique museum, across the road to the east of the R&A Clubhouse, was opened in June 1990 and tells the story of the history of golf. There is an unrivalled collection of golf memorabilia on loan from the R&A collection, and other features which are so important a part of St Andrews past and present.

St Andrews Golf Club

This men's club was founded at a meeting in the Town Hall in September 1843 as the Mechanics Golf Club. The leading lights were Andrew Carstairs, cabinet-maker, and D. Todd, painter. After one or two moves, it made its headquarters in Golf Place and in 1922 acquired Links House. It now has a membership of over 1,700 members, local and from all parts – a testimony of its success.

The New Golf Club St Andrews

Early in 1901 Herbert M. Singer called a meeting in the Royal Hotel. A group of golfers had been considering starting a new golf club. Mr Robert Officer, Captain of the Thistle Golf Club was in the chair. (You will find no trace of a clubhouse of the Thistle Club which was started in 1817, ended in 1939, was re-formed in 1865 and still exists.) A committee was elected: Mr Singer, Arthur C. Aikman grocer, James Pirie china merchant, C.A. Donaldson hatter. After a series of meetings they decided to form a new golf club. The problem was to find premises, but by chance Herbert Singer heard from a Cupar man that his mother-in-law might consider selling 3 Gibson Place (a typical St Andrews happening). Somehow the money was raised, and a hundred people had subscribed and showed willing to join the club. Ex-Provost John MacGregor chaired a meeting in the Council Chambers on 6 February 1902, and the New Club was born. 'The New' had its own permanent clubhouse before the St Andrews Club (R and A) had theirs. Plans were drawn up by Mr Gillespie, and the house was altered with room for an extension. The Club's premises were opened on 17 July 1902 – no time had been wasted.

In 1923 the Club bought 4 Gibson Place, and the extended clubhouse was opened in 1929. Five years later 2 Gibson Place was acquired. So this spacious clubhouse faces both south and north. In May 1941 the RAF had already taken over the Grand Hotel, Rusack's

Hotel, West Park Hotel and the Imperial Hotel as living quarters for Staff and Cadets. The New Club was also commandeered and a rental of £325 settled. This was a great setback, and, when the Club was handed back in August 1944, James Murray and David Cooper fought a hard battle to get it on a firm financial footing. As T.G. Jarrett wrote in his history of the New Club, 'It had its share of rough and bunkers.' But its empire continued to grow – as early as 1938, lady visitors were allowed the use of The Blue Room, and later a mixed lounge was provided. All attempts to introduce lady members have been foiled. In 1959 the Club bought 5 Gibson Place and ten years later 6 Gibson Place.

Herbert Singer certainly started off a big enterprise. For twenty years he was a butler at Westerlee, Kennedy Gardens, and later had boarding houses in Gibson Place and in Murray Park. Though not a good golfer himself, he had a passion for organising. I now learn that he also founded the St Andrews Cycling Club and the St Andrews Cricket Club, of which I can find no traces.

The New Club has had many members who have played not only golf but also important roles in St Andrews.

The Ladies Golf Club

I will write more fully about the history of this Club than of the other golf clubs, as it indicates the change in the status of women. This is also apparent in the story of other societies. In the early 1860s some members of the Royal and Ancient noticed that a few ladies were practising putting, using two clubs only, on the piece of ground where Rusacks was later built. This was then a public drying green, and a few holes had been made there for the use of caddies. A move was made by the gentlemen to acquire a short course for the ladies, and this they achieved very quickly. It lay between the two foot-bridges over the Swilcan and 'the Rocket Pole' and did not interfere with the other courses. Mr T. Burn and others drew up a set of rules, and old Tom

Morris was appointed to look after the course. A committee was formed with Colonel R.T. Boothy President, Miss Boothby Vice-President, and Mr D.L. Burn Honorary Secretary and Treasurer.

The first prize competition was held in September 1867. There were fifteen short holes placed from 3 to 7 or 8 feet apart. In her delightful small book *History of the Ladies Putting Club* (1992), Marjorie Moncrieff quotes from *The Scotsman*'s account of 8 October 1867 on the St Andrews Ladies Golf Club: 'To practice this game it requires no stress or muscular power, and is a most graceful, interesting, recreative game. The implements required for practice are a putter, cleek and a ball. We are sure that it will become a favourite game, not simply among the ladies of St Andrews, but throughout the kingdom.' How right this prophecy proved to be. A report in the *St Andrews Gazette* of 4 January 1868 remarks 'the novelty of the Ladies Golf Club – quite in every way preferable to croquet – is a great success. It has seriously interfered with the Archery Club, which was mainly kept up by Ladies.'

Initially the Club was restricted to a hundred ladies and fifty gentlemen (who were associate members), but such was the pressure that this limitation was abandoned. However, for decades now there has been a long waiting list. It is said that vacancies for this prestigious club only occur on the death of a member! The Ladies Golf Club became 'one of the most flourishing institutions in the city'. From 1870, winners of competitions were presented with awards suitable for ladies: crosses, rings, earrings, brooches, bracelets, bangles, a handsome chatelaine bag, gloves, a dagger fan, a silver putter. In 1876 His Royal Highness Prince Leopold gave a gold locket. In 1922 the Prince of Wales, while Captain of the R & A, presented two silver cups, and in 1930 the Duke of York also presented two silver cups to the Club. A fine array, not to mention club medals and club prizes in money.

The course was soon extended to eighteen holes, and competitions were played over two rounds – thirty-six holes. There were natural hazards, water and whins; at all times players were permitted to ground their clubs anywhere. In 1885 there was a serious legal action which went to the Court of Session. The legality of the Ladies Club using the ground, which was owned by Mr Cheape of Strathtyrum, and keeping the Club private, was challenged. Of course some of the gentlemen of the R & A took up the ladies' cause; the findings were in favour of the ladies, and an agreement was made to pay a small rental to Mr Cheape.

On 5 September 1868 twenty-eight couples competed for a Ladies Club gold medal in front of a large crowd of spectators, among whom was the cream of St Andrews and Fife Society, and some from as far as London. The lowest score, at 107, was by Miss L. Lamb. In September 1886 there were 92 entries for the monthly medal! The members of the R. and A. rejoiced in acting as caddies and as markers. The Club had an office in Bell Street. For the competitions a large tent was erected by the course, which was a source of anxiety when the winds blew hard. In September 1898 a shelter was erected as a clubhouse, with a verandah on all four sides. This served well until it was replaced in 1968 by the present building.

There are many familiar names of early participants either in play or on the committees of the Club, among them Colonel and Mrs and Miss Boothby, General and Mrs and Miss Moncrieff, Dr Robert Chambers and Miss Chambers, Colonel William Playfair, Edith Lady Playfair and the invaluable Mr Burn. The annual ball came to be one of the social events of the year.

The Junior Golf Club was an offshoot of the Ladies Club and was first mentioned in *The Citizen* of 27 May 1871. The members of this club played competitions over eight holes of the course. 'The Children's Links were situated between the railway line and the old main road, bordered by a wall'. This Junior Club continued to flourish. It is interesting to see that the first Secretary was Master Charles Grace, aged fourteen, later Honorary Treasurer to the R & A.

The Ladies Club weathered two wars, changed its name to The Ladies Putting Club, and has continued to flourish. Miss Moncrieff's conclusion to her book gives a good idea of this: 'We now celebrate the one hundred and twenty-fifth year of our club's life.' She gives all credit to the excellent greenkeepers and the fine state of the course, then writes,

> We are also up to date in that ladies and gentlemen can compete on equal terms, the only sport other than croquet and the equestrian arts to do so. We begin with tiny tots wielding pint-sized putters on to teenagers who in turn become students in search of an hour to unwind in the pressures of examinations ... Last year 50,000 visitors played around the course and the pleasure evidenced by them is ample reward to the Presidents and Committees who carry on the Club's traditions with great pride.

The course is now usually known as 'The Himalayas'; the undulating green turf a joy to behold and a challenge to master.

St Rule Club

Captain Boothby presided over the Annual General meeting of the Ladies Golf Club in October 1898. One of the items discussed was the possibility of forming 'a long links for ladies'. (Some of the members of the Ladies Club thought this notion to be 'rather fast'.) The site being considered was between the New Golf Course and the sea. There was also a proposal to form another ladies golf club. It was agreed that Colonel Boothby would hold a further meeting with those who were interested.

On 10 April 1897 the new 'Ladies Course', later known as the Jubilee, was ready. In 1898 St Rule Ladies' Club was founded as a recreational and residential club with a golfing section. Ideas about ladies' golf began to change from views such as: 'the wielding of the club assumes a milder form under the sway of the gentler sex, and has never extended beyond the simpler strokes of the putting green.' From this it has developed to the game played by Joyce Wethered and a long line of other lady champions. The St Rule Club never looked back. It continues to fill its role as a welcoming social club and a golf club, with its clubhouse in The Links (next-door to St Andrews Golf Club). Apart from golf, members enjoy bridge, lectures, a book club; meals, drinks and snacks are also available.

St Regulus Ladies Golf Club

This Club was started by a group of Madras College former pupils (FPs), who had their meetings at the College. In 1915 the Army took over the College, and when the Club was later reconstituted, the Rector of Madras did not wish it to be associated with the FPs (whose numbers it exceeded). So this Golf Club used premises at Seton House, City Road, until 1932 when – as St Regulus Golf Club – it obtained 9 Pilmour Links as its clubhouse.

For a Newcomer to the Golf Scene

Arriving at Golf Place, where there are two handsome houses recently acquired by the R. and A. for offices, you see the tidy bulk of its clubhouse before you. Turn into the Links; if you stand in front of the Tom Morris house and shop, the Kingdom of Golf lies around you. Next door to the Tom Morris is the ex-Woollen Mill, now a very large extension to the R & A clubhouse. To the west is St Rule's clubhouse, and next door to it is St Andrews Golf Club. Further west is Rusacks Hotel, intimately connected with golf, as is the Old Course Hotel, looming obtrusively further west on the edge of the Links. The New Club, whose entrance is in Gibson Place, has a long history, dating from 1905; in 1977 it extended its premises into a large basement next door. So here you see three men's clubs and two ladies' clubs, each with the finest view possible, each with a large membership, each with its competitions and trophies and traditions. Stretching further than you can see, there are now six interwoven golf courses, the public Links clubhouse, the Eden Course clubhouse and distantly the offices of the Links Committee. (It was not until 1894 that the management of the Links came to the Town Council, who formed a Links Committee. In the 1920s the public was admitted to play on the putting course. Right up to 1947 the citizens of St Andrews played on the Links courses free of charge.)

Some Personal Memories

It would be unusual to live in St Andrews and be untouched by its importance as 'Golf City'. After 1880 it brought 'rank, fashion and ardent golfers', as well as firms making golf clubs and balls. In the 20th century it increasingly attracted tourists and players from all over the world, and gave to its citizens a shared interest and excitement – and space on television, The first championship I ever watched was the Walker Cup in 1934. My friend Elizabeth Barker and I followed Cyril Tolley and Roger Wethered round. At one point Barker managed to twitch out a thread from Roger Wethered's tweed jacket, which she wove into a miniature four-coloured plait, made of silk threads from the tassels of trenchers, and worn from the button-hole of her scarlet gown.

I have been a spectator at all the Open Championships here from 1950 to 2000. I can visualise Sam Snead in a yellow sweater and a cowboy hat, Henry Cotton always accompanied by his neat wife, Bobby Locke, Peter Thomson and many more. The Open Championship was at first played on three courses only – St Andrews, Prestwick and Musselburgh (soon replaced by Muirfield). Then the circuit widened. Most people would agree that the Open is the best championship of all for the spectator. Often the result hangs in the balance until the 17th or 18th hole or into a play-off. I think of the 1960 Open when Kel Nagle just managed to hold off Arnold Palmer who had a birdie at the 17th. I think of the tension and stillness ('Quiet please') and the excitement – cheers and waves of clapping –

when Tony Lema just beat Jack Nicklaus in 1964, and when Jack Nicklaus, a great favourite with local people, beat Doug Sanders in 1970 in a play-off, and was again the winner in 1978. Seve Ballasteros was a popular winner in 1984. In 1995 Daly beat Constantine Rocca in a four-hole play-off. Then there was Nick Faldo's record-breaking win in 1990.

Walking out to the loop, climbing up high on the stand which faces west(ish), you look down on the procession of big-name players battling their way round the four holes below. An occasional burst of distant applause, and the friendly stranger and golf sage next to you will know what that is about. One year, seated there in brilliant sunshine, we were suddenly enshrouded in a cold relentless haar. Before long we rushed all the way back to the Woollen Mill to buy the thickest jerseys we could lay hands on. Another time at the Open we were so hot we abandoned the play and lay down for a time in the blessed shade of a wall by the old shepherd's cottage on the Eden course. Whenever you moved from one place to another you met genial spectators, delighted to give you the latest news of the rise and fall of the heroes. What dramas there have been, and what sudden plumettings in steady scoring, when competitors have played for the seventeenth green (cries of 'It's bunkered' or 'It's on the road').

Then there was the year of the flood. All was going merrily for the huge gallery when the heavens opened and released an avalanche. We ran along the Scores and took shelter at the house of friends. The celestial taps were turned off as suddenly as they had been turned on. So, back to the Links and an amazing sight: a river running down the Scores and a waterfall down the steps of the R & A, turning the 18th green into a swimming pool for gulls. The announcement that play was suspended until the next day, and that entry would be free, brought joy. Yes, there have been many strange incidents in the history of golf here – but perhaps none so dramatic as one in the early days of the Ladies Club. A cattle beast, which was being driven, broke loose at the corner of Gibson Place and made for the Ladies' Course where a match was being played. One competitor was wearing a red petticoat, and this put fear into the hearts of the ladies who ran faster than was ever thought possible to shelter and safety. The Links must have been colourful in those days, especially when the gentlemen of the R & A sported red jackets.

The Tom Morris property has been owned (and still is) by successive generations of the Morris family. The front windows of the house overlook the 18th green of the Old Course. My friend, Bunty Mould, lived there for many years, and on the final day of the Open she used to have a fine party. Henry Longhurst sometimes dropped in; what an interesting and entertaining man he was, and an unsurpassed commentator. Bunty and I took up golf in the early 1960s (and after ten years abandoned it for graveyard research). I remember walking out on the Eden with the song of larks and the sweet smell of the whins. One day both our balls landed in a deep shell bunker; we played alternate shots, in vain, until we had each played twelve, when Bunty collapsed in a fit of laughter. We ignominiously replaced our balls on the turf and recorded shameful scores. When we got handicaps, for a time we played in as many competitions as we could. One day we were in a team to play a match at Crail. Mrs Murray Mitchell arranged that three of us would meet outside the shop in Market Street. She told us, 'I'll leave the rear door of the green van open – just load up and get in; I'll be out as soon as I can.' We got there and put all the gear into the van. A man stood there looking at us curiously, then he said, 'Excuse me – but that is my car!' The air at St Andrews must vibrate with the thousands of golf stories that have been told. Golf may be about achievement, but it also about friendships and laughter and fun. The recent book by Michael Tobart, *Pilgrims in the Rough*, is refreshingly entertaining.

I will end with a most moving occasion. I was fortunate enough to be at the ceremony in 1958 when Bobby Jones was given the freedom of the City. He was in his wheel chair. When the time came he stood up and made a wonderful speech which ended with words that are immortal: 'I could take out of my life everything except my experience of St Andrews and I would still have a full rich life.'

The St Andrews Curling Club

The Curling Club was instituted in 1846, but there are no details to be found about its early days. There was a curling pond on the land of Mr James Cheape, off the Guard Bridge Road near where the old railway station was. In November 1905 there had been no curling there for some time, and it was decided to create a new pond on a more suitable site. With permission from Mr James Younger, a pond was made in a shady spot near the Law Mill, just off the road to Mount Melville and on the north edge of what is now the Bogward estate.

The Club is listed in the St Andrews *Directory* of 1926, and also in 1932 and 1935 with the following officials: Charles Maitland, H.C. Wilson, G.H. Moncrieff. The Chaplains were Rev Wallace and the Rev G.N. Price. (Why this Club had two chaplains, I don't know!) In 1939 the President was G.H. Moncrieff and the Secretary A. Duncan. This pond was filled in some years ago to make a children's playground with provision for skateboarding.

St Andrews Bowling Club

The first meeting to form a bowling club in St Andrews was held in the Council Chambers on 28 February 1887 when a committee, with Bailie Ireland as convener, was elected. Various sites for the Club were discussed; the one chosen was the property of the Skating Club on the corner of Kinessburn Road and Pipeland Road. An agreement was made to pay £45 for the property including the existing house (demolished in 1957), and a 21-year lease of the ground was granted. By March 1887 there was a list of 83 intending members. Here is an extract from The Citizen's account of the opening on 8 June 1888:

> The green of the new club was finally opened on Wednesday. It is true that some of the over-enthusiastic players had played on it last year, but the green being in its infancy and players just learning, regular play on the turf can really only said to have begun on Thursday. Mr. J. Wilson, florist, had charge of the work, and a finer bit of turf could not be seen. D.S. Ireland, President, owner of the Argyle Brewery and of Denork estate, declared the green open to nearly one hundred members.

Mr Ireland was President for three years; he died in 1900. Other 1887 committee members were J. W. King (banker), Dr Browning, K. Bruce (grocer), G. Freeman (music teacher), James Gillespie (architect), J. Hutton (upholsterer), A.T. Reid (jeweller), J. Wilson (aerated water manufacturer), J. Wilson (solicitor), R. S. Millar (watchmaker), W. Nisbet, J. Petheran and A. Pitcairn. The good mixture of skills!

The first-sown seed did not prosper, but turf was obtained 'for the lifting' from the lands of Kincaple. Tom Smith, greenkeeper of Hawick, supervised the laying of the new green. The green suffered some severe damage from an air raid on the Nelson Street area in 1942. In the dry year of 1959 the Firemaster, John Gillespie, obtained the services of the Fire Brigade, and during that summer and other hot ones the green was watered from the Kinnessburn by means of hoses. In October 1981 a sprinkler system was installed at a cost of £2850, comprising of a 600-gallon water storage tank installed and four sprinklers, one to each bank. In May 1983 additional land to the south was purchased, and here an extra three rinks were eventually established.

A serious set-back came in the spring of 1984. No play took place after the opening day. The green was seriously affected by *Fusarium* (snow mould). Investigations by turf specialists did not establish the cause of the original fault. The green was out of commission for fifteen months, during which time play took place at Craigtoun and finals were played at Guardbridge. The principal contractors, Souter of

Stirling, were paid nearly £10,000 for laying out new ground and re-seeding it, removing old hut and hedge, adjusting green levels and building boundary walls. In August 1986 it was agreed to appoint Arthur Crichton of Carnoustie as greenranger (an administrative post) and greenkeeper.

The first pavilion was erected from cash raised at a Grand Bazaar in 1902. It was lit by gas. A new pavilion was built in 1961; the joiner, plumber, plaster, roughcast, electrical and painter work was done by voluntary work of club members. The great day was 3 May 1962 when T.M. Law, Honorary President, officially opened the splendid new pavilion. It was extended in 1971 and 1984, and many improvements have been made over the years.

The membership diminished during and after the 1914-18 war, but was up to 90-100 between 1928 and 1941. By 1987 there were 189 men and 69 ladies. 'The first ladies observed were in the 1914 matches versus visitors.' It was as late as 1962 that it was at last decided to have a Ladies' Section and also a Social Section. The ceiling for each of these was to be thirty, but by 1984 there were 70 ladies. The Ladies were admitted to the Tayside League in 1981 and became very active. The officials on the first Ladies' committee were: President Mrs D.H. Mitchell, Vice-President Mrs D.M. Hutton, Secretary Mrs J.M.Allan. In 1981 Juniors (children of members) were admitted.

The Club joined various associations: in 1893, both the Fife Bowling Association and the Three Counties Bowling Fellowship; in 1934 the Scottish Bowlers Association; in 1966 The District Carpet Bowling League. It donated a medal to the World Bowling Championships at Aberdeen in 1984, and this was presented to the winner by President John Gillespie. A rink of players from St Andrews (Hugh Thomson, skip) reached the Scottish finals at Queen's Park. The Club was twenty-five times winner of the Martin Whyte Cup (St Andrews Burgh trophy). The Club also joined the Tayside Bowls League and won eleven times between 1953 and 1971. In 1964 the Ladies I. Mitchell, F. Cation, W.E. Dick and H. Gillespie were winners of the Fife Rinks. The same year R.Hendry and F. Cation were winners of the North East Fife Pairs (Ladies).

These are only a few facts I have extracted from an excellent handbook published in the Club's Centenary year (1987.) There are lists of Presidents, of many successes in competitions, of individual champions and of long-serving members. Some outstanding members are listed, including Alex Gilchrist who was Secretary 1929-45 and Honorary President 1945-87. There are many others with records of such loyalty.

I think the following gives the spirit of the Club; the writer is referring to the many match fixtures.

> It is difficult to analyse the origin of some matches, but some are because of nearness, others the result of friendship or kinship or direct challenge, but there is no doubt that some lasting friendships accrue. There is a deep down latent current of feeling beneath the surface which ebbs and flows like a ceaseless tide, which gives more satisfaction than the mere competitiveness of the play itself. This is friendship.

The Lade Braes Rifle Club

This was established in 1897. The range was along the Lade Braes in the old quarry south of the New Mill. In 1904 the President was T. Neilson, and there were 120 members. This Club won the Aston Cup in 1906, 1907, 1909 and 1911, and the Fifeshire Cup in 1909, 1910 and 1911. There was also an indoor rifle range at the old brewery buildings in Argyle Street. The Club moved to a range at Higham Toll, four miles south of St Andrews and continued right up to 1974 when the Club range was in use every night by its members and by the University Rifle Club, and on Tuesday and Thursday afternoons by younger members.

In 1982 Mr David Mitchell received the National Gold Award for being twenty-four years in office as Secretary to the Fife and Kinross Rifle Association.

St Andrews Clay Pigeon Shooting Club

This is first listed in 1932 with Captain How as President. Mr Rogers of Netherlee, Lade Braes, was also involved. No further information has been found.

Swimming: the sea and the pools

The Victorian and Edwardian visitors to St Andrews (and some of the citizens) braved the cold waters of the North Sea for the good of their health. Old photographs show green and white bathing huts on wheels, dotted along the West Sands. These were pulled out by a horse to the right depth of water; the lady occupants might descend for a healthy bracing dip without exposing their legs. In 1810 'Ladies Baths hot, cold and tepid, with changing rooms' were erected on the cliff edge just west of the Castle – a sort of mini-spa. In 1895, below the Ladies Baths and on the shore, a Ladies Swimming Pool was made by erecting a wall and putting up bathing boxes. St Leonards School took this over in 1920 and used it until an indoor swimming pool was built for the School. Recently the Spa buildings were demolished, and on this superb site the house and garden of 'Ladies Lake' were created.

Men swam at the Step Rock beach; there are letters in *The Citizen* of 1900 complaining bitterly of men and boys undressing in the open – 'a disgrace to St Andrews'. The Step Rock pool was built in 1902-3; it was 300 x 100 ft. Movable shelters in which bathers could change were brought to the pool for the summer, but in May 1930 permanent shelters were erected. There were also terraces for spectators and sunbathers, but the Town Council laid down strict regulations that sunbathers and bathers must wear 'full regulation costumes at all times'. One of the annual big events of the summer was the Step Rock Gala. Mindful of the history of wrecks, a St Andrews Humane and Swimming Club was started in the mid(?) nineteenth century, its objective being to train members in life-saving. One of the judges of the competitions of this club was a descendant of John Honey, the student who rescued the crew from the wreck of the 'Janet' from Macduff and was given the Freedom of the City for his heroism.

The Step Rock Amateur Swimming Club

This Club was formed in 1928. Jack Humphries was the first President, and A.B. Paterson was on the committee. In the records of the Torch Club there are references to the meetings of this Club in the rooms at Louden's Close. Learning to swim was important, and competitions were fiercely contested. I have vivid memories of the ordeal it was to swim in the icy waters of the Step Rock pool, but two St Andreans were noted for swimming all the year round: one was ex-Provost Aikman (1846-1932). At seventy-six he continued to take his daily swim in the Step Rock pool. The other was Professor Rose; I recall him cycling home, wearing a macintosh with his towel hung round his shoulders.

In 1957 the size of the pool was halved – a measure of economy, as the upkeep of the walls was a drain on the Town Council's resources. In 1970 the pool was in dire need of repairs, and the Council met to hear that the cost would be £4,300 which was not acceptable. There was demand for a heated pool. The Step Rock pool was not used for swimming after 1976, and it was sold to a firm which in 1989 set up a Sea Life Centre, an added attraction to visitors. The Step Rock Swimming Club used the St Leonards pool for a time and then the new swimming pool at Kilrymont School (Madras Junior).

On 9 June 1971 the Town Council voted that plans for an indoor pool should go ahead, but time went by without any action. Eventually a site along the East Sands at St Nicholas Farm was found, but negotiations were protracted until the spring of 1986. Then some of the residents of the new houses at the farm steadings objected to the plans for the East Sands Leisure Centre and car park. The case went to the Court of Session and was eventually settled. Meantime, Andrew Dawson had headed a Pool Fundraising Committee. One of the ingenious ideas had been to sell to passers-by buckets of water from a lorry parked in the main thoroughfare. Business was brisk. By the end of several years the committee was able to hand over to the Council the sum of £35,000 which paid for the water flume.

The East Sands Leisure Centre was opened on 22 April 1988 by Michael Forsyth. There was a surprise splash to end the proceedings: David Niven with two young members of the Step Rock Club jumped into the pool and were the first swimmers. Although the pool is not competition size, the design is pleasing and it is much used. There is a grand water flume, spa and steam baths, sunbeds, squash courts, snooker and pool tables, table tennis, and a café and bar. It is a fine place for the young Step Rock members to learn to swim. It is a place for enjoyment – and what I enjoy most is watching the babies in their small lagoon, floating blissfully on the calm blue water.

Kinburn Park: Tennis and Bowling

Kinburn House was built in 1856 as the home of Dr Buddo, and was subsequently owned by Provost Paterson. The Town Council bought the house and grounds in 1920 for the sum of £10,000; the grounds were turned into a public park with an eighteen-hole putting green, a bowling green and nine 'blaes' tennis courts. A tennis pavilion was erected, and for refreshments there was Kinburn Tea Garden. For some years the Hay Fleming Library was in Kinburn House, then this valuable collection was moved to the Town Library in Church Square, and again in 2001 to the University Library. In July 1991 Kinburn House became the Council's St Andrews Museum.

The first tennis club in St Andrews was the Kilrymont Club which had the use of three hard tennis courts at Bowling Green Road, south of the bowling green. In the winter the courts were flooded and became an ice rink – I remember the fun we had skating there. In 1932 Colonel Torquil Macleod was President of this Tennis Club, and Brigadier General Fellowes was Secretary. In the late 1930s the membership was about sixty, with the Rev Alexander Howell as President, Ronald W. Kerr Secretary and Miss Doris Keir Treasurer. The lease held by this club expired in 1939, and there are no records of its revival after the war. In 1973 the St Andrews Lawn Tennis Club (at Kinburn) was gifted the balance of funds from this old club.

Season tickets for members of the public to play tennis at Kinburn were issued by the Town Council from 1920 to 1972. The first ever Scottish Hardcourts Tennis Championships were held at Kinburn in August 1922 and were a great success. Between then and 1981 fifty-three of these tournaments were played at Kinburn. It was a competition which attracted international players, some of whom excelled at Wimbledon. Over the years there were many winners who were members of the St Andrews Club. However, with the conversion of the courts from blaes to all-weather, the venue of these championships was moved to Broughty Ferry.

At Kinburn a St Andrews Lawn Tennis Club was started, probably in the early twenties. It is entered in the St Andrews *Directory* (1932): 'St Andrews Lawn Tennis Club, President M.T. Anderson, sec. Mrs MacDonald, Treasurer J. Foster'. In 1935 the officials were Professor Donald Baillie (President) and Dr W. Crosby, J.B. Hughes and A.B. Rogers. Ian Kirkcaldy was Secretary in 1939. After the war the Club was revived on the intitiative of Susan Inglis; Dunsmore Hotchkis, Miss J. Solman and Miss J. Lawson were leading lights. The Club seems to have ceased some time in the mid-sixties, and until 1971 tennis was played at Kinburn only by holders of season tickets.

Recently I went round to Kinburn Park on a lovely sunny summer's evening. I turned past the hut where Mr Kay used to reign. There were white-clad teenagers in earnest action, and the evocative sound of ball on racket. I went into the clubhouse where two girls were serving home-made cakes and lemonade. (It took me back seventy years to Saturday afternoons at the tennis club in our village; 'Who's on teas next week?'). I was surprised and delighted to find that there was a booklet, *St Andrews Lawn Tennis Club; Anniversary Booklet 1971-1991,* written by Ian Palfrey in 1991. I quote from it part of a letter written by Catherine Schoeden.

> Summers at Kinburn were synonymous with enjoyment and friendship. We played enthusiastically at every opportunity. Season ticket holders certainly got their money's worth. In those days – late twenties and thirties – both the University and Madras College used the courts. All this activity made Kinburn a very busy place. Matches were played on courts 1-3, whilst School usually had 6-9. Louise Spence was a fine player and a pillar of the Club. Many of the Staff at Madras were keen and coaching was not confined to games periods. The Rector, Mr McPetrie, was himself an enthusiast and was wont to drop in of an evening and offer help and advice. The seniors from Madras proved the mainstay of the Club.
>
> Everything connected with tennis seemed worthwhile ... We played in all possible tournaments – the Barns-Graham Medal, Junior Scottish Hard Courts, and the handicap events at the Scottish and so on. Umpiring was not omitted.

Mary Brown, writing of the past, mentions Myra Haxton, Kathleen Niven and Nancy Grimond (sister to Jo Grimond). 'The Scottish Hardcourts Championships were the highlight of the season. My mother supplied the white tablecloth for the trophy table, the Bulletin Cup for the Men's Singles being the largest.' She also recalls the courts being flooded: 'Sacks were used to mop up. We had a wringer at home and this was taken to Kinburn to wring out the sacks.'

In 1971 a meeting was held in the Town Hall for the purpose of forming a tennis club for the members of the public in St Andrews:

> The present St Andrews Lawn Tennis Club was born with Colin Risk, James Murray and David Robertson elected President, Secretary and Treasurer respectively. 1972 was the first playing season and the membership was 56 juniors, 31 seniors and 4 students. At first the Club had the use of courts 1-3 and the use of the others when not taken by the public.

In the seventies there was considerable trouble with the surface of the courts. This led to a two-phase resurfacing with a polymeric all-weather called Elasatosol which was not completed until 1982. It meant that it was possible for tennis to be played all the year round. It also brought a sharp increase in membership – from 74 in 1980 to 144 in 1981.

Ian Palfrey gives details of some of the members who contributed a great deal in these early years, by their service on committees, their part in negotiations with the Council, in coaching the Juniors, in captaining teams, in fund-raising and in the social activities of the Club. Mary MacFarlane and Colin Risk were made Honorary Life Members in 1989. Other prominent members were James Murray, Marjorie and Barry Neild, Mhora and David Robertson, Jean and Graham Neilson, Fergus Muir, Fay Taylor, Anne Oliver, Vicky Christie, David Eglinton and Ian Palfrey, who have all taken a major part in the running and the activities of the Club. Ian Palfrey stepped down at the AGM in 2000 after twenty-six years of service, for which he won a Scottish Sports Council Award. In 1987 a group of members took on a three-year lease on behalf of the Club, and this was renewed by a twenty-one-year lease in 1990. In 1989 plans were lodged by

William Low for the construction of a supermarket and a car park which would involve building on the tennis area. The compensation offered was four courts, a car park and a clubhouse at Petherum Bridge. James Murray, Iain Donald, David Eglinton, Fergus Muir, David Robertson and Ian Palfrey led the campaign against the development. A petition 'Save Kinburn' contained 5,642 signatures. Success followed: the plans were finally withdrawn in June 1990.

Ian Palfrey's book gives detailed information of the prowess of young members in the eighties: Alastair Caithness, Roderick Christie, Philip and John Rowlands, Karen Christie, Bruce McIver and Eilidh Smith. The list of activities up to October 1991 indicates the healthy state of this Club.

There has been a series of increasing successes under Mike Aitken, winner of the Over-35 Men's Scottish Championships in 1997 and 2001, of the Scottish Hardcourts Men's Doubles in 1998 and of the Men's Over-35 singles at the 2002 Scottish Vets Open. In 2002 the Kinburn Girls 15-and-under team came third in Britain in the National Junior Club League. The Juniors retained the Midland Junior Super League title for the fourth year running. The Men's Team won the Midland 1st Division for the second time and the Mixed Team won the Midland Henderson vase for the second time. Individual champions 2002 and up to early 2003 are now listed:

Scottish Hardcourt Championships:

Men's Singles	Graeme Hood
Men's U-21 Singles	Graeme Hood
U16 Boys Singles	Graeme Hood
U18 Boys Doubles	Euan Forbes
U16 Girls Singles	Susannah Roy

Scottish Indoor Championships:

U18 Boys Singles	Graeme Hood
U16 Boys Doubles	Graeme Hood

U18 Boys Doubles	Graeme Hood
U14 Boys Doubles	Steven Birrell
U16 Girls Doubles	Susannah Roy
(2003)	
U18 Girls Singles	Susannah Roy
U18 Girls Doubles	Susannah Roy

Susannah was also winner of the Iron Bru Classic 16-and-under, and Steven Birrell played for the Scotland U13 Team in the annual Four Nations Competition.

In view of past achievements, the Club was given 'Performance Club' status by the LTA, receiving a grant of £2000 towards the development of future young players in the next three years. How is that for a comparatively small club with no indoor courts? It says a lot about the young folk and the enthusiastic seniors.

The Kinburn Bowling Club

Go along to Kinburn Park on a fine summer evening and you might see a bowling club match – as I did. Small groups of white-clad figures stood at either side of the immaculate green. It was like a silent ballet. One from a group stepped forward and took aim. All eyes followed the spinning course of the bowl as it sped towards the target area, lost speed, came to a stop. Players changed ends. In the background the trees in full leaf glimmered with light from the lowering sun.

I sat down on a bench beside a man called Ernie Duffus. He told me that this was an annual match, Visitors versus Kinburn, which he had inaugurated in 1954. He pointed out a lady visitor who had played in this match in the 1950s; the young man partnering her this evening was her grandson!

I learned more about Ernie Duffus later. He was a founder member, elected to the committee at the inaugural meeting of the Club at the Town Hall on 15 October 1952, chaired by Mr H. Shields, Postmaster.

Ernie Duffus was President of the Club in 1954, 1959, and 1980. He was one of a team of twelve who won the Three Counties Tournament in 1958. He donated the Duffus Shield for the annual match with the Visitors and the Duffus Cup for Pairs (Visitors v. Kinburn). He donates trophies each year for winners and runners-up.

Ernie was made a Life Member. Another Life Member is Margaret Finlay who has devoted many years to the Club; she joined in 1957. Three years later the Ladies Team – Mrs J.A.S. Duncan, Mrs R. Gillespie, Mrs E.S. Allen and Mrs H.N. Kirk – won the Scottish Public Greens Championship at Perth. In 1972 Margaret Finlay was elected to the committee; in 1974 she was appointed Ladies Match Secretary and has kept that post until recently. She was interim Secretary for the whole club for five periods between 1977 and 1985. And then, after a course of training, she became official coach to the Club. In 1978 she took the leading part in forming a Ladies Tayside League of which she was President in 1979 and again in 2001. She continues to play in this as a skip. In 1994-95 she was President of the Scottish Public Ladies Bowling Association. This meant that the finals, held on the last Saturday of August, took place at Kinburn as the President's Green.

The Kinburn Club has many internal competitions, singles, pairs, trebles and rink. They also play friendly games with seventeen other clubs. They are members of the (Men's) North of Fife Bowling Association, and the Men and Women's Fife Bowling Association, Scottish Public Bowling Association and the Tayside League.

The St Andrews United Football Club

The Club was started in 1919 and was the idea of the late Jimmy Alexander. A group of young men who had recently been discharged from the Army met in the Whey Pat at the West Port and decided to take up the idea Jimmy Alexander put forward – that St Andrews should have an official football team. The names of these founder members were Gourlay, P. Hutchison, Burns, Dawson, Hay, Anderson, Carstairs, Cuthbert, Davie, F. Hutchison, Wilson, and of course Jimmy Alexander. The name of the team was settled as St Andrews Football Club, soon to be changed to St Andrews Comrades, and yet again in the 'twenties to St Andrews United Services; the word Services was later dropped. The team's colours were also changed three times in the early days, the final choice being white tops and black shorts. At first the players bought their own kit and contributed 1/- to the running costs of the Club. In 1920 the Club turned junior and entered the East Fife League and the Scottish Junior Cup. By the 1926/7 season they were doing well, winning the League Championship, the Fife Cup, the East Fife Cup, the Fife Shield and the Martin Whyte Cup. For the next two seasons they repeated these successes. But with the outbreak of war, a meeting was held and it was decided 'to disband the club until the present operations were over'.

A start was made again when, at a meeting on 27 March 1946, it was agreed that Junior Football should return to the town. In the 1952/3 season St Andrews United won the first trophy for over twenty years when they beat Crossgates 6-2 in the League. In 1957/8 they won the Cowdenbeath Cup, in 1958/9 the West Fife Cup and the Daily Express Cup. In the following year, on 21 May 1960, came the greatest day in the Club's history: St Andrews United went to Hampden Park to play in the final of the Scottish Junior Cup, and won. On their return to St Andrews the players were welcomed by cheering crowds of over two thousand. A reception was held in the Town Hall and there were great celebrations. The players were J. Lister, W.P. Penman, Captain J.H. Hughes, W. Crookston, G. Davidson, T. Wills, T. Carmichael, J. Fraser, J. Smith, W. Penman and Romeo Borella. Twenty-five years later, in 1985, an Anniversary Reunion was held, and all those players save four returned. Two had died, and two others – one in Australia and one on Canada – did not attend. It was a terrific party! Dennis Martin produced a booklet for this occasion giving a history of the Club.

St Andrews United return from Hampden Park with their trophy
(St Andrews Preservation Trust)

During the period 1947-1960 there were three outstanding officials: Jock Wilson, Chairman 1958-1983; Jimmy Spence, Chairman 1949-1951 and then Secretary for 27 years; and Nat Dewar, Treasurer 1958-1973. In the history of this Club, as in most of the St Andrews clubs, success has depended on a small core of members who have put in a huge amount of work and enthusiasm. They in turn depend on fund-raising and on the backing of other club members and supporters. Another common feature is that almost every club has had its ups and downs. In 1973 St Andrews United F.C. came close to folding. The record of the team had been good up to 1970 and had then dropped. John Wilson, the Chairman, decided to bring in ex-player Brian Cook, who saved the day – he brought in younger members and the situation improved: in 1975/6 the team moved up from bottom to fifth in the League. But the pitches were in a poor state; with the help of a loan of machinery from the Links Department and a group of dedicated workers, it became possible to sow new grass each season.

In 1977 there was a cash crisis, so the Committee started several fund-raising schemes. By a great effort the Club raised over £3000 and embarked on the ambitious project of building new changing rooms. This was made possible through a £1000 donation, and many more from firms and from friends. With all this and a loan of £3000 from the Hamada Trust it was possible to embark on the scheme under the leadership of Jim Spence. The demolition of the old buildings began at the end of May 1980. Local tradesman helped by giving their time free. Teams worked at weekends and evenings and the modern new pavilion was completed in March 1981.

But this was not the end of the improvements. In the late 'seventies an ambitious project was being discussed – that of building a Social Club. David Donaldson came on to the committee, and was a great help through the months of discussions and planning. The digger moved in on 14 June 1982. It seems incredible that this new Club was ready in four months and was opened on 15 October, with Archie

Finlay Chairman of the Football Club and David Donaldson President of the Social Club. By May 1985 there were 1500 members of the Social Club – by far the largest local membership of any club in St Andrews. In 1986 an extension was built. There is a bar, a lounge, a function hall, facilities for all sorts of indoor games – snooker, carpet bowls, etc. – and there are bingo sessions three times a week. The Social Club continues to thrive, with a stable membership of over a thousand.

In 1982 the Football Club started an under-18 team (which was later changed to under-19). This was a success, and several of the youngsters graduated to the Saints (the popular name for St Andrews United F.C.). As for the team, the record from 1987-95 was good. It won the East Coast Windows Cup 1987/8, and also the Fife Cup and the Laidlaw Shield. In 1988 they won the Fife Cup, the Laidlaw Shield and the East Coast Windows Cup. In 1989/90 they won the Fife Junior League without losing a game, the Fife Cup, the East Coast Windows Cup, the League Cup and the Rosslyn Cup. In 1990/1 and 1991/2 they won the Cowdenbeath Cup, and in 1994/5 the Fife and Lothians Cup.

St Andrews Colts Football Club

If you want to read a cheering, an interesting and an admirable success story, get hold of a copy of the above Club's 25th Anniversary Booklet, 1976-2001. Colin Mackay had already written up the history of the first ten years of the Colts, and this was reprinted with an addition to bring it up to date by Don Burnett, under the chairmanship of A.J. (Ian) Dochard who has chaired the Management Committee for the last twenty years.

Early in 1975 Matt Sinclair and Colin Mackay decided to go ahead with an idea they had discussed – that of starting a team composed of young football players from many areas. After 'trials and scouting missions to Cupar and Fife's fishing villages', a team was formed. Matt Sinclair applied for membership of the 'St Andrews Colts' in the

Dundee and District Sunday Boys' League at Under-15 level. On Sunday 22 August 1976 this team travelled to Kennoway to play the first league match of the season. 'It was proud moment and exciting, not only because of the prospect of a win but because this meagre beginning might lead to greater things.' The score was 2-2. The team spent its first season about the middle of the League. Successes were to come, and so were 'greater things' and with an amazing speed.

From being a team, the Colts became a Club with the necessary officials and committees. In 1977/8 a new team, the Under-13s, was formed with Bill Kirk as coach. I quote: 'A greater ability in football, a stronger sense of loyalty and belonging, and a general awareness in self-discipline could be generated by the introduction of younger teams.' This belief proved to be important in the Club's development. The Under-15 team progressed to the Under-16 level. The Club needed training facilities, and these were found at the Cosmos Youth Centre. 'Literally hordes of young lads thronged the playing areas during the week.' St Andrews United offered its facilities. Dave Johnson of Dundee F.C. joined the Club managers to offer expert advice. *The St Andrews Citizen* began to give its regular reports on the Colts, for example: 'St Andrews Colts kept up their recent fine form with a splendid performance that completely overwhelmed a very competent Dundee Social Club side in the Sunday Boys Under-13 League game.' One of the team, Brian Bachelor, could have played for an Under-10 side; this was the beginning of a very successful football career for Brian. In this season the Under-16 team took a place in the top half of the League. In 1978/9 a third team, Under-14, was started. The colours were now red, white and black. Each team had two dedicated adult members as mangers.

The next season a Parents' Association was formed, and this expanded into a flourishing supportive organisation. Over the years it has made a huge contribution towards the running costs of the Club. The first transport was a van – with park benches for seats! In 1979 a Parents' football team raised enough to buy two mini-buses. The boys themselves have joined in various fund-raising efforts such as sponsored runs. One valuable aid was the formation of a group of ladies who washed the football strips.

The 1980/1 season was billed by *The Citizen* as 'Colts Best Ever Season'. The Under-15 team won the Heath Cup, and the Under-14s took the League Championship, winning the T. McGovern Shield. In 1981/2 the newest Colts, Under-10, made a sensation. 'Their brand of football lifted one of the Dundee League cups at the end of the season and a notable performance was "calculated" against Dundee Everton. The score was 27-0!' The response to Under-10 level was so great that Eric Gillespie, assisted by Dave Stewart and Jim Mackie, ran weekly coaching sessions for all those who were not in the team. 'So widespread were the social and playing activities of the Club that a host of adults were involved. In one or two cases the Club almost became a full time job!'

There was, of course, a close link with Madras College. Cups and trophies were donated. A special one is the Drew Brown Memorial Cup, introduced to perpetuate his memory. 'To receive this trophy a player must be a member of the youngest team, and show good behaviour, loyalty, support and must take good care of his kit and appearance.' Another, The Matt Sinclair trophy, 'in recognition of his valued contribution to youth football', is awarded only when the Management Committee is of the opinion that there is a deserving case. 'The recipient can be a member of the management team or, preferably, a young Colt who has been with the Colts for at least three years. The award criteria relate to loyalty, support to the Management team, good behaviour, dedication, application and positive attitudes and kit care, all upholding the good name of the St Andrews Colts.' Among the adult winners of the Drew Brown have been Ian Donaldson, Nettie Donaldson, Wray MacArthur and Ian Dochard. Young winners have been William Donaldson, Martin McKechnie, Ross Watson, Kevin Taylor, Greg Dochard, Marc Archer, Alex Raeside, Derek Long, David Wilson, David Mathewson, Reon

Juskowiak, James Aird and Kevin McMullan. In 1999 the Colts Under-15 went as visitors to Loches in France, played three successful matches and, with their pipers, led the 400-strong Easter Parade. Teams have played matches in England, and were taken to Holland by Ian Donaldson and Ricky Skelding. Dave Bachelor took a Sunday Boys' Select to France, the Colts being represented by Christopher Nicoll. Many of the players have gone on to junior and senior clubs. In the booklet, the player selected for the profile 'Champion Colt' is Robert Raeside. He has played for Leven Royals, Wraith Rovers, St Andrews United, Dundee, Irish champions Shellbourne, and Arbroath, and is now with Greenock Morton in Scottish Division 1. The Editor writes that at the present time 'there are now four teams with Manager, Treasurer, Chairman and so on, all contributing to a healthy young football scene in the town.'

St Andrews Sailing Club, and Sand Yachting

The origins of this Club go back to 1955 when the harbour at Dysart was no longer operable and there seemed little prospect of repair. The fishing fleet was laid up and, hearing of this, W.K. (Wink) Watson of St Andrews went over and bought one of the yawls. This was 'a 17-foot boat with high unstayed masts and dipping lug sails'. Mr Watson took people out in this yawl, and soon there were half a dozen of the Dysart boats with new St Andrews owners. In December 1950 this group started the St Andrews Boating Club, 'with the object of encouraging amateur sailing, rowing and motor boating'. (In 1966 the name was changed to St Andrews Sailing Club.) At a meeting on 27 January 1957 W.K. Watson was elected Commodore, a committee was elected and various sub-committees were formed.

This Club sailed off very smoothly, apart from the first regatta which had to be cancelled owing to a very strong easterly wind – only too familiar to all St Andreans. Fund-raising led to the purchase of three rowing gigs which were stored in the stables to the south of harbour.

Through the Town Council the Club set up headquarters at 'The Auld Hoose' nearby and set it to rights. They then bought the 'Green Hut' from Leuchars; members dismantled, transported, reassembled it, then laid on electricity, and it was used for storage and gear.

By 1968 Club membership had reached 133. It has kept steady, and today is about 120. Members began to build their own boats from kit, the first a Yachting World Senior and an Enterprise, and then an Osprey and a Heron. Later, the Enterprise and Mirror Classes were the most popular. Dugald MacArthur, who was University librarian and a keen sailor, wrote an outline of the history of the Club from its start to 1981. From the 1960s to 1980s, the Club had a fleet of Airbournes which had been used for Air/Sea Rescues in the war. These unique boats raced regularly. Some are now in maritime museums.

In the 1980s the Club owned a fleet of Mirror dinghies, many built by members and Madras College pupils. These were mostly used for training purposes. Recently the Club bought its own boats for training and for members' use. Miss Marian Whyte (sister of Herbert Whyte, farmer at Boarhills) had a taken a keen interest in the Club and left a legacy to buy a Wayfarer dinghy for training purposes. The training fleet was expanded in the 1990s to include Toppers, Laser 3000s and Enterprises. Ann Morrison wrote: 'This fleet forms a good foundation for an RYA recognised training programme for youngsters and adults. It has been a major factor in the good health of the Club.'

The present clubhouse was originally the lifeboat house. The Club rented it and was soon able to buy it outright from the Town Council. In 1973 considerable rebuilding and extension work on the east and west sides was carried out, much of it by Club members. An upper storey was inserted with balcony, race boxes and an extension to the kiosk. This kiosk is a good source of income. A new slipway for dinghy launching from the beach was finally completed in May 1970, 'when the Commodore and chief planner, K. Purdom were duly launched at the end of the ceremony'. Life membership was conferred on K. Purdom and J. Hunter for their part in the work.

A vital part has been fund-raising, by means of draws, discos in the 1970s and 1980s, jumble sales (the result of one is recorded as '£173.28½ and one button'). Letting of the clubhouse for various functions out of season brought in money. One entry runs, 'Club room will be let to one Henry Cotton for a reception. The Ladies have agreed to spring clean the place before the event.' In the early 1960s memorable events were two huge fetes, joint efforts of the Club and the Harbour Trust. Several 'Harbour Weeks' were held; one in 1961, held jointly with the Step Rock Swimming Club, featured helicopter demonstrations, castle-building and fishing competitions, canoe races and treasure hunts.

Sailing events began early in the Club's history. In 1965 the Club won handicap races in the Russell trophy for racing, entered by Elie, Earlsferry and St Andrews Clubs. In the early 1970s R. Pyper and D. Webster appeared in prize lists in various parts of Scotland. The Club hosted the Scottish single-handed championships in 1979 and the Scottish Junior Championships of 1980. Other associations have also held their Championships at St Andrews. In the 1970s, in mid-season, 'The Fleet sailed as far south as Holy Island and as far north as Norway. P. MacAlinden reached the Faroes in 1973, while others, such as Hugh Barkla and T. Lamb were regular visitors to the West Coast by the Caledonian Canal, Cape Wrath or by Lorry'.

Many successful regattas have been held. From 1980, Club racing was confined to weekends. For non-sailors, the Club's activities have greatly enlivened walks on the East Sands and the cliffs.

Sand Yachting

In her book, Lady Irvine records that, when her son Nigel was an undergraduate, he constructed a sand yacht which he called the Dulcibella IV. It was fitted with a motor-car steering wheel and gear, and four car wheels. The bodywork was a skeleton. The mast was about four feet high, and the sails were made by a sailmaker at

Anstruther. 'The Dulcibella achieved a speed of forty miles an hour on the long stretch of golden sands at St Andrews.' Many years later, there was a Sand and Land Yachting Club, and at Easter 1972 the British Sand Yacht titles were held on the West Sands.

Badminton

Badminton was played in the past in the Volunteer (Recreation) Hall and the church halls. In the 1932 St Andrews Directory there are records of three clubs: the St Andrews Badminton Club, President Dr McTier; the New Badminton Club, President Miss Spence; and the Eden Badminton Club, President E.M. Ness. Since the Volunteer Hall was demolished, I can find no clubs listed, but badminton is not played at the University Sports Centre except by students, or at the East Sands Leisure Centre.

St Andrews Motor Club

This Club was very active before and in the 1950s, two of the leading lights being Alex Gillespie and his brother Peter, who was well known as a driving instructor. There is a longer history of motor bicycle races being held on the West Sands, St Andrews. Some members of the Motor Club took part in this.

The Club had regular evening meetings when they had talks on technical subjects. One move the members made was to have a statue erected to Jim Clark, the racing driver whose tragic accidental death occurred in 1968. David Annand, sculptor, was commissioned to carry out the work which is erected at Kilmany, birthplace of Jim Clark. There were also other subscribers to this very fine work of art.

The Motor Club seems to have come to an end in the 1960s. I was surprised to read in an old *Citizen* that a motor car rally was held in Cockshaugh Park in 1977.

Chapter 12

YOUTH GROUPS

The 1st St Andrews Boys' Brigade

The Boys' Brigade was founded nationally in October 1883. On 14 March 1894 a meeting was held in the Good Templar Hall in Castle Street with the purpose of enrolling boys to form a branch here. The initiative was taken by Sergeant William Smith, the School Board Officer, who became the Captain. A total of 88 boys were enrolled; the Brigade was at first attached to the Scottish Coast Mission. William Smith played a vital role in the following years, and in 1909 received a knighthood for his work.

Weekly drill in the Artillery Drill Hall was taken by Sgt Major Blake. By the time the second parade was held on March 1894, there were 118 boys on the roll. On 24 June 1984 a church parade was held at the College Church, the boys assembling at the Roundel and marching along North Street accompanied by the City Flute Band. Six officers, 13 NCOs and 80 privates took part. Soon the Company was equipped with rifles, which at that time were part of the uniform. In 1924 the Company won the Fife Challenge Drill Cup.

The scope of activities widened: sports, limelight entertainments, concerts and plays annual outings and annual camps. A Bible Class was held weekly, and for some time Professor (later Principal) Duncan of St Mary's College gave the sermon. Under Captain George Jackson the project to build a hall with gymnasium and reading room was begun. The foundation stone for the Boys' Brigade Drill Hall in Greenside Place (actually now in Kinnessburn Road) was laid with a masonic ceremony on 18 May 1899. A Grand Bazaar raised £1360 towards the costs. The Hall was ready by 25 October 1900. There was no bridge over the Kinnessburn then, so access was by wooden planks. Nor were there any houses in the area.

In 1914-15 there were 150 boys on the roll, and the number remained high during the First World War. The Hall was occupied by the Highland Cyclist Battalion, so the Company had to use the Artillery Drill Hall in narrow Market Street. On Christmas Day 1914 the boys were drilled on the West Sands and marched back to the Hall after being out for 2½ hours!

After the war, annual outings and annual camps took place. Andrew Thom was recruited to the Company by Captain Weir-Breen, took over in 1924 and held the post of Captain for the next 45 years. The achievements of the Company during his office were remarkable. The number of individual awards were as follows: 60 King's Badges; 58 Queen's Badges; 17 Gold, 25 Silver and 13 Bronze in the Duke of Edinburgh Award Scheme. Several times they won the County Sports Shield and the County Pipe Band Shield. BB football teams, athletic teams and gymnasts have also had successes.

Captain Thom died in 1969. J.K. Robertson, in his editorial in *The Citizen*, wrote: 'No other individual in the present century has done as much for St Andrews.' A tribute to him was the erection of the Andrew Thom Memorial Cottage in Kirkton of Glenisla, and this has been a centre for outdoor activities in Angus. The many officers are all listed in the centenary booklet; I have only space to give the names of four long-serving Company Captains: Andrew Thom 1924-69, David McGregor 1970-80, Tom Donaldson 1980-91, and George Donaldson from 1991. There have been very many loyal officers in the century of its history. In 1994 the Rev Charles Armour had been minister to the Company for over forty years. In 1947, there being no representative of the Scottish Mission at St Andrews, it was decided that the Company should become affiliated to Holy Trinity Parish Church, but that the minister of each church would take a turn of being Chaplain for a year. That arrangement still holds.

The St Andrews BB Pipe Bands have had may successes during the past eighty years. The records kept by Pipe-Major Andrew Kirk are held in the archives of the University Library. He has carefully entered the engagements of the BB Pipe Band from 1921 to 1951.

1920 and 1921: The Ceres Games, Ladies Golf Club, Blebo Craigs, the Games at Newburgh, Strathkinness, Kenley Green, Guardbridge, Tayport and Cupar.
(I will not repeat these engagements, but they occur throughout the years.)
The Band took part in a Services Concert in the Town Hall in aid of Widows and Old Folks.
31 December, 'Playing out the Old and in the New'.
(This also occurred annually.)
1922: There were now nine pipers and six drummers.
Concert at Balcarres for the coming of age of Lord Balcarres.
Games as far away as Aberdeen.
1923: Played at the presentation of the play 'Rob Roy' in the Town Hall. (Dr Playfair took the part of Rob Roy.)
Played at the University War Memorial Service.
1924: Full-size pipes were now issued.
Played at Dr P.M. Playfair's funeral; 2 nights at the film 'Annie Laurie' at the Picture House; at the Pittenweem Parade; at the St Andrews Horse Parade; at St Andrews Football Match; at Boxing matches; at University House fête and garden party; at the Crail Fancy Dress.
1925, 1926, 1927, 1928: Played at the Burns Club supper, and at the Black Watch dinner.
11 December 1926: 'Mr Lothian of the Leith BB Company advised Captain Thom to apply for the Band to play at the Royal Albert Hall. Mr Keir of Glasgow inspected the 1st St Andrews Boys Pipe Band and agreed that they should try for London.'

27 May 1927: 'London Council Officials said that the Band had played at its best. The Band were masters of the Contest, winning 16 points more than the Band which came second.' The Band had seventeen engagements in 1927, and the numbers were similar in 1928 and 1929.

1930: Captain Rusack inspected the Band.

30 October, 'Miss Georgina Smith, aged twelve, got first prize in the Fife Girls under-18 section.'

1931: Played at Dundee Police Sports. There were 27 engagements this year.

1932: Alexander Geddes won the Lady Stewart Sandeman Cup and a medal.
The Band played marches, reels, strathspeys, slow marches, retreats. (Pipe-Major Kirk lists the whole repertoire including those he composed.)

There is now a gap in the records until 1947. However, we know from James R. Bone's excellent book, 1st St Andrews Company the Boys Brigade 1894-1994, that the band went on from strength to strength. In 1933 the Boys attended the Golden Jubilee Royal Review in Hampden Park when the Duke of York reviewed 33,000 members of the Boys Brigade.

1947 and 1948: The Band played at the Kate Kennedy procession, on Charities Day, and at the Inter-Varsity Pipe Band Contest. St Andrews won. There were fourteen in the BB Band.

1951: The instructors were Pipe-Major Kirk, Drum-Major Wallace, Cadet Pipe-Major T. Sprunt and Drum-Major Harry Black.

There were three royal occasions at which the Band played: at the wedding of the Duke of York to Lady Bowes-Lyon; on the visit of the Prince of Wales to St Andrews; on the visit of H.M. Queen Elizabeth to St Andrews.

When Pipe-Major Kirk retired after thirty years of great and successful service, Pipe-Major Bill Watson took over. In 1988 he announced that he was hanging up his pipes; he had been in office for thirty-seven years and brought the bands to many successes. He was made Honorary President of the Company in 1992. Pipe-Major John McPherson succeeded him.

Further events

At the King's Jubilee in 1935, 1st St Andrews BB was selected to take part in relay-running from St Andrews to Pitscottie. The Company won the Fife Drill Cup for squad drill and the Kilmaron Shield for athletics. The football team had a good record. From 1939 to 1945 the Boys made a contribution to the war effort.

One of the great events was when, in 1963, 600 officers of the BB attended the World Conference in St Andrews. The BB Band played, but not only that – the Boys gave a performance of *The Masque of St Andrews* by A.B. Paterson. The Brigade continued successfully for at least another 25 years, and the programme widened in its indoor and outdoor activities.

But in October 1993 it transpired that the Brigade was no longer flourishing. Captain George Donaldson was invited to address the St Andrews Community Council concerning the problems facing the youth organisations in the town. He expressed his concern over the loss of teenagers to drink and drugs, and appealed to the Council to take the lead once again in getting all youth groups, most of whom were facing the same problems, round the table. He told them that the BB numbers had held steady for the last three years, but were well down several years ago. The biggest problems were with the 14-16 year olds. He had support from several councillors.

Since then a big drive has been made. Towards the end of 2001 a meeting was held with parents, and the Executive has announced the good news that various offers of help have been made. Stephen Donaldson is the new Acting Officer in Charge, Allan Milne Chairman of the Executive Committee, Bill Sutherland Secretary and

Rev Dr Henderson Chaplain. There is a minimum of staff, but a new Pipe-Major has been found for the Band, which has been in abeyance for some time, and it will be re-formed if a Drum-Major volunteers. A fund-raising committee is in action, and it is hoped to begin a Friends of the BB Group. All three sections are starting up: the Company section, the Junior Section and the Anchor Boys (ages six to eight). There is a lot of goodwill towards them. Many of us associate the important, the stirring, the entertaining events in our City with the splendid BB Bands and the generations of youngsters of whom we were proud,and whose characters had been moulded by the years of training and enjoyment in the lst St Andrews Boys Brigade. By early 2003 the BB is gathering strength.

The Girls' Brigade

The old Girls Guildry was formed at Holy Trinity Church by a group of ladies: Miss Playfair, Mrs Allen, Miss Guild (of the Episcopal Church), and Mrs Everard of Kennedy Gardens. These names indicate that this was in the 1920s or earlier.

In the 1950s the Guildry was absorbed by the Girls' Brigade, which still continues. Some of those in charge have been Miss Ethel Joy, Mrs Betty McQueen and Mrs Marna Cunningham.

Scouts and Cubs

Robert Baden-Powell became a national hero for his 217-day defence of Mafeking in the South African war of 1899-1902. When he returned to England in 1903, he was appointed Inspector General of cavalry and the next year he established the Cavalry School. Having learned that his military textbook, Aids to Scouting (1899) was being used for training boys in woodcraft, Baden-Powell ran a trial camp on Brownsea Island, and he wrote an outline for the proposed Boy Scout movement. Troops of Scouts were started all over Britain. The immediate response to Baden-Powell's book Scouting for Boys, published in 1908, must be one of the greatest success stories ever; within a year 111,000 copies had been sold. A central organisation was set up in the same year, and in 1909 the first rally was held at the Crystal Palace which was attended by 11,000 Scouts – and a few girls who were wearing a similar uniform to the boys. Baden-Powell noticed these girls and, through his sister Agnes, the Girl Guides Association was formed in 1910. In 1912, aged fifty-five, he married Olave Soames, who in turn devoted herself to Guiding and was elected World Chief Guide in 1918.

In St Andrews the Cathedral Eastern Cemetery contains a monument to Warington Smyth Baden-Powell who died in 1921. He was the founder of the Sea Scouts and an elder brother of the Chief Scout. Warington's wife's parents farmed at Boarhills, and she had a second cousin Captain Ian Wilson (Kilmallie), who was an early Scout Leader of the 8th St Andrews Troop. This troop was founded sometime in 1913 and was listed as the St Andrews and District Boy Scouts Association. The Honorary President was Sir James Donaldson, the Chairman Colonel Sprot and the Secretary E. J. Balfour. A granite fountain in Kinburn Park is inscribed 'Dedicated to the Memory of Major General R.S. Baden-Powell and other Immortal Heroes of Mafeking. 18th May 1900'.

By 1920 there were almost a quarter of a million Scouts, and in August the first World Jamboree took place at Olympia, London. It was here that Baden-Powell was declared Chief Scout of the World, to the acclamation of eight thousand Scouts from twenty-one countries, among them large contingents from America and Holland, and four Scouts from Siam and two from Japan! The second World Jamboree was in Denmark and the third in 1929 – the 'Coming of Age' – was at Birkenhead. It ran from 31 July to 14 August, ending with a massive display. Massed pipe bands, eighty-four strong, played in front of the Royal Box. There were Highland games, inter-team relays, obstacle races, tug-of-war competitions, five-a-side football and camp fires.

There was a display of dancing, with 'Flags' halfway through; so important was the timing that the performers were warned: 'One man going to sleep upsets the applecart.' Were any of the 8th St Andrews there? At least one was; in his retirement David Niven jotted down some notes as follows.

Joined the 8th St Andrews Scouts in 1925.
1929 Went to Jamboree at Birkenhead. It rained all the time. Hungarian Scouts made excellent cooking fires. Met Australian Scouts.
At camp at Stravithie Dr Fyfe and Deputy-Constable McPhee came.
Camp at Yetts of Muchart. Major Lumsden visited the camp.
Went 1st class walk from Tayport, stopping at Balmullo, then walked home.
Passed Cook tests at West Sands. Capt. Wilson was the examiner. On Saturdays nearly always went to West Sands and put out whins fires.

Captain Ian Wilson was Scoutmaster of the 8th Fife (i.e. St Andrews up to 1935 and was succeeded by James Thomson, Group Scout Leader (GSL), who retired in 1964. Others associated with 8th St Andrews in the early days were Ian Caldwell of Madras College, A.B. Paterson and Alex Thom. At a Scout Reunion Dinner on 24 April 1933 at MacArthur's Restaurant, the toasts were to Mrs Ian Wilson and Dr G.M. Fyfe.

James Methven was prominent in the movement. He was a Cub Scout before the Second World War and his sons Ian, Alistair and Gordon were all Scouts in the 8th Fife. Ian together with Ronald Smith, J. Hulbert, R. Orr and Trevor Royle were Queen's Scouts. In the 1957 reorganisation Boy Scouts became Scouts, and Wolf Cubs became Scout Cubs. The Venture Scouts (16-18) worked for the Queen's Scout Badge, and the 15- to 16-year-old Scouts for the Duke of Edinburgh Award.

Headquarters

The first Scout headquarters were in a hut in the football grounds. In 1964 James Methven and Mr Angus were responsible for negotiations with Mrs Ian Wilson, daughter of Captain Wilson, about the ground for the new headquarters in the Scores behind Old Admiralty House. Mrs Wilson donated this ground to the Scouts. She opened the large hall which was erected and which served as headquarters for the various different Scout groups and also for Sea Rovers. In the late 1970s the Committee faced considerable expenses when necessary repairs were made to the hall, including rewiring, plumbing and re-equipping the kitchen. In 1989 there was a meeting to discuss the erection of an extension to the hall. The Venture Scouts were very keen to have a den of their own and had raised money to subscribe to the extension. Plans were drawn up, and the addition was built.

The Scout cottage at Kilry near Alyth was much used at weekends and holiday times. The St Andrews Scouts kept it in good order, and money and labour went into repairs, painting, etc. In 1987 there was bad news about the cottage. It had been decided that the key would no longer be kept by the 8th Fife Scout Troop, but by Mr D. Smith for availability to the Scouts and to other groups.

From the start, transport was necessary and a series of vehicles came and went. A Scout van which was acquired in 1969 could take twelve boys and tents. It did 1,000 miles in the two summer months! It was soon replaced by a Bedford Work-o-bus which did not last long and was not replaced.

Structure

The numbers of Scouts and Cubs has stayed fairly steady throughout the years, with Cubs outnumbering Scouts, and often a waiting list for Cubs. By the end of 1964 there were enough Scouts to form another troop. Leonard Angus, who had been with the 8th for some time, took this in hand, and the 113th Fife was founded in January 1965 in conjunction with Rev Mr McLellan, minister of St Leonard's Church. The Scouts met in the attic part of the old coach house in the garden of the Manse, and the entrance was by a hatch in the ground floor ceiling. Leonard Angus remembers that the boys were disappointed when a proper entrance was made. He left after three years or so and became District Commissioner. He was succeeded by George Davidson who acted as GSL and Scout Leader for twenty years. Each summer the boys went to camp in Perthshire for a week; parents were ready to help. Mary Neilson was Cub leader. When George Davidson became Chariman of the St Andrews and District Council, Len Zukowski took over the Scouts. A student, Callum Farquhar assisted and later got a post with the Scout Association. When St Leonard's Manse was sold recently, the Scouts were told that they could no longer have the Scout Hut there, so they disbanded. Now only the Cub Scouts make up the troop; they meet in St Leonard's Church hall.

To return to the 8th Fife: in 1975 there were 100 boys in all, and in 1985 there were 55 Scouts and 30 Cubs. There were two patrols of Scouts, the Oak and the Acorn, each with a Group Scout Master (GSM), and an Assistant GSM, the patrols meeting on different nights. Wolf Cubs were started by Baden-Powell in 1924, but I have no date for the first St Andrews Cubs. They were also divided into two packs, Oonai and Seeone. In the earlier times Bob Houston gave dedicated service to the Cubs, and also Jean Orr. In December 1986 she started a third colony, The Beavers, for 20 boys. Venture Scouts were boys aged 16 to 18 years old. Robin Orr, who had been Scout leader and Cub leader, then became Venture Scout leader for about nine years. Andrew Wilson succeeded him. The Venture Scouts disbanded in 1977, but re-formed in 1986 with Mr S. Miller.

Activities

The public are no doubt aware and proud of the St Andrews Scouts,

Cubs and Venture Scouts, the Scouts Pipe Band, and the parades on Armistice Day and other important City occasions, and on Founders Day and Thinking Day.

Camping was an integral part of scouting, 'not just to learn the benefits of outdoor activities but for enjoyment'. Scouts and Cubs and Rangers attended the Discovery Camp at Scone, regular summer camps at Lochearnhead, and at many other places, including Dunstaffnage, Dunbarney, Glenisla and Glen Tilt, and nearer to home at Lochore Meadows and Spinkie Den. Older boys went to London, to the French Alps, to Luxembourg, to Switzerland, and to the jamboree in USA. They enjoyed camp fires (inter-district camp fires were well attended), cycle rides, hikes, skiing, sand yachting, sailing and football.

The Sea Scouts also had use of the Hall. In 1963 it was recorded 'the Sea Scouts are now afloat'. An old whaler had been bought; however it did not serve long and was replaced by dinghies. The Scouts also enjoyed sailing, and in 1967 built three canoes. It was then necessary to obtain a rescue dinghy. For some years there was an Air Force Scout troop under the leadership of Mr W. Marr GSL.

Scouts and Cubs have done various services for the town: planted the trees in Abbey Street, cleared up the Kinnessburn from time to time, also Cockshaugh Park, the West Sands and the Castle beach. In 1957, to celebrate the 50th anniversary of the Movement, the Scouts planted an oak tree in the south-east corner of Cockshaugh Park. It flourishes, but I can find no plaque.

There may be earlier records extant, but those I have seen date from 1959 to 1990; they contain minutes of committee meetings and Cub Record packs. The latter have an individual record for each boy, with the tests he passed and his other achievements. The wide range of tests included swimming. I noted that one troop was studying signalling, seamanship and meteorology. One Scout, Angus Stewart, went to London in 1958 to receive the Queen's Award (the highest there was). In the 1960s he was in charge of the St Andrews Sea Scouts.

Going through the minute books of the committee covering these years, I am left with the following impressions. An enormous amount of work was done by adults, which brought a great deal of success and enjoyment to Cubs and Scouts. There was a never-ceasing struggle to find enough funds, and a great deal of time and energy was expended on fund-raising. It had always been policy to involve parents, and one important result was that a 'Supporters' group was formed in July 1982. The members of this group did splendid work and raised a lot of money. The upkeep of the Hall, of vans and boats, of tents and essential equipment involved steady expenditure. The aim was to keep the scout subscription as low as possible, and to ensure that nobody was barred from membership or activities through lack of money. One drain was the necessary capitation fee to Headquarters, and this fee increased as the years went by. It has been necessary for the committee, the supporters and the boys to take part in a great number of fund-raising events. They have held raffles, jumble sales, coffee mornings, car washes, the Mile of Pennies, and sale of Christmas cards, ... The Venture Scouts did a sponsored leapfrog across the Tay Bridge and raised £450 – half towards the construction of a hovercraft and half to the Mentally Handicapped. And of course we all have memories of the annual Bob-a-Job week. In 1983 the Scouts made £526, one boy having done fifty-five jobs. That year the Cubs made £178. I remember one Bob-a-Job week in the 1960s, when I had my nursery School in Argyle Street. One morning in that week, young Patrick Carstairs and a friend were in the cloakroom 'making an aeroplane' from bits of wood. There was such enthusiastic hammering that I went to check progress. The two workers had driven several dozen nails through the carpet into the wooden floor. None of us could prise them out. Elder brother Jeremy and another Scout arrived in the early evening to see if I had a job for them. I had! They removed all the nails, well earning the money. Another way the Scouts raised money for charities was by running a 'Christmas Post' for ten years; they delivered letters and cards all over St Andrews for sixpence an item.

The second problem was a staff shortage. When one of the leaders retired it was proving difficult to replace him. In 1963 there were 70 boys and 10 leaders; in 1971 there were 120 boys and 4 leaders. This crisis was met, but recurred in the 1980s and is now worse than ever. University students have made a most useful contribution and continue to do so. In fact this year (2001) the running of the Scouts rests on the help of students, and when they are away for the long vacation one troop cannot function. GSM Ranald Barrie soldiers on.

Balancing this is a long record of quite extraordinary loyalty to scouting, of long service of adults as Chairman, Secretary and Treasurer of the Committee, as GSL, Assistant GSL, as Scouter in Charge. Some names appear above, but in addition surely the following should be remembered for their contributions – in the 1960s Mrs Gladys Hind and Gillian Hands. Jean Orr worked with the Cubs for thirty-eight years, and in 1963 she was the originator and Cub Master of a third pack, the Beavers. Archie Strachan was Cub Master, Group Scout Master and founded the Air Scouts. Mr and Mrs Joy, Ian Firth and Helen Firth, Phil Gribbon, Bruce Baillie, R. Harris and D. Smith were all involved for many years. Robin Orr has fine record as Cub Leader from 1970 and Venture Scout Leader to 1975, and many years as a Scout Leader and GSL. Michael Zochowski became Cub Master of the Seeonee pack in 1959. From 1973 to 1990 he was Scouter in Charge and committee member, and during that time also Acting GSL for some years. On his retirement in 1990 he was presented with the Silver Acorn.

Guides and Brownies

As with the Scouts, the Guiding movement spread rapidly. Before 1920 there were forty companies in Fife. The registration date for the 1st St Andrews Guide Unit was 11 July 1919, and the name entered was Miss A. Craig. Further records list the following Guiders: 4.6.1958 Miss A. Provan; 26.2.1962 Patricia Thomson; 30.1.1964 Norma Smith; 10.11.1966 Eileen Tyndall; 6.7.1968 Elizabeth

Crawford; 10.1.1973 Betty Christie; 16.11.1977 G.H. Paterson; 24.5.1991 Mrs Janet Douglas. Members of the Trefoil recall three sisters who were long-serving guiders – Sarah Watt, Nancy Watt and Betty Watt. Sarah ran the Sea Rangers at St Andrews.

The first premises the Guides used were the Scout Hut at the Football Club ground. In 1922 there was a change of premises to the present guide hut in Greenside Place, which had previously been a toy factory. Pat Ramsay tells me that this hut was bought with the help of Trefoil. There were two patrols, Rose and Ivy. In 1927 a 3rd St Andrews Pack was started at St Leonards School and Lady Baden-Powell visited. When the Prince of Wales came to St Andrews in 1922, the 'Girl Scouts' and Boy Scouts lined up at the Town Hall. In 1925 Baden-Powell addressed the Fife Guides, but in her book *Girl Guiding in Fife 1910-1977* Doris W. Coyne does not mention the place of this meeting. In October 1927 the lst and 2nd Guides and Brownies were inspected by the Duchess of York.

In 1933 the St Andrews Guides got into the final of the County Cup Competition at Weymss Castle and won the cup. That year the 1st St Andrews joined the 1st Kilrenny at a camp at Brig o' Turk. There were annual camps locally and the chance to go to international camps. In 1948 Olave Lady Baden-Powell paid a visit to Fife Guides. By 1950 there were four St Andrews Companies. In 1953 a new Guide Hut was erected at Greenside Place with help of a grant from Trefoil St Andrews Association. In 1966 a new uniform was introduced. In the years 1968-78, St Andrews University Guide and Scout Group gave invaluable help to the Guides.

County Commissioners were as follows:

1914-46	Lady Wemyss
1946-48	Miss E.C Sharp
1949-60	Miss A.M. Pilkington
1960-70	Mrs R. Purvis
1970-75	Mrs W.N. Thomas
1975-	Mrs P.D. McFarlan.

The Trefoil Guild

This Guild is part of the Guide Association. Letters were sent to ex-Guides to see if there was sufficient interest to start a Guild, and on 21 January 1970 a number of ladies turned up – enough to ensure going ahead. The first meeting, on 10 March 1970, was held in the St Leonard's Church Scout Hut. Seventeen members attended and Mrs Duncan, Lawhead Road, was nominated President. Mrs Cutherbertson succeeded her. The Guild transferred to the Guide Hall for sessions 1972-73 and thereafter.

Mrs Pat Lindsay gave me this information and writes:

> They were an active lot and we have always tried to follow their example. We still have two of the original members, Miss Isobel Brown and Miss Joyce Cuthbert.
>
> Trefoil is for anyone over 21 years of age. Most of us are ex-Guides but we are open to non-Guides. Trefoil help where they are needed, fund raising, badge testing, campfires, tea and coffee making. We attend national and international outings, and visit various Guide houses. Today's Trefoil partake in the Discovery Award. Our aims are to keep the spirit of Guiding, to keep the promise and the laws and take this into communities, also to give financial and moral support to Guiding and Scouting.

The Brownies

Various people have been Brown Owl or in some way helped a great deal with the Brownies in St Andrews. Among them were Margaret Mitford, Bid Provan, Ena Pirie and Marigold Spiers. (I asked Marigold if she had any vivid memories from Brownie days. 'One was the Winnie the Womble competition', she said. 'The eggs were

supposed to be hard-boiled but many proved to be soft and runny!')
Unfortunately I can find no further information.

The St Andrews Boys' Club

This Club was affiliated to the Scottish Association of Boys' Clubs. The minutes are from 1942, but there is reason to think that there was a previous Boys' Club; it may appear in church records. The 1942 Club was founded by Professor Dickie, who was elected Chairman, and the Rev George Johnston, Secretary. Professor Dickie was succeeded by Dr Paton, Dean W.S. Andrew, Cllr W.P. Tulloch, Dr Jack, Rev John Thornton, Andrew Thom, Tom Roche and the Rev Scott. The Club initially offered membership to boys aged 13½ to 15½ who did not belong to any other organisation. The age went up to 18, and for a time over-18s who did not want to leave the Club were accepted.

Through the years there were recurrent difficulties to overcome. These were met with fortitude and with help from friends. The part that a few St Mary's students played was vital to the continuance of the Club. At the start, temporary premises were offered at 22 Market Street. The next year the Club moved to rooms at 98 Market Street, which were offered until the end of the war. Provost Bruce saw to it that the rooms were free of rent and rates. The Ladies' Committee decorated and furnished these premises. In 1948 there had to be another move – this time to bigger clubrooms on the corner of South Street and Abbey Street. The Ladies set to work again. The Club increased in numbers and in its range of activities. The last move took place in 1957 to the disused East Infants' School in Gregory Place. By now the 'Ladies' had been replaced by a Mothers' Group who in turn made the premises very attractive.

The second problem was that there were many changes in the post of Club Leader. They were young men who had to move on to full-time work, or who were called up to National Service. I will list them; that the club thrived indicates their calibre. It was hard to lose them;

I was intrigued by the phrase used in the Annual Report in regard to one Leader: 'we cannot but bemoan his way-going'.

1942 Captain Robert Simpson
1944 Duncan Mitchell
1946 Sgt Major Humphries who was assisted by two St Mary's students
1951 D. Valentine
1952 M.T. Hudson and Mr Tulloch
1953 Marshall Gibson, a St Mary's student
1955 James L. Bruce
1957 Angus Scott
1958 Robert Simpson assisted by W.T. Humphries of St Mary's
1959 W.T. Humphries; Tom Roche assisted the Leader until:
1968 D.R. Allen and R.L. Husband
1969 Mr R. Kennedy, Area Youth Leader, stepped in
1970 Angus Stewart

It was always hard to make ends meet, but there were legacies from Mr Philip Boase and from ex-Provost Tulloch, and handsome donations from Miss J. Moir and Provost Fordyce, and gifts of money and equipment from supporters.

At the start, meetings (7 p.m. to 10 p.m.) were held in the clubrooms on two evenings a week for boys of 14+. When the numbers increased to fifty-nine at the end of 1947, the 14-18 group met on two evenings and the 12-14 group on two other evenings.

In the early days of the Club, Mr Croll had offered an evening gym class at the Burgh School, and some of the boys attended regularly. This offer benefited the Club for many years. Football was one of the major interests and, until they could muster a full team, the boys played five-a-side, with matches against B.B. teams. Mr Rennie took joinery classes. Courses in First Aid and demonstrations in fire-fighting appealed, also, later when the equipment was available (1960), snooker and pool, badminton, table tennis, darts and – being St Andrews – *Golf!* The first dance was held in 1944, and sixty-three attended a party in 1948. At Abbey Street the Club got a catering licence. In 1959 some of the boys started a jazz club. Others organised a jumble sale and with the proceeds got strips for the football team. Thirty boys went on a day trip to the opening of Dalguise House near Dunkeld, a new training centre and camp; some stayed there in later years. By 1965 some were skiing, hill-walking and mountaineering. In 1966 a boat-building section was offered by Donald Chisholm. The first of 21 sessions began in January, and the small group of Boys' Club and Torch Club members built a mirror dinghy. It was completed in May, and the seven boys and four girls began sailing. They were very keen and decided to build a second dinghy.

The last set-back was in 1969 when the clubrooms at Gregory Place were broken into and seriously vandalised. Both billiard tables were badly damaged. Club members set to and did all the redecorating. There were about seventy members now. In late 1970 the Boys' Club committee met the committee of the new Cosmos Youth Club. So the Boys' Club as a separate identity ended, and a new club began.

The Torch Club

I am told there was an earlier club for girls which was started to provide for young girls who came to residential posts as maids, and had nowhere to spend their half days. There was certainly a girls' club which needed premises; it approached The Preservation Trust when the South Street Louden's Close property was being restored and obtained headquarters there. The annual reports and minutes of the Torch Club are in the archives. The President was Lady Sandeman, and the members of the management committee were Mrs Hall Stewart, Mrs Peterkin, Miss Herbert, Miss Eleanora Aitken, Mrs

Rennie and Mrs Jean Tynte, all familiar names in the town. The Torch Club had a far smoother run than the Boys' Club. When the Preservation Trust bought the derelict property of 146-148 South Street and the houses in Louden's Close behind it, there was an agreement that the ground floor of the South Street House would be a hall for the Torch Club and the two small houses behind would be clubrooms. The hall was completed in 1941, but the clubrooms were not ready until the war ended. The Torch Club was grateful for the gifts and for furniture from the Social Club.

The Leader from 1948 was Miss Wishart, who was supported by Miss McCubbin. Miss Robertson, the Assistant County Youth Organiser, became Leader in 1952 and stayed for ten very successful years.

In 1948 there were two age groups: the Seniors of between twenty and thirty in number, and the Juniors eighteen to twenty. The girls focussed on helping others. Before Christmas they were busy making gifts which they delivered to old people in the Gibson Hospital and in the Home of Rest. In spring they gathered primroses which they took to the old people. They took presents to the children in the Convalescent Home at Dyer's Brae, and to the children at St Michael's. They ran a jumble sale, and then a dance in the Town Hall, and used the proceeds for giving a party for the sixteen children at St Michael's. They made glove puppets and produced a play. It was a great achievement when, together with boys from the Boys' Club, they put on in the Holy Trinity Church Hall three one-act plays written by A.B. Paterson. For this they made the scenery, the programmes and some of the costumes. The Torch Club had been given a sewing machine, so some of the girls had classes in dressmaking. They also acquired a cooker and had cookery lessons.

Miss Robertson took some of the girls on expeditions to the Highland Show in Edinburgh, to a Club Conference at Aberfoyle, to Falkland Palace and to the Glen Prosan cottage. She took small groups on holidays to Cornwall, to Norway, and to Austria. The Juniors went to the beach and the putting green on summer evenings. The older girls enjoyed singing and dancing. In 1960 they had a dinner dance at MacArthur's. There was a phase of square dancing, when they invited Boys' Club members to come along. Then jiving became the thing, with boys from the Boys Brigade, to music by the 'Nuclear Band', but unfortunately this band 'split up'! Occasionally the Boys' Club shared a film evening at the Torch Club.

Seven girls began working for the Duke of Edinburgh Awards; they found it hard, but three were successful. Others entered a home-making competition. The Seniors had their own committee. From 1956 there were enough members to hold three club nights a week. In 1963-4 they held 'Juke Box Jury' and 'This is Your Life' programmes.

Times were changing, and 1966 is recorded as 'a year of depression'. Mrs Horrex was now Chairman of the Club, and a great source of strength. It was decided to cater only for the older age group. At a conference, leaders and others were told of new policies for youth clubs: 'we are no longer trying to impel youth into action, but into situations where they would benefit'. As Dr John Thomson of Madras College wrote, 'Young people were now "doing their own thing".' His remarks were to the effect that they were abandoning traditional ideas, and this might be alright, but not if they threw out the principles. Miss Robertson was able to give only one night a week now, but on the other evening the Boys' Club Leader, Mr Ramsay Allen, took the two groups together.

The following year Miss Robertson resigned. Mr Kennedy was the new leader. Some girls attended an orienteering course at Montrave and Aviemore. In 1969 interest was waning. Mrs Jean Tynte had played a large part on the committee of the Club for many years. Mrs McKirdy and Mrs Burbage did what they could. In June 1970 it was decided that membership would be suspended, and notice was subsequently given to The Preservation Trust that the Torch Club wished to end its lease. The new Cosmos Club was beckoning.

The Ichthus Youth Club

The Ichthus Club (Ichthus means 'fish' in Greek, the letters standing for Jesus Christ) for boys and girls aged 14-18 began at Hope Park Church in 1966 with the sanction of the Rev Wilfred Hulbert and on the instigation of two St Mary's students, Ron Ferguson (who in 1981 became the Leader of the Iona Community) and Willie Salmond. Run by these two students and the Church Youth Fellowship, the Club met on Saturday evenings for a dance night with epilogue, and on Sunday evenings for discussions, talks, folk singing, etc. By 1967 the membership had grown to 137. In December 1968 the Club was dissolved as it was felt the facilities at Hope Park were insufficient. It was very soon re-formed as the Ichthus Youth Club when Father Gordon was good enough to allow the use of the church hall at St James'. The new committee was: Chaplains Rev. I.M. Paterson and Father Gordon, Leaders Ron Ferguson, John Nicholson, Lawrence Moonan, Marius Felderhof, Chairman Norman Spittal, Secretary Nicola Allen, Treasurer Ron Gatherum, Social Convener Sandy Kinninmonth, Helpers' Supervisor Miss Pat Harvey, Committee Adviser Jean Law, Acting Member Bob Smith. The aims were 'to provide a place where young people can meet and enjoy themselves in a Christian atmosphere; to present the message of Christianity in terms relevant to young people; to find opportunities for Christian service; to extend a helping hand to anyone in need; to train young people for leadership of the Club.'

A youth club needs its own premises. Father Gordon had left St Andrews, and in early 1969 notice was received that the Club must move elsewhere. In the summer of 1969 Ichthus was without a home. The St Andrews Youth Development Committee and the adults involved in the Ichthus Club wished to keep the club alive so that it could form the basis of a new club which was being planned. The old railway station buildings were vacant and might be converted into club premises. The above committee acquired free use of these buildings. Mr Harvey (who had the agricultural engineering works in Greenside Place) now became involved, and he and others went to work with great enthusiasm and made a magnificent job of transforming the buildings into well-equipped club premises. Altogether the work took 1,146½ hours; the cost of materials was only £250. Pat Harvey gave me a vivid description of the transformation of the old station. 'There were quite a few boys who were painters and so on, but my father said we needed a few joiners. Voluntary help came. The Station Master's office became a café and was also used for table games. The left luggage was made into a cloakroom, the waiting room and ticket hall into a hall for discos and games. People were generous in giving equipment (such as a cooker).' Pat remembers a dance when, by a timing device, the new lighting went on and off in time to the rhythm of the music. The clock from her bedroom had disappeared – its innards had become a vital part of the ingenious timing mechanism. The discos were held on a Sunday evening, Friday and Saturday nights being avoided.

The Club was now run by Leaders E.P. Harvey, Pat Harvey, Ian Baker, Ron Gatherum and a Members' Committee, each of whom had a job to do. It was self-supporting and self-governing Club. The rules about discipline were firm. And it was a great success; in 1970 there were two hundred members. The range of activities had continued to widen. The indoor programme included table tennis, chess, dominoes, film shows, folk-singing and dancing. For a time there were two football teams, then three, and also a girls' football team; the coaches were Mr Martin and Mr J. Menzies. Through the Army Youth Team, members enjoyed weekend camping, skiing, climbing, canoeing, country runs and youth hostelling. They even used the steep cliff at the old station to practise rock climbing.

There might be as many as a hundred at a disco, and the income helped the Club to donate to charities. On 25 April 1971 a 24-hour Marathon Darts Match was held. A.B Paterson threw the first dart, and T.T. Fordyce the last three. A world record of 876,998 points was made. It wasn't only the players who were tired – the support team had a lot of work to do, too! The proceeds went to help handicapped children at Strathkinness Youth House. Each Christmas time the members made up food parcels which they took to the old people.' In Pat's file there are some letters of thanks for these gifts. One recipient wrote rather touchingly, 'It was a real surprise, that's the first one I have ever had. God bless you.'

These young people worked hard on behalf of those less fortunate. They held a summer fete in 1970. There were pony rides on the old station platform. Someone had a bright idea and filled in and turfed part of the yard's siding to make a mini-golf range. The proceeds went to the Save The Children Fund. In 1971 twenty members did a sponsored walk and raised £140 for Holidays for PHAB (Physically Handicapped and Able-bodied Young People). Another sponsored walk enabled the Club to send £82 to the St Andrews Shelter Group. Donations were also sent to the Sea Rangers Unit and the Boys Brigade.

It is sad to write of the end of such a fine club. The new Cosmos Youth Centre in Abbey Walk had been opened in 1971. The committees had always expected that the members of the Ichthus Club would form a strong nucleus. The lease of the premises at the station was by no means secure (and later they were demolished when the Petherum car park was laid out). Another factor with the Ichthus was that the adults could not continue giving up such a large amount of time. Very unwillingly on the part of the older members, it was decided by the end of 1972 that the Club must come to an end, and members who wished should join the Cosmos Centre. After the Club had disbanded, the proceeds remaining were used to purchase trophies. These were presented to the Cosmos Youth Centre, together with miniatures for use in the first year.

There are many people living in and away from St Andrews who have happy memories of Ichthus.

The Cosmos Youth Centre

St Andrews Churches Youth Council Committee (set up in October 1966) met on 17 April 1967 to consider the need for a youth club which would be available for all. There were representatives from nine churches, and Mr Lewis, Secretary to the Fife Union of Youth Clubs, was there to give advice. The proposal to set up a St Andrews Youth Centre was discussed and agreed. It was decided to inform all congregations of the scheme and to ask for young adults to volunteer to take a series of training sessions. Fifteen young people responded and these sessions began forthwith. It was visualised that Ichthus and the new club would join up.

An Advisory Committee was set up and met on 26 May 1968. There were representatives from Ichthus (Mr Harvey and Pat), the Torch Club, the Boy's Club, Martyrs' Church Saturday Youth Fellowship, and Mr J. Lewis as adviser. The plans were that the Club would be directly controlled by a responsible committee which would own the buildings, furnishings and equipment, and lay down the policy on which the Centre would be run. This was The Youth Development Committee and was chaired by Dr D.E. Watt from May 1969. Dr Watt later chaired the Management Committee until September 1973.

The first search was for premises; after negotiations with the County Council and the Town Council it was agreed that the Centre could be established by a conversion of some of the buildings at the old Burgh School in Abbey Walk. Terms were agreed with Fife County Council for a twenty-year lease (later extended) and a nominal £1 annual rent. Plans for alterations and additions, by Messrs Walker and Pryde, were accepted. The old gym would become an indoor sports area (75 x 40 ft) and a new sports hall would be built (75 ft with two bays of 15ft). Meantime the financial aspects had been worked out. The name was chosen from a long list of suggestions: Cosmos meaning harmony and order, and also membership open to all-comers in the area.

From 1968 Roddy Kennedy, a professional youth leader working in St Andrews, gave his help and advice to the committees. The initial costs for the building, furnishings and equipment came to £40,000. Grants of £20,000 from Fife Council, £10,000 from the Scottish Education Department, and £6000 from the St Andrews Town Council were augmented by donations and by fund-raising (Mrs Dewar was in charge of this, assisted by Mrs Horrex and Mrs Braid). By 1973 the whole debt on the Cosmos enterprise was cleared. It was estimated that the running of the Centre would cost £1000 per annum, apart from grants (the salaries of the Warden and the Depute Warden were paid by the Fife Education Department). The Centre was to be self-supporting from membership subscriptions, charges for entry to dances, etc., the café, and fees obtained from outside bodies for use of the Centre. It was estimated that the membership would be about four hundred.

The building programme began on 5 January 1970, and by 6 June that year the outer walls of the Sports Hall were completed. It seems amazing that it was possible to open the Cosmos Centre on 20 February 1971. Mr Ian Fraser was appointed as Warden, and the Assistant Warden was Mr G.D. Boffey, a local youth leader. The official opening by Princess Anne took place on 1 July 1971. There was a membership of 400 in the first months, but this level was not sustained. Cosmos was open four afternoons and evenings a week. The proposed range of programmes was based largely on those of the Ichthus Club. To run the Cosmos a three-tier system had been set up: the Youth Development Committee, the Management Committee and the Members' Committee. Officials on the first (Interim) Management Committee were Dr Watt Chairman and Mrs Dewar Treasurer. Mrs Horrex, who later became Chairman, was a member.

Mr Boffey resigned in February 1972 and was replaced by Bill Mitchell in February 1973, but both he and Ian Fraser resigned on the 1 July of that year. The Comos was closed for a few weeks until Bill Foston took over, to be replaced by Sandy Kininmonth in 1974. All this disruption must have been very disappointing, as a good programme had been set up and the numbers had stayed steady at 350. The most popular activity was judo, coached by Mr Rutherford, and also karate. There were dances/discos for two age groups, one on Friday evening, one on Saturdays. Unfortunately there was occasional trouble in or after the discos. Under-18 and under-16 football teams played in matches at Cockshaugh Park. Mr Pennington took two sub-aqua courses, and Mr Donald Chisholm supervised the building of white-water slalom canoes. In addition, there were all the options that had been offered by the Ichthus Club, plus netball and volley ball.

Various faults developed in the building, and the remedies were costly. In phases, the building was re-roofed, and a new kitchen and coffee bar were installed. Floods did great damage to the floors of the hall and involved extensive replacements.

The Cosmos Youth Club had been set up according to Government policy. With the findings of the Alexander Report of the Scottish Education Department in 1979, policy changed. It advocated the establishment of Community Centres. The Cosmos Youth Centre was already catering for many groups who held their meetings there. Accordingly, its name was changed to Cosmos Centre, and then in 1994 to Cosmos Community Centre. Bill Sangster, who had been a member of the Management Committee for eleven years and succeeded Hugh Grey as Chairman, told me that the committee made a decision to widen the scope of the Centre. Negotiations were carried out with Glenrothes College, and in 1995 classes were started in the upstairs classrooms of the building. Through an amalgamation with Glenrothes College, Fife Council and the Cosmos, there was sufficient funding to demolish the old school buildings behind the Cosmos, and new classrooms were built.

The Cosmos Community Centre

I was taken round the Cosmos Community Centre by Kathy Kirkcaldy who has been an official there for about twenty-five years and is the present Manager. I also met Tricia Ryan who is the Youth Education Officer. When possible, six youth workers, working part-time, are on the staff. The premises have recently been refurbished and are in gleaming first-class order. There are modern kitchen and bathroom facilities, a snack bar and comfortable seats. A 'Parents, Babies and Toddlers Group' was enjoying the morning session. The dance hall was bright with big toys and small smiling faces. Recently it has been the scene of two wedding receptions and is often hired for dances. The Stroke Club meets here – carpet bowls and bingo are popular. Home Start (voluntary members) holds its sessions here, and young families who have children under five years old and who are in difficulty receive help and encouragement. A weekly lace-making class is also held here. Other sessions are Line Dancing, Spiritual Enlightenment, and a club for children with special needs. The Centre runs Youth Clubs for four sessions a week.

We went through to the fine sports hall which is used for badminton, football, basketball, volleyball and karate. Classes from Greyfriars School next door have gym sessions in this hall. In addition, there are three small rooms for quiet activities and committee meetings. Also, a range of education classes is run by Glenrothes College; these include English-speaking for foreigners, preparation classes for those going back to work, adult basic education and computer management.

A minibus was standing outside; this was a lottery award. Every afternoon children of primary school age are collected from their schools for the after-school club. From 35 to 40 children attend daily, Monday to Friday, and I hear they greatly enjoy it. It is of course a vital help to those parents who cannot finish work at 3 o'clock. Sometimes a class of schoolchildren come for a day because their teacher is on an in-service course.

CONCLUSION

At the beginning of the twentieth century, St Andrews was a small place with a long history. The population was 9,600. The industries were fishing, which ended mid-century, and the manufacture of golf clubs which lasted until 1985. The Kinessburn was the boundary to the south; the building of handsome houses was taking place to the west. The University and the schools gave St Andrews a reputation for good education. From the time the railway line to St Andrews was laid, people chose to come to live here in their retirement, attracted by the seaside and golf, by the clubs and societies, the comfortable size of the place, its natural beauty and by the presence of the University which increasingly brought fresh life to the town. The town's population, excluding students, increased to 14,600 by 1991 and may be about 18,000 in the 2001 census. There is a healthy tourist industry.

One might think that the increasing number of residents would increase the membership of societies, but their decline (except for sports clubs, which continue to flourish), and in some cases termination, are trends common to most places. In seems that one cause is the lack of volunteers to take on the necessary work involved in being an official. People say that they 'have not the time'. Why? One obvious answer is that nowadays most wives have jobs; neither do households have 'the staff' who, in the earlier part of the twentieth century lightened the load of house and garden keeping. Another cause might be the time-consuming activity – for children and adults – of watching TV, playing computer games and surfing the net. Also, with public transport and cars, interests and entertainment can easily be found away from the home town. A further factor in St Andrews: in 1968-69 Clarke Geddes set up for the University's Extra-mural

Department a two-term programme with a series of Friday evening lectures. This led to an increasingly wide range of lectures and activities provided by what became the University's thriving Adult Education Department. By 2001-02 there were 32 different courses offered.

The goodwill and the public-spiritedness of the citizens of St Andrews in the twentieth century (and before it) are evident in many chapters of this book. The church congregations and many societies shared the aim of helping other people. The records show that many other clubs – sports clubs, youth clubs included – regularly donated money to various causes. The causes now are worldwide, are overwhelmingly numerous and demanding.

This study has also shown how the people of St Andrews – a self-contained community – set up and took part in a wide range of lively activities. I have been impressed by the time and energy given by many individual volunteers, and by the fellowship, the stimulation and the fun enjoyed by the members of the different groups.

BIBLIOGRAPHY

Books

Calder, J. — *Wealth of a Nation.* Edinburgh: National Museum of Scotland, 1989

Clark, Eric D. — *History of St Andrews Golf Club 1843-1993.* St Andrews: West Port, 1993

Coyne, Doris — *Girl Guiding in Fife 1910-1977.* Kirkcaldy: John Stevenson & Son, 1977

Hackney, Stewart — *Bygone Days on the Old Course.* Dundee, 2nd ed.,1990

Jarrett, T.G. — *St Andrews. History of the Golf Links: The First 600 Years.* Mainstream, 1995

Leneman, Leah — *A Guid Cause: The Womens' Suffrage Movement in Scotland.* Aberdeen University Press, 1991

Magnusson, Magnus — *The Story of a Nation.* Harper Collins, 2000

Rivers, W.H.R. — *Instinct and the Unconscious.* Cambridge University Press, 1920

Robertson, J.K. — *St Andrews Home of Golf.* St Andrews, 1967.

Salmond, J.B. — *The History of the Royal and Ancient Golf Club.* 1956

Smout, T.C. — *History of the Scottish People 1560-1830.* William Collins, 1969

Tobert, Michael — *Pilgrims in the Rough. St Andrews Beyond the 19th Hole.* Loath Press, 2000

Booklets and directories; photographs with text

Anderson, James M. *A Quincentenary Handbook of the 500th Anniversary of the Foundation of St Andrews University.* 1911

Bennett, J.M. *St Andrews Bowling Club 1887-1987.* St Andrews: Quick Print, 1987

Bone, James R. *1st St Andrews Company The Boys' Brigade 1894-1994.* 1994

Campbell, Alex *St Andrews Directory, a Classified List of Trades and Professions in Fife 1820-1870,* 2 vols., 1894 (typed). Kirkcaldy

Cant, Ronald G. *The Parish Church of the Holy Trinity St Andrews. A Short Account of its History and Architecture.* 1992

Cant, Ronald & Coulthard, W.L. 'The Churches of St Leonard's at St Andrews'. *Church Service Scottish Annual.* No. 23, 1953

Docherty, Ian *Something Very Fine: A History of St Andrews Baptist Church 1841-1991.* 1991

Fordyce, T.T. *Hope Park Church, St Andrews: A Concise History 1738-1994.* Supplement by D.E.R. Watt, 1994

George, Judith *All Saints Church St Andrews. A Handbook.* St Andrews, 1975

King, Peter *The Catholic Church of St James, a Short History 1884-1984.* 1984

Linskill, J. *The Ghosts of St Andrews.* St Andrews, 1911.

Lyle, David *Shadow of St Andrews Past.* John Donald, 1989

Lyle, David *Images of St Andrews Past.* St Andrews: St Nicholas Press, 1994

Mackay, Colin & Burnett, Don — *St Andrews Colts Football Club 1976-2001.* 2001

Marford, Charles — *The Byre Stormers.* St Andrews, 1949

Moncrieff, Marjorie — *History of the Ladies Putting Club.* St Andrews, 1996

Palfrey, Ian — *St Andrews Lawn Tennis Club Anniversary Booklet 1971-1991*

Paterson, A.B. — *The History of the World's Smallest Theatre.* St Andrews, 1939

Paterson, A.B. — *The Byre Theatre Through the Years.* Kirkcaldy: Litho, 1983

Paterson, A.B. — *The Tale o' the Toon St Andrews Through the Eyes of A.B. Paterson 1925-1981* (3 vols). Kirkcaldy: Litho.

Reid, Ruby — *Discovering Old St Andrews.* Morgan Services, 1985; 6th reprint 1995

Thompson, John — *St Andrew St Andrews 1689-1993.* St Andrews, 1994

Tucker, John — *The Bute Medical Buildings 1899*-1999. St Andrews: School of Biology, 1999

Warren, Robert A. — *A Short History of the Congregation of Martyrs' Church 1843-1993*, revised by David Sinclair, 1993

Wilson, George R.T. — *History of Lodge 'St Andrew' No. 25.* Joseph Cook & Son, 1894

Wilson, George — *Official St Andrews Directory 1894, 1898, 1907, 1909, 1913, 1926, 1932, 1935, 1939, 1940.* St Andrews Times

Wolfe, Christine M. — *A New Guide to the Parish Church the Holy Trinity.* St Andrews, 1998

INDEX

Cover and Layout: Stephen M.L. Young .
stephenmlyoung@aol.com

Font: Adobe Garamond (11pt)

Copies of this book can be ordered via the Internet:
www.librario.com

or from:

Librario Publishing Ltd
Brough House
Milton Brodie
Kinloss
Moray IV36 2UA
Tel /Fax No 01343 850 617